Praise for
The Power *of* Trust

"You can't buy it. You can't sell it. You can't even see it. But if you had more of it, your employees would work harder, and your customers would stay with you longer. Trust is one of the most valuable intangible assets that a company can have and this book will show you how to get more of it. Packed with wonderful stories and practical examples, this book is a great read. TRUST me!"

—Erin Meyer, INSEAD, author of
The Culture Map and coauthor of *No Rules Rules*

"The 2021 Edelman Trust Barometer found business is the most trusted institution. Business has a new mandate to lead as the world combats ongoing crises and widespread mistrust. Against this backdrop, *The Power of Trust* is a must-read. Both scholarly and practical, it draws on fields from ancient philosophy to modern management theory to analyze and deeply examine the core elements of business trust while taking a lively journey through real-world cases of trust won and lost (and won again). Professor Sandra Sucher and Shalene Gupta make a vital contribution to the trust conversation and provide a compelling call to action for CEOs to build trust by embracing a broader societal role."

—Richard Edelman, CEO, Edelman

"Full of fresh insights brought to life by compelling examples, *The Power of Trust* is a rich and rewarding read. It's also extremely timely. With more and more companies today pledging to balance the interests of all of their stakeholders, and not always put their shareholders first, Sandra Sucher and Shalene Gupta make clear that the driving question executives should be asking themselves every time they make a major decision is, 'Will this enhance trust among those we claim to serve—or betray it?'"

—Rick Wartzman, author of *The End of Loyalty:*
The Rise and Fall of Good Jobs in America

"Unveils a new understanding of the business, economic, and societal importance of trust."

—Jeffery Weirens, global financial
advisory leader, Deloitte

"With vibrant and compelling insights, Sandra Sucher and Shalene Gupta break important new ground about trust as a key foundation for both human relationships and business. Their illuminating and exciting exploration of what it takes to build trust, combined with vivid storytelling, make this page-turner a critical companion for any business leader."

—Hubert Joly, former chairman and CEO,
Best Buy, and author of *The Heart of Business:
Leadership Principles for the Next Era of Capitalism*

"Trust is at the foundation of sustainably successful enterprises in business, government, and any organization, for that matter. *The Power of Trust* does a great job explaining the how and why of building trust, including fairness, one of my favorite issues."

—David M. Cote, former CEO, Honeywell,
and author of *Winning Now, Winning Later*

"Sandra Sucher and Shalene Gupta offer a comprehensive blueprint for companies and leaders who want to build or regain the trust of their stakeholders. Their work provides an insightful trust model that underpins moral leadership—looking at competence, motives, means, and impact. A brilliant resource for anyone who wants to truly understand what trust is, how it works, and what they can do to incorporate it into their leadership practice."

—Celia Moore, codirector, Centre for Responsible
Leadership Imperial College Business School

The Power
of Trust

THE POWER

of TRUST

HOW
COMPANIES
BUILD IT,
LOSE IT,
REGAIN IT

Sandra J. Sucher
& Shalene Gupta

PUBLICAFFAIRS

New York

Cover design by Pete Garceau
Cover image by Pete Garceau
Cover copyright © 2021 Hachette Book Group, Inc.

PublicAffairs
Hachette Book Group
1290 Avenue of the Americas, New York, NY 10104
www.publicaffairsbooks.com
@Public_Affairs

Printed in the United States of America
First Edition: July 2021

Published by PublicAffairs, an imprint of Perseus Books, LLC, a subsidiary of Hachette Book Group, Inc. The PublicAffairs name and logo is a trademark of the Hachette Book Group.

The Hachette Speakers Bureau provides a wide range of authors for speaking events. To find out more, go to www.hachettespeakersbureau.com or call (866) 376-6591.

The publisher is not responsible for websites (or their content) that are not owned by the publisher.

Library of Congress Cataloging-in-Publication Data
Names: Sucher, Sandra J., author. | Gupta, Shalene, author.
Title: The power of trust : how companies build it, lose it, regain it / Sandra J. Sucher & Shalene Gupta.
Description: First edition. | New York, NY : PublicAffairs, [2021] | Includes bibliographical references and index.
Identifiers: LCCN 2020049224 | ISBN 9781541756670 (hardcover) | ISBN 9781541756663 (ebook)
Subjects: LCSH: Organizational behavior. | Trust. | Corporate culture—Moral and ethical aspects. | Leadership—Moral and ethical aspects.
Classification: LCC HD58.7 .S87 2021 | DDC 302.3/5—dc23
LC record available at https://lccn.loc.gov/2020049224

ISBNs: 978-1-5417-5667-0 (hardcover), 978-1-5417-5666-3 (ebook)

LSC-C

Printing 1, 2021

For my family, where trust began. —SJS

To my parents and Usheer, both trusted and beloved. —SG

Contents

INTRODUCTION

A Moment of Trust "in the Small"

FITTINGLY, A BOOK ON TRUST BEGAN WITH A MOMENT OF trust when my new research associate suggested that perhaps I was missing the big picture. Shalene Gupta asked me whether I* wanted to shift the focus of my work from how companies can retain trust after a layoff, to a bigger question. Rather than a limited look at an important but still short-term problem, isn't the question more of a strategic issue of how companies build and maintain trust in the long term?

It was January 2017 in Tokyo, cold but not Boston cold. Shalene and I were in the lobby of our hotel: picture purple velvet-clad banquettes, dim lighting, a space designed for waiting, meeting, and greeting. We had come to Japan to research Recruit Holdings, an astonishingly capable technology and services company that hosts platforms on everything from planning your wedding to buying a house, changing your job, ordering takeout, and getting your nails done. You'll learn more about Recruit later, a spectacular story of trust regained, a "fallen angel" that redeemed itself.

---

* With one exception the first person is used throughout the book when Sandra Sucher relates a personal story.

I was sitting in that lobby, leaning against pillows that kept sliding away from my back, with Shalene, a bespectacled, curly-haired writer (she of Fulbright fame, former reporter for *Fortune*) who had started to work with me as a research associate at Harvard Business School. We had finished making our to-do list of next steps for the case on Recruit, when Shalene turned to me with her question about the thread I was following in my research. This was a moment of trust "in the small" as it were, trust between two people. Shalene and I had only been working together for five months. We were just finding out things about each other like whether we liked our eggs scrambled or hard-boiled, tea versus coffee, and yet here she was, asking me whether I wanted to reconsider the focus of my work.

What Shalene was demonstrating at that moment was trust. One crucial aspect of trust, as we'll see later, is a willingness to make yourself vulnerable to the intentions and actions of others. First question: How vulnerable was Shalene in asking that question? Answer: Very. We hadn't been working together very long, and the question she asked is one I might hesitate to ask a colleague I've known for years. Second question: How might I have responded? I could have decided that someone who would presume to know me better than I knew myself on the strength of only five months of interaction was a little too sure of what she believed, and a lot less interested in trying to understand me before coming to judgment. I might have concluded this is not someone I wanted to work with on a long-term basis, because I no longer trusted her.

[*SHALENE*] So, WHY DID I open my mouth and ask Sandra about changing the narrative arc of a book she planned to write? Because during our week in Japan, I had built trust in Sandra—in more ways than one. I had a deep respect for her compassion for other people and her acute ability to home in on what mattered to them, as well as her ability to identify companies that delivered excellent products and services while doing right by all of their stakeholders.

At the time I was burned out on large organizations, where I'd worked as a writer in everything from government to media to non-profit. Too often, I'd found, politics took precedence over competence, and injustices took place behind closed doors. However, I had to pay rent, so here I was in Japan working for Harvard Business School, even though I wasn't exactly sure why we were studying Recruit. It is a fascinating company to be sure, but I was still trying to put my finger on how it related to Sandra's research. But I kept my mouth shut. I'd learned the hard way at other jobs to tread carefully.

Sandra, it turned out, was dead-on about Recruit as a company worth studying. Part of why it recovered from a giant scandal in the 1980s to become a tech behemoth is a host of processes that are practical and psychologically astute, designed to motivate and empower employees to do their best work. For example, one of Recruit's core principles is that managers constantly ask employees a fundamental question: Why are you here? At Recruit, a good manager is one who designs tasks that couple an employee's passions with activities that improve Recruit's bottom line and benefit society. As we continued our work at Recruit throughout the week, a deeper story—one that went way beyond Recruit—started to percolate.

So, at the very end of our trip, with all of this bubbling through my mind, I forgot everything I knew about power dynamics at work and blurted, "Do you want to shift the focus of your work? I think your research has a much bigger and more important story."

There was a long pause. I wondered if I was going to have a job the next day. The pause became interminable.

Sandra turned to me and said, "I think you're right."

AND THAT'S HOW *THE POWER of Trust* was born. We were supposed to rest and go on a tour of Tokyo, but we were so excited, we munched on snacks (a very important part of our relationship) and kept talking. When Shalene and I came back to Boston, we spent hours walking through my career, my research, and teasing out the connective tissue holding together my body of work, as well as planning our investigation of other companies. As we talked, we realized all of my prior work on moral leadership, process excellence, corporate responsibility, and fairness were part of the much larger concept of trust.

I've spent eighteen of my twenty-two years at Harvard Business School teaching The Moral Leader, a course that uses books, novels, and historical accounts to help students develop their own definition of moral leadership to turn to in the future, and ten years teaching Leadership and Corporate Accountability, where MBA students learn how to grapple with the tough dilemmas business leaders face, when there are multiple right answers or, worse, situations where the choices are bad all around.

Recruit is not the only wonderful company I have conducted research on during my more than twenty-year career at Harvard Business School. It turns out I had developed a goldmine of research about how companies and leaders make decisions that retain the trust of their constituents.

I have researched operations processes and teased out what makes for excellent customer service (you'll read about this when we discuss The Ritz-Carlton). I've conducted a host of field studies on companies and leaders, like Dave Cote of Honeywell, who asked themselves how they could do the best by their employees during the Great Recession of 2008–2009 and came up with smart and compassionate solutions. I have conducted field studies on other companies, like Michelin, that broke the trust of employees and the public so thoroughly that the European Union wrote a law to make sure the same situation could never happen again. A disaster—except, Michelin used the experience to build a new process for strategic change that made it best in class.

My journey for understanding what trust is has taken place over several decades, with experiences that include one of the worst days ever encountered by investors.

When Shalene and I met, I was in the third act of my work life. I'll skip over my first job, the brief stint in a nonprofit drug program in Harvard Square called the Sanctuary. (No, we didn't sell drugs to people for no profit; we tried to help people who were using drugs.) This allowed me to exercise my desire to help people, but I realized I was more interested in being in businesses that could help people by filling their needs and wants with wonderful products and well-designed services, wowing them with great customer care, and building a good environment for the people who worked inside the business. A material girl in a material world.

To make the switch, I went to Harvard Business School, joining the MBA-doctoral program because I knew I wanted at some point to teach. I left after getting my MBA since I'd never actually worked in a business and couldn't imagine how I could teach about something I hadn't experienced myself. After ten years in fashion retailing at Filene's (and, I confess, probably something like a hundred scarves later), I moved to Fidelity Investments. There were several moments at Filene's and Fidelity that taught me about the importance of trust, but the one that made the deepest impression happened shortly after I joined Fidelity in 1986.

The 1980s had been a down and up economy, with recession in the early part of the decade followed by a strong recovery.[1] For Fidelity, one of the main opportunities and business drivers was the recently approved 401k retirement savings plan, which allowed employees to set aside pretax money for their retirement (often matched to a certain level by their employer). All of a sudden, the world of investors with an appetite for risk was joined by ordinary people who wanted to save for their retirement, greatly increasing our customer base.[2] But we knew the good times couldn't last forever.

And sure enough, on Friday, October 16, 1987, all hell began to break loose. In 1987, the Dow Jones Industrial Average (DJIA) had risen 44 percent in just seven months, raising concerns of an asset bubble.[3] By mid-October, rumors of shaken investor confidence began to circulate; they grew worse with the announcement of an unexpectedly large US trade deficit, which caused the value of the dollar to fall.[4] Individual markets began tumbling on October 14, and on Friday, October 16, the Dow lost 108 points, which was the single largest one-day drop ever recorded at the time.[5] That Friday turned out to be a mere windup for when things really hit the fan the following Monday, when the Dow dropped 22 percent.

At Fidelity, we felt the first shock wave of customer panic that Friday, in a rising tide of calls to our 1-800 phone operation (yes, this is how customer service worked in the pre-internet era). I was one of the senior leaders who ran Fidelity's individual investor phone operations. At that time, I supported the several thousand employees who worked in Fidelity's customer call centers by heading up three functions: training, internal communications, and quality call monitoring. We decided we had no choice but to make this an "everyone to the phones" moment. Everyone, and that included me, would be trained to be on the Quote Line, on which you told callers the daily value of each mutual fund they owned.

I took my turn at what proved to be a nerve-wrackingly hard job of quickly locating each customer's mutual funds from the day's printed pink sheets of net asset values, which listed hundreds of funds. However, customers had other questions—questions, I, for sure, wasn't prepared to answer. What happens to a mutual fund if everyone pulls their money out of it? How secure is Fidelity as a company? What keeps Fidelity afloat at a time like this? How long will this go on?

I realized we could put our resources to use helping all the people who were working the phones by getting them answers to those difficult questions. We asked the quality monitoring staff to keep track of all the questions that customers were asking. We ranked those most frequently asked, had members of the training staff hunt down reasonable answers, and distributed the answers to the people working the phones. In addition, we turned the data into an hourly report and gave that to the senior staff managing the phone operation, and to Chairman Ned Johnson and his executive staff. At the time, it was one of the only windows we had into the mindset of our customers.

One major lesson stands out as I look back on that crazy time through the lens of our research on trust: processes were at the heart of creating customer trust in Fidelity. All of us on the phones had the best of intentions and wanted to help customers, but we needed a process to make good on those intentions. Thankfully, customers weren't holding Fidelity responsible for the market correction itself. But talking with them on the phone, it was clear that they were painfully aware of how much they needed us to be trustworthy.

We need these kinds of deeply embedded processes about trust to be pervasive: where companies take responsibility and create processes to foster trust with all the groups they interact with. Not only will it help steer us through crises, but it can also help us prevent them or lessen the impacts of a world where markets are collapsing, pandemics are rampaging, and climate change is imminent. If you consider how we've handled past crises, it's clear that we could be doing so much more and so much better to build trust in companies and the institutions of our societies.

The problem, however, is that trust can be a meaningless buzz phrase, a concept that is poorly understood and hard to execute. To paraphrase the words of one Supreme Court justice used in another context, people know it when they see it. But there is a gap between vague recognition and truly "getting it" and giving trust a spine by pinning it down, discussing it, and scaling it up. Together Shalene and I built a trust model. Its four elements have the goal of helping companies understand what trust is, how it works, and what they can do to fold it into their thinking from everyday decisions to long-term strategies:

- *Competence*: Your ability to create and deliver products and/or services through a combination of process excellence, technical know-how, managerial smarts.

- *Motives*: Your good intentions for doing what would be best for all the people and groups you interact with. And, when confronted with the necessity to make painful decisions, thinking through how to balance the needs of different groups to cause the least amount of harm.
- *Means*: The fairness of your processes and treatment of people when distributing rewards and pain points. Ensuring that your processes allow for open and transparent communication so that people affected by a decision can weigh in.
- *Impact*: The overall effect, both intended and unintended, of your actions on other people. And when the consequences are unintended, do you stand up and take responsibility?

Overall, the business world has done a terrible job of understanding the importance of trust. Time after time, our community has flunked trust tests and failed to learn from its mistakes. October 1987 was not just a panic-inducing gyration for investors and the companies, like Fidelity, that served them. It is now recognized as the beginning of the first global financial market correction, as losses from the United States were mirrored by losses in capital markets around the world. And none of the responses to the 1987 crash were enough to prevent the Great Recession of 2008, which was another trust test, which the US banking community—aided and abetted by a host of players in the private sector and in government—flunked. They flunked because their actions led to the longest recession since World War II, officially beginning in December 2007 and ending in June 2009. It took until 2013 for the economy to return to slightly above its previous peak.[6] Trust in business is easily shaken, and regaining it can be a long slog.

During the winter of 2008, when the US government was just beginning its first bailouts, I was teaching the MBA course Leadership and Corporate Accountability. Our class one day raised the question of how a company should think about the tension between "offshoring" a business to a country with lower labor costs and the commitments it had, if any, to local workers. The majority of the class prioritized lower costs over commitments to local workers: a painful illustration of the kind of thinking that helped create the Great Recession.

However, there was a note of hope. After class I was approached by two students, Elana Silver and David Rosales, who were dismayed by the cavalier attitudes shown by their classmates about the effects on employees who would end up being laid off, and on the communities where they worked when their plants were closed down. This research ultimately led me to Tokyo where, perched on banquettes in a hotel lobby, Shalene and I discussed how to broaden my research into a larger strategic question about trust.

Today, the need for business to focus on trust is clearer than ever before. We're past the Great Recession, but the conditions that now shape the landscape have brought trust directly to the forefront of conducting good business.

There is of course the shift to a service economy. Trust changes when an economy relies on services rather than products. I like to think of the difference between products and services as the difference between owning a car (product) and using Uber (service). While a product-based business requires trust at specific times (when I buy my car, or repair it), I am roughly assured of a similar experience each time I use a product, unless it breaks. However, every time I call an Uber I may have a different experience. There are opportunities to betray trust *each time* the truster uses the service. Trust is harder to maintain in service-based businesses because of the sheer volume of interactions. Moreover, the needs of users can vary in ways you can't even begin to imagine.

Second, the extensive deployment of technology has changed the very nature of business, with strong effects on the potential for trust to be enhanced and also betrayed.

In the early, optimistic dawning of the technology era, it seemed like a dream come true. Technology could help companies better manage the problems inherent in a service economy. It could scale far more efficiently than humans could on their own. It would also be more reliable because it could standardize service interactions in ways that imperfect humans never could. Most exciting, technology created opportunities to personalize services for customers. In addition, the porous boundary that separates a service from its users has become nearly invisible, given how willing people are to share aspects of their personal, familial, social, professional, and communal lives through the social media, search, and e-commerce platforms they use.

The ability to share their lives with others through technology has enhanced connection in so many positive ways—connections to individuals known (Hello Mom) and not known (OkCupid), to information about products, services and their creators, and information about historical and contemporary events. It also, as we know, has enabled the dissemination of fake news, and has provided a way of broadcasting and amplifying calls for violence against people. This, of course, is where the problems with technology and trust begin. Many ethical and practical problems haunt this space, but I'll point out just three.

First is the question of data privacy and ownership. Either customers own their data, requiring opt-in or opt-out features that allow them to decide which data are sharable and which are kept private. Or the data are the property of the companies that build the platforms customers use. Tech companies have done a lousy job of spelling out the rules of engagement for data use and sharing, but an excellent job of siphoning data off us and using it to make a healthy profit.

A second ethical problem is the potential for systematic bias and discrimination in the algorithms, based on big data, used to direct services to individual people. Financial institutions like banks can pinpoint the needs of customers based on a fuller understanding of their lives to deliver better services and products. On the flip side, the algorithm could also charge higher interest rates for borrowers who fit nontraditional profiles, creating discriminatory outcomes.[7] Similar problems are encountered in the public domain, where a pre-crime algorithm named PredPol was designed to predict when and where crimes would take place.[8] A study determined that PredPol sent officers to neighborhoods that correlated more with the presence of racial minorities than with the true crime rate of the area.[9]

A third ethical problem is the effects of technology on the future of work. Some experts claim that robots and machines will progressively take over unskilled, semiskilled, and then the bulk of even skilled human jobs,[10] creating a future in which there is less and less work for people to do. Even without such dire consequences, the shift in labor and economic forces will be highly disruptive to the global economy, with a tendency to increase income inequality as the chasm between high-paying jobs and low-paying jobs grows ever larger.

We are facing problems that require cooperation and trust on an unprecedented scale. For example, the tipping point for damage wreaked by global warming will arrive sooner than climate scientists had thought, as early as just twelve years.[11]

A special report of the UN Intergovernmental Panel on Climate Change (IPCC) stressed how important it is that global warming increase only 1.5 degrees Celsius rather than the 2.0°C target set in the 2015 Paris climate accord.[12] The report laid out two paths forward: mitigation and adaptation. Mitigation means actions designed to prevent an increase in global warming, while adaptation refers to actions that accommodate rising global temperatures, such as lowering the demand for energy.[13] The IPCC report concludes with a section devoted to what it will take to limit climate warming to 1.5°C. At its heart are partnerships between the public and the private sectors, investors, government, and academia. It notes that our only chance at saving the planet, and indeed, saving ourselves, will come down to our ability to work together and trust each other.

Finally, much of this book was written during the COVID-19 pandemic. We are witnessing one of the greatest natural experiments of all time, when we can see how the particular combinations of government leadership and cultural preferences for, say, rugged "I don't care about you" individualism, or a willingness to cooperate for the greater good, or unquestioning compliance to authority have created vastly different outcomes. Layer on different attitudes toward science and facts, and internal political, racial, and social tensions, and the world is as uncertain and uneven a place as it may ever have been.

For individuals, rising income inequality in some countries across the world creates a very uneven playing field. On its peaks are people who can retire to summer (or mountain) houses to limit the risk of contagion, nearly all of whom can work from home and have solid healthcare plans. Just below them are families who may now have two people working from home and kids to watch over. Below them are people who live in spaces so small there is no way to quarantine the sick, who need to take public transportation, and must choose between earning an income and being exposed to the virus or losing their income and who may or may not have healthcare. On the valley floor are the newly jobless, the homeless, and all the people whose lives are defined by what they now don't have. In the midst of the peaks and valleys is business, which has the power to reduce these inequalities that undermine society. As we write, we keep monitoring the news to see the latest that companies are doing to help or hinder the safety of employees and customers, and whether they are helping relieve communities that have been hard hit.

We have large problems looming ahead of us. Businesses have the power to help us through this, gaining our trust and our willingness to interact with them, or to cause undue suffering and lose our trust as we saw in the case of the Great Recession. We've written this book because we believe in the potential of business to be a force of good. However, this requires businesses to weave trust into decisions that impact the people and groups they interact with. We developed the trust framework of competence, motives, means, and impact to help businesses do a better job of being trusted. If businesses fold trust into their processes and make it a driving factor in their decision-making, we could unlock a world of potential. Not only could we weather economic and environmental disasters better, we might be able to head them off altogether. Trust, once understood properly, is a powerful force that can change the world for the better.

ONE

WHAT IS TRUST?

He who does not trust enough will not be trusted.

—Lao Tzu

T HERE ARE FEW STORIES ABOUT COMPANIES THAT HAVE lost the trust of the public that have a fairytale-like ending. One of the few classics is the story of Johnson & Johnson's Tylenol recall in the 1980s. In 1982, seven people in Chicago died after taking Tylenol from bottles that had been tampered with and laced with cyanide. Experts predicted Tylenol would never recover. And yet, within two months, Tylenol was back on shelves. Its market share, which had been 37 percent before the crisis, dropped to 7 percent immediately afterwards, but a year later it was back up to 30 percent.[1]

James Burke, Johnson & Johnson's CEO, immediately took control of the situation. He pulled Tylenol from the shelves, recalling 31 million bottles at a time when recalls were rare. Johnson & Johnson designed a new tamper-evident seal for the bottles.[2] In total Burke spent $100 million on the recall: an overreaction, some experts said. Perhaps, but the Tylenol recall established the gold standard for crisis management, Burke made his way onto *Fortune's* list of the ten greatest CEOs of all time, and the recall cemented people's trust in Johnson & Johnson.

Or so we think. The story, however, has a sequel. Between 2009 and 2010, Johnson & Johnson's subsidiary McNeil Consumer Healthcare (which had to execute on the recall after the Tylenol poisonings of 1982) had to issue recalls for several popular children's medications including Tylenol, as well as Benadryl and Motrin. This time the company flubbed badly.

Starting in the early 2000s, McNeil replaced senior leaders in quality control with more junior members, some of whom were contract workers. In 2006, Johnson & Johnson bought the consumer healthcare division of Pfizer, promising substantial cost savings from the merger. McNeil was removed from the pharmaceuticals group at Johnson & Johnson, where stringent quality control and regulatory compliance were essential processes, and was moved to the merged consumer business. Cost reduction targets to justify the merger were described by a McNeil manager as "mind boggling," and "unheard of."[3] Layoffs reduced the workforce. At one facility the workforce dropped by 32 percent between 2005 and 2009 and all employees of the corporate compliance group were let go. Several of the processes for quality testing were truncated. Johnson & Johnson paid a price for this.

In 2009, McNeil issued a recall after discovering bacteria in raw materials at one of its facilities. By April 2010, it would issue another four recalls as customers discovered a moldy smell in the packaging, while others reported that taking the medicine caused them nausea, vomiting, and diarrhea. In January 2010, the FDA finished its months-long inspection of McNeil and concluded that McNeil had not conducted a formal investigation into the likelihood of chemical contamination, despite receiving 8 complaints about gastrointestinal problems from its medications as early as 2008, and 112 complaints about odor between April and August 2009. The FDA roundly criticized Johnson & Johnson for not "assur[ing] timely investigation and resolution of these issues."[4] In May, Congress hauled Johnson & Johnson in for a hearing. There,

Johnson & Johnson revealed it had conducted a "phantom" recall of some 88,000 packages of the pain reliever Motrin, manufactured in 2008, that its own tests had identified as defective. It had a contractor hire a subcontractor to send employees out to purchase the medicine from drugstores while acting like regular customers. In June and July 2010, Johnson & Johnson issued two more recalls. Sales for Johnson & Johnson's pain relievers fell by 56 percent, and its liquid pain relievers (including Children's Tylenol) fell by 96 percent. Overall, the recalls cost Johnson & Johnson an estimated $600 million in revenue: it had lost the trust of the public.

No matter what you may have done in the past, if you don't continue to behave in a trustworthy manner, you will lose the trust of the public. Trust, it turns out, is not a constant: it waxes and wanes, and good behavior in the past does not guarantee protection from mistrust in the future.

What Is Trust?

On a personal level we tend to equate trust with reliability: "I never have to worry when Suzy is on the case since I know she always delivers." Reliability is of course important but does not actually get to the heart of what makes trust so vital. To trust fundamentally means to make yourself vulnerable to the actions of others. We trust because we believe they will do right by us.[5] When we choose to trust someone, we willingly give them power over us, trusting that they will not abuse this power. Trust is a special form of dependence, and is predicated on the idea that we can be more than disappointed: we can be betrayed. Say, for example, you ask Suzy to do some essential number crunching the night before your board presentation. There is always the chance that Suzy could drop the ball and your presentation flops. You are vulnerable because you've placed faith in Suzy to deliver. If there is no possibility of betrayal, then we are not talking about trust, we are talking about reliability, a simpler type of dependence that can lead to disappointment, perhaps, but not that terrible, wrenching feeling of having been betrayed.

Understanding how this works in personal relationships is, it goes without saying, important. However, it becomes even more important—and more complex—when we talk about companies. When we interact with a company, we are also making ourselves vulnerable to it. When we buy a product or a service, we trust that it will work as promised and will not harm us. When we take a job, we trust that a company will treat us fairly. When we invest in a company, we trust that they will give us truthful information to make investment decisions. As members of the public we need to trust that a company will not use its powers to cause undue damage to us. To better understand what trust is and how it works we will dive into the four elements—competence, motives, means, and impact—that make trust actionable. But it is important to clarify four background concepts that help us understand the context trust operates in.

First, we tend to make the assumption that trust is an all or nothing proposition. The reality is much more complex. In actuality, trust is a limited relationship with three parts: the trusted party, the trusting party, and the action the trusted party is expected to perform.[6] We trust people to behave in certain ways based on the customs of the societies we are part of. We also trust people because of the roles they play. For example, we (the trusting party) trust plumbers (the trusted party) to come into our houses because it is their job to fix a leak in a water line (the expected action). We will tell our doctors about our bodies and submit to physicals because we trust the profession of medicine. However, if our plumber was to probe deeply about our health or our doctor about the detailed workings of the kitchen sink, we would have questions.

Zeroing in on the specific role trust plays in our relationship with others is the product of a collaboration between Robert C. Solomon, an American philosophy and business professor who taught at the University of Texas at Austin for over thirty years, and Fernando Flores. Flores is a Chilean who survived three years of imprisonment for his role as finance minister for Salvador Allende, the president of Chile who died following the military coup of 1973. Flores went on to seek refuge in the United States where his achievements spanned philosophy, computer science research, entrepreneurship, and communications. (You are forgiven if you are asking yourself, as I did when I read about Flores's many and varied accomplishments, "And what have I done in *my* life?")[7]

Trust can be between countries, stretching over time and subject to twists and turns as each country takes actions that the others can agree with, or violently dispute. (Think about what the relationship was like between the US and the UK during the late 1700s versus today's so-called special relationship.) The relationship can be between individuals such as the relationship we have with our doctors or plumbers. And, most important for our purposes, trust can be between companies and other people—customers, investors, suppliers, community members, employees, or organizations—be they in companies or countries.

Recognizing that trust is a relationship is powerful because it means you can think about trust as something concrete and real that you can do something about. That's what happened for James Burke as he proactively managed Johnson & Johnson's relationship with the public. The recall showed the public that Johnson & Johnson prioritized customer safety above profits, and its new tamper-evident seal demonstrated to the public that Johnson & Johnson wanted to ensure that poisonings could not happen again because customers could tell if the seals had been broken.

SECOND, WE TEND TO THINK that trust is a result of managing our reputations. In actuality, trust is built from the inside out. While reputations are important, they tend to be built because the company is solid through and through.

This is reflected in virtually all the trusted companies in this book. It was the principle I used, when I was a quality officer at Fidelity, to draw process flows that mapped out all the steps and departments that were involved in creating a positive result for customers. The logic is the same: to build trust you work backwards from the outcome.

Picture the number of steps and processes it takes to research and develop a medication such as Tylenol, manufacture it, and then bring it to market so customers can purchase it at their local drugstore. Lots of hands touch each bottle, and if you want to ensure each bottle is safe, you need every person whose hand touches that bottle to be careful and committed to achieving a high level of quality. The conditions for these feelings on the part of employees are set, in large measure, by the amount of trust that exists between the employees and their employers. In other words, to establish trust with your customers, you need to first establish it with your employees and create processes and standards internally to ensure your products or services are up to standard.

Consider what was happening at McNeil before the 2009–2010 recalls. McNeil had gutted its quality control processes while tests that were hard to meet were removed. One employee recalled that internally some parts of the quality control department were called "EZ Pass System."[8] It was simply a matter of time before something below standard made it to market.

Meanwhile, McNeil had decimated its workforce through layoffs and relied on contract workers. Layoffs are known to have devastating impacts on the morale of surviving employees. What kind of trust could employees have in McNeil when their colleagues were being laid off? In turn, what would that do to their engagement and the amount of care they put into their work, especially when processes for quality control were being curtailed? So, just as trust is built from the inside out, distrust also flows from the inside out, eventually reaching the customer in the form of products and services that are not up to standard.

THIRD, ALL TOO FREQUENTLY WE think trust once lost can never be regained. The truth is more complex and actually difficult to execute: trust once broken can be rebuilt, but only with time and real effort as we saw with the 1982 Tylenol recalls. (And we'll have more stories later that speak to this.) Regaining trust is a long game. You have to persuade the people whose trust you betrayed that you are motivated to get that trust back. You can't just say, "Trust me," and expect anything substantial to result from your encouragement. Trust is earned by listening and responding in an appropriate way to the concerns of others. But in addition to trusting again in your motives, people need to trust in your actions and their impact—another distinction we'll discuss at a later point in the book.

Annette Baier, a philosopher who taught at the University of Pittsburg for most of her career, began a conversation about trust in a seminal article written in 1986.[9] She wanted to answer the question, "Whom should I trust in what way and why?"[10] and goes on to concisely describe the kind of trust we exhibit every day: "We trust those we encounter in lonely library stacks to be searching for books, not victims."[11] Baier reinforces the idea that "some tact and willingness to forgive on the part of the truster and some willingness on the part of the trusted...to be forgiven...seem essential" if trusting relationships are to be sustained over time.[12]

So, be warned: the actions required to regain trust may sometimes stretch your notions of the right thing to do and of what fair treatment looks like, a recognition of the fact that trusting relationships are forged between fallible human beings and the institutions they create.

FINALLY, ROBERT SOLOMON AND FERNANDO Flores also describe the idea that trust creates new opportunities. Solomon had been studying medicine at the University of Michigan when, as he later described to a class at the University of Texas at Austin, he wandered into a lecture by Frithjof Bergmann. Bergmann was lecturing on a question posed by the work of Friedrich Nietzsche, the German philosopher: If given the opportunity to live your life over and over again ad infinitum, forced to go through all of the pain and grief of existence, would you be overcome with despair? Or would you fall to your knees in gratitude? For Solomon, the decision to move from the exacting world of medicine to the haunting questions of philosophy was made that day.[13] And one of those questions, eventually, was about the special force of trusting relationships and the unexpected opportunities they could unleash.

How Does Trust Work?

If you were to take the advice of scientists and researchers, you would make trust a top priority. According to the data, trust has a sizable impact on the economy and people's well-being. In a study of twenty-nine market economies across one decade by the World Values Survey, a 10 percent rise in trust correlated with a 0.8 percent rise in economic growth.[14] Economists Stephen Knack and Philip Keefer built a model that shows that a 15 percent rise in the number of people in a country who think others are trustworthy raises average income 1 percent a year for every single year trust increases. The additional 1 percent of income creates new jobs and more resources to invest in business, which in turn begets more wealth. Conversely, Knack and Keefer's model shows that countries with trust levels below 30 percent are caught in a poverty trap: the lack of trust makes it impossible to do business and create new opportunities.[15] After all, how can an economy grow if people don't trust each other enough to exchange even basic goods and services?

Trust in leaders has an outsized impact on team performance. In a 2000 study of thirty NCAA basketball teams, researchers found that trust in a leader was more important to winning than trust in one's teammates.[16] Teams that trusted their coaches won 7 percent more games than teams that didn't. And the team with the highest trust in its coach won the national championship, while the team with the lowest trust in their coach only won 10 percent of their games. As one player commented, "Once we developed trust in Coach ——, the progress we made increased tremendously because we were no longer asking questions or were apprehensive. Instead, we were buying in and believing that if we worked our hardest, we were going to get there."

This trust in a leader can translate to profits. In a study of 6,500 employees at Canadian and American Holiday Inns, respondents ranked a manager's behavioral integrity (how closely "words and actions aligned") on a 1–5 scale. An eighth of a point score improvement translated into a 2.5 percent increase in revenue. In dollars, that 2.5 percent amounted to $250,000 more in revenue per hotel. Out of all the aspects of manager behavior the researchers studied, trust had the largest impact on profits.[17]

Profits aren't the only benefits of trust. In a meta-analysis of four decades of trust and leadership studies, Kurt Dirks at Washington University in St. Louis and Donald L. Ferrin at State University of New York at Buffalo revealed that trust in leadership positively impacts outcomes such as job performance, overall job satisfaction, commitment to the organization, commitment to a leader's decisions, and overall satisfaction with a leader.[18] The research shows trust has a huge impact on individual behavior, but also on entities as large as national economies, as Knack and Keefer found.

Yet companies do a miserable job of earning trust. According to the Edelman Trust Barometer, an annual survey of trust and credibility that captures data from more than 34,000 respondents in twenty-eight countries,[19] over the past decade trust in business has hovered between 43 percent and 53 percent. In the 2020 barometer, businesses were rated as competent but not trusted to be ethical.[20] (In later chapters we'll discuss how competence is one part of trust but not all of it.) Business was actively distrusted in twelve countries and trust had declined in eight more,[21] while 56 percent of respondents felt that capitalism as it exists today does more harm than good.[22]

Part of the problem is that historically CEOs haven't realized how important trust is. PricewaterhouseCoopers has been surveying CEOs since 1997 to understand what is on the minds of business leaders, but it didn't ask about trust until 2002.[23] This is not a coincidence. The questions were inspired by the collapse of the dotcom bubble and a scandal-ridden environment. In 2001 executives at Enron, a US energy and utilities company, falsely inflated Enron's revenue even though it was losing money, eventually costing shareholders an estimated $74 billion.[24] The following year, WorldCom, a US telecommunications company, filed for bankruptcy because it had cooked its books: it reported profits of $1.4 billion instead of an overall loss.[25]

Yet despite these giant scandals, in 2002, when PricewaterhouseCoopers asked CEOs what they thought about trust, only 12 percent of the surveyed CEOs thought there was a sizable decline of public trust in companies, and only 29 percent believed the reaction to corporate wrongdoing posed a serious threat to business. However, nearly a decade later, some of them were beginning to take notice. In 2013, following the financial crisis and the subsequent slowdown in economies around the world, 37 percent of surveyed CEOs thought that declining trust in business would hurt their companies' growth. By 2017, that number had leapt to 58 percent.[26] The increase is heartening, but it's not enough. Our very economy depends on trust. So, what can companies be doing better?

How Do People Decide Whether to Trust a Company?

My research over the past decade and a half on how companies earn, lose, and regain trust forms the foundation for a framework to help companies understand what trust is and how to earn it. The framework helps explain dilemmas like why we continue to use Uber even though we are angry about how it treats its employees and even when we have the option of downloading Lyft. Or how is it that Recruit Holdings, a Japanese company, can survive a scandal so large that the prime minister and his entire cabinet have to resign, and yet go on to earn $20 billion in revenue?

Each of trust's four components—competence, motives, means, and impact—can be a reason why your company may (or may not) be trusted. We've framed each as the kind of practical questions that customers, employees, investors, suppliers, or government officials might ask themselves to decide if your company is worthy of their trust.

Our goal is to provide you with a road map you can use in your own organization to build, improve, recover, or sustain the trust of the people and groups who rely on you, and whom you rely on, to build a thriving business.

The Four Elements of Trust: Competence, Motives, Means, Impact

Is your company competent? Does it have the ability to innovate, produce, and deliver products and services and to navigate external circumstances? We generally think of a company's competence as being applied to external customers, but a great deal of highly influential work goes into becoming competent at innovating, producing, and delivering processes and operating systems directed at your employees and organization. You might even say that the ability to do this inside work is a prerequisite to building an organization that is capable of being competent on behalf of its external customers. This echoes one of our principles of trust: that trust is built from the inside out. In our next chapter, we'll examine how Uber was able to capitalize on competence to build a company that changed taxis as we know them, and how at the same time, operating on competence alone was not enough to make us trust Uber.

Are you motivated to serve the interests of others as well as your own? The motives of companies, like individuals, play a role in whether they earn our trust. People don't just care about what companies do; they also care about why they are acting as they do, and whose interests they are serving.

Machiavelli makes several appearances throughout the book with his advice that it is better to be feared than loved.[27] His additional warning, however, is frequently, and dangerously, overlooked: "But the prince must none the less make himself feared in such a way that, if he is not loved, at least he escapes being hated."[28] Machiavelli's lesson is that some actions can be taken for motives that are so unacceptable that no response is possible except to hate the person (or company) who made them. We'll see how this plays out in the chapter on competence with the story of Uber, where self-interest led to Uber's poor treatment of employees, customers, and industry players such as regulators and competitors. In the chapter on motives we will analyze the basic promises that customers, employees, investors, and regulators expect from companies. We'll introduce HDFC, an Indian home financing company, which built a reputation for trust by investing in the competition, and Honeywell, which took unprecedented actions during the Great Recession in order to protect its employees and create the road to a fast recovery.

Do you use fair means to achieve your goals? If motives explain why someone should trust your company, the means you use are your "how." They are the way you show you can be trusted because you treat others fairly. Fairness isn't unitary; in fact, there are several different ways by which people can be treated fairly (or not).[29] We'll break down the four different types of fairness: informational fairness, distributive fairness, procedural fairness, and interpersonal fairness. We'll also go on a trip to France, to see how Michelin, the famous tire manufacturer, used all four of these types of fairness in the wake of layoffs that landed them in so much hot water they had to rethink their entire approach to restructuring.

Do you take responsibility for all the impacts you create? The last and arguably most important element of earning trust is the impact of company actions. Impact has a two-part test that helps determine whether a company can be trusted.

First, what impacts have company actions led to? What are the concrete, real, and observable impacts the company has had on the individuals, communities, societies, and countries where it operates?

Second, does the company take responsibility for these impacts, both those that were intended and, even more importantly from the standpoint of trust, those that were *un*intended? The issue here is not about companies' feelings of responsibility. It is about whether and how they act on these feelings to respond to the impacts they create.

We'll discuss both intended and unintended impacts by comparing how Facebook and Pinterest handled the unintended impacts when people used their platforms to post false information. Facebook has been slow to take responsibility for the issue. Pinterest, on the other hand, has given us an entirely new way to think about what it means to take responsibility for the spread of misinformation.

Each of these elements involves a different set of behaviors that you can take, and that others can judge, to help you become trusted. As you think about the four pieces of the trust framework, you may be wondering how the pieces fit together. Do they work like an engine that needs all cylinders to be firing? Not exactly. Rather, the elements are separate components like the drive shaft, brakes, and steering mechanisms in a car, each of which needs to work, but can work—or not—even if other parts aren't. This means you can be trusted on some elements but not on others, as we will see. However, cars run best when all of their elements are working, and trust is similar. The more elements on which you perform well in the eyes of your employees or customers, the better.

In addition, since much of how companies earn trust is tied to how leaders behave, we'll also take a chapter to discuss what trusted leadership looks like and what it doesn't look like. Our journey will take us through a variety of venues as we develop a clearer understanding of trust, from Saudi Arabia to learn how a young woman turned around the country's largest investment bank, and time-traveling back to the 1970s to learn how Katharine Graham, the publisher of the *Washington Post*, used these trust elements to navigate the Pentagon Papers and the Watergate scandal.

Finally, we'll conclude by painting the vision of trust's true potential: the possibilities trust unlocks, from creating movements to total transformations of individuals, companies, and even industries. Trust, once understood properly, is a powerful force that can unlock unprecedented change.

TWO

COMPETENCE

The Art and Science of Excellence

It is easier to do a job right than to explain why you didn't.
—MARTIN VAN BUREN

COMPETENCE, WHICH REFERS TO SKILL OR ABILITY, IS the *sine qua non*—the foundation of trust. Without competence, it is unlikely you will win other types of trust. Once you are trusted for competence, it's the go-ahead for building other types of trust. Although a foundation is the starting point for building a house, it still needs walls and a roof to make it complete. Competence alone, as we'll see in the case of Uber, is not enough to build and maintain trust.

Uber, the uber-popular ride-hailing app, is perhaps the best illustration for understanding the importance of competence in establishing trust, but that by itself it is like a house lacking walls and a roof. Bear with us for a second and no eye-rolling, please, since we understand that, at first blush, Uber and trust can seem like oil and water. But, as we'll see, Uber's story takes us a long way down the road of understanding how trust is built... and lost.

According to company legend, Uber was born in 2008, when two friends, Travis Kalanick and Garrett Camp, were attending a conference in Paris on a cold night and couldn't find a cab.[1] Since both were tech moguls, instead of throwing up their hands, they came up with another solution: build an app that lets you book and pay for a ride by pushing a few buttons. In 2010, Uber launched its first ride in San Francisco.[2] Five years later, Uber had reached 1 million drivers, and launched in 360 cities across the globe.[3]

It was easy to see why Uber had become wildly successful. Instead of trying to flag down a taxi that may or may not stop, where the driver may or may not bark at you while overcharging you, or worrying about calling up a dispatch service that may or may not send a cab in time, Uber offered a completely different experience. The app let you book a ride instantly, see the price upfront, track the car on a map so you knew where it was, and automatically pay through a stored credit card. Uber offered a lot to love.

However, for anyone paying attention, there were a lot of reasons to worry about what kind of company Uber was. A few of the highlights: Uber earned a reputation for ruthlessness because it turned on surge pricing—a feature where the price of an Uber increases when there's more demand—during several emergencies. During a 2013 snowstorm in New York City the price of an Uber ride went up by as much as seven times,[4] while Uber's surge pricing kicked in for customers fleeing from a hostage situation in Sydney.[5] In December 2013, an Uber driver ran into a family in San Francisco, killing a six-year-old girl and injuring her mother and brother. The family sued Uber and the driver, but Uber decried responsibility saying that since the driver didn't have a passenger and hadn't accepted the next ride, they technically weren't working for Uber at the moment.[6] (Uber did eventually settle and change its policy to cover drivers who had the app activated but had not accepted a ride, while the driver was charged with vehicular manslaughter.)[7]

In 2014, a passenger was raped by an Uber driver in Delhi, leading Delhi to temporarily ban Uber in the region and raise questions about whether Uber was doing enough to vet drivers.[8] The same year, news broke about Operation SLOG, Uber's ruthless scheme to poach drivers under Lyft's nose, which we'll cover later.[9]

This, however, all occurred during Uber's golden era, when things were going relatively well.

Uber's fall came in 2017 when it went through a blood bath. One disaster followed another. The year began with a social media campaign to delete Uber, which an estimated 200,000 people actually did. In February, Susan Fowler, a former Uber employee, published a whistleblowing blog post about sexual harassment at the company, a culture that was toxic for women, and full of political back-stabbing.[10] In the same month, Waymo, Google's self-driving car project, sued Uber for stealing trade secrets.[11] In March, the *New York Times* broke the Greyball story: For years Uber had used a tool called Greyball that specifically targeted city officials and showed them a fake version of the app in cities where they were banned. The city official would see icons of cars on apps but be unable to book an actual car and ticket it.[12] In June the news broke that Uber executives had illegally obtained the medical records of the Delhi passenger who had been raped.[13] During the same month, the law firm Perkins Coie, which had been hired to investigate Fowler's claims about sexual harassment, found 215 human resources claims of sexual harassment, bullying, and bias. In 100 cases no action had been taken, and 57 cases were still open.[14] At the same time, former attorney general Eric Holder, whose law firm had also been hired to conduct a separate investigation of Uber's broken culture, released his report and strongly recommended that Travis Kalanick's role be reallocated.[15] Throughout the first half of the year a wave of executives were fired or asked to leave due to charges of sexual harassment, stealing medical records, and sexism, culminating in CEO Travis Kalanick's ouster in June 2017.[16]

The depth of Uber's fall from grace can be seen in its loss of market share to its competitor Lyft. In January 2015, Uber controlled 90 percent of the market share of ride-hailing in America, while Lyft had about 9 percent.[17] Three years later, that had dropped to 69 percent while Lyft's market share had risen to 28 percent.[18]

In 2018, Uber had been preparing for its IPO. Despite the trials and tribulations of the past year, bankers foresaw a rosy future for Uber. The likes of Morgan Stanley and Goldman Sachs calculated that Uber's debut could hover around $120 billion. Experts wondered if Uber would outperform Facebook's 2012 IPO at $104 billion.[19]

And yet, Uber's road to an IPO was rocky. Its biggest investor, Japanese firm SoftBank, funded competition in China and Latin America—a huge blow since Latin America was Uber's fastest growing market. Meanwhile, SoftBank poured money into the American company, DoorDash, one of Uber's competitors for its food delivery service. Uber's growth began to slow, blunting investor appetites. Meanwhile, early investors who had acquired Uber's stock cheaply were put off by the now higher prices.

On May 10, 2019, Uber went public and fell flat on its face.[20] Uber set the price at $45 per share, but when the day began the price started at $42 and dropped to below $42 per share. Uber closed the day valued at $69.7 billion.[21] Uber's IPO made history for a different reason: the gap between its expected value and its actual valuation was larger than any other American company's initial public offering since at least 1975.[22]

Like many others, we've gone through our own tortured relationship with Uber—we hate Uber one week and love it the next, which illustrates the powerful yet limited ways in which trust in competence works.

In 2017 Shalene was one of the 200,000 users who deleted their accounts when #DeleteUber went viral.[23] When President Trump issued an executive order banning all foreign nationals from seven different Muslim-dominated countries, the New York Taxi Workers Alliance declared an hour-long ban on pickups at JFK airport. On the same day, Uber tweeted that it would be turning off its much-reviled surge pricing, where the price of an Uber increases as demand for rides spikes—a move that the public saw as Uber trying to capitalize on the strike so it could gain more business. As a result #DeleteUber started trending, encouraging people to delete the app.

A year later, Shalene moved. Her new apartment was farther away from public transit and she didn't have a car or a bike. Her only option for getting to work was to walk—which was fine, until it rained or snowed, and since we're in Boston, that's not infrequent. Shalene hesitated, stuck with Lyft, and then when a particularly snowy week hit, and Uber offered her a promotion that meant she could ride to work for a couple of dollars, she capitulated. Cringing, she redownloaded the app and ordered an Uber.

Shalene isn't alone. In 2014—before the crest of the Uber scandal wave—the *New York Times* published an article on "Uber angst," the phenomenon of using Uber or wanting to use Uber while dealing with guilt over its policies.[24] Yet, in 2017, despite the slew of bad press and scandals, Uber powered over 4 billion rides, with an average of about 75 million active riders per month.[25] We love Uber. We hate Uber. And we can't walk away. Why?

Trust Starts with Competence

In a word, because Uber is competent. Competence is a company's ability to create and deliver a product or a service. In the case of Uber this means getting a customer like Shalene from her apartment to her office at Harvard Business School. Competence is the bedrock that trust rests upon. Without it, a company will not get off the ground. This looks like an obvious and almost humorously "duh" insight. Why would anyone trust a company that's *not* competent? Yet, competence has its limits: it's a big part of trust but not all of it. Competence can take a company a long way—but not all the way, as we saw with Uber, because it turns out, trust is multifaceted. It relies on several different elements.

Scholars have long wrestled with the nature of trust. This perhaps is because our understanding of trust is flimsy: we bandy the word about and use it to refer to a potpourri of characteristics. In the days of togas and laurels, Aristotle argued that in order to gain the trust of listeners a speaker had to have ethos (character), pathos (emotion), and logos (logic). Ethos refers to the moral character of the speaker, pathos to the emotions the listener feels, and logos to the sound logic of the argument.[26] In other words—there's more than one way to gain trust, and these ways vary vastly from the moral domain, to the emotional, to the logical.

Many centuries later, specifically in 1995, three management researchers—Roger C. Mayer of North Carolina State University, James H. Davis of Utah State University, and F. David Schoorman at Purdue University—reviewed over twenty academic studies to understand the elements of trust.[27] They came up with a list of trust factors that included words like ability, integrity, goodwill, benevolence, and openness. While this might sound like a word salad, an overall theme of two types of trust emerged.

First, there's competence-based trust: trust that's based on skill and expertise. This kind of trust is logic based—or logos based if you want to get your Greek on—and comparatively amoral. Here we're not concerned with whether someone is right or wrong, just whether they are effective. For example, think of a customer who is on a budget and looking for a way to get from her apartment to her office quickly.

The second type of trust is bound up in our ideas of morality and has an emotional aspect. This is trust based on our sense of how we are being treated: Do we believe the other party cares about us? Are they fair and principled? What is the overall impact of their actions on us? For example, think of a customer who wants to know that when she pays for a taxi ride, those dollars go to a company that cares about environmental sustainability and treats its employees well. We will be covering the different elements of this kind of trust in the next three chapters, where we discuss trust based on motives (do we believe the other party cares about us?), trust based on means (do we believe the other party treats us fairly?), and trust based on impact (what is the effect of the other party's actions on us?). However, for now we'll just focus on competence.

To really understand competence's role in trust, we'll start with one of our core trust principles: *trust is a limited relationship*. To have trust in a relationship we do not need to assume that the other person will be competent in *every* way. If you're running or working in a company, this should be good news. Strategy 101: no company can be good at everything. However, while companies don't have to be good at everything, they do promise to be good at certain things, and they must live up to those promises. For example, this means we trust Uber will get us home from work, or from home to the theater. It does not mean that we expect Uber to safely move our furniture or watch our children or pets if we happen to leave them behind in the car.

Shankar Ganesan, a business professor at Notre Dame, conducted a study to examine why companies develop long-term relationships with their suppliers.[28] He found two key factors fostered long-term relationships: dependence and trust. Dependence makes sense: if you run a peach jam factory and only one farmer sells peaches, you're stuck buying from the farmer even if you think she treats her employees terribly. In part, this explains Uber's appeal. Uber provides transportation between destinations that are not linked by public transportation, often at the lowest price in the market. (Anyone who has spent an hour on the Boston subway, which operates on a hub-and-spoke model, will well appreciate the magic of Uber. Instead of spending an hour traveling from Cambridge to Jamaica Plain—which is all of six miles by road—an Uber can take you there in twenty minutes, often for a much cheaper price than a taxi.) However, Ganesan found dependence was not enough. Trust was required to develop a long-term relationship.

But what kind of trust? Ganesan broke trust down further into cognitive trust (trust in a vendor's expertise and reliability) and affective trust (trust in a vendor's motives and actions). He found that a vendor's expertise and reliability was the most important aspect of trust between buyers and vendors, and that makes sense. In order for buyers and vendors to do business with each other they had to believe in each other's competence. Buyers and vendors needed to trust that the other party would stick to their commitments and that they were good at their jobs. This applies to Uber too: we may not trust Uber's good intentions, but we're still willing to use it because it can get the job done. If Uber didn't work and didn't send us a car whenever we ordered one, we would stop using it.

Competence, then, is the necessary first step for building other types of trust. Daniel J. McAllister, a business professor at the National University of Singapore, studied how trust between managers and their peers worked. He surveyed trios of business managers and professionals on their "cognition-based trust" and their "affect-based trust." To measure cognition-based trust, McAllister surveyed the managers about how they felt about each other's ability to do their job, including whether or not they were perceived as dedicated, created more work for others, or needed to be monitored to ensure they would produce.[29] To measure affect-based trust, or how managers treated each other, he asked them whether they shared ideas, if they could speak openly to each other, and if they trusted each other to respond constructively and caringly to the other managers' problems. He found that, overall, managers had more cognition-based trust in each other than in the affective aspect of trust, which is consistent with the idea that the ability to do one's job is the foundation that affective trust is built on. However, he found that higher levels of cognition-based trust also tended to result in higher levels of affective trust in each other. McAllister explained that people will not invest in others or develop deep relationships unless there's a baseline of trust in one's ability to do one's job. Once that baseline has been met, people will start to develop other, more complex types of trust.[30] For example, managers who developed these deeper types of trust took each other's needs into account while making decisions that affected both parties, considered problems to be communal and a shared responsibility, and refrained from tit-for-tat thinking and worrying about who got credit for work.[31]

While trust can be divided into different categories, the same is true for competence. On one end of the spectrum there's Uber, that can make a car arrive at your door with the tap of a button, but leave you feeling rather slimy. On the other end, there is The Ritz-Carlton (yes, they prefer that the *T* is capitalized), which has spent so much time thinking about how to provide excellent service that its care for people is palpable. Uber and The Ritz-Carlton are examples of competence that manifest in very different ways.

Technical competence is a company's ability to produce a product or a service, which Uber and The Ritz do extraordinarily well. However, there's a second type of competence: managerial competence. Managerial competence is a company's ability to adjust to shifting conditions and manage relationships with different groups in order to accomplish set goals.[32] Uber's take on managerial competence was purely self-interested, while The Ritz coupled managerial competence with a genuine care for employees and customers to deliver incredible results. We will explore how both types of competence manifested in both companies.

Technical Competence: The Science of Process Engineering

I joined Fidelity Investments, as I noted earlier, after a ten-year stint in fashion retailing. I continue to get excited about the rise and fall of hemlines, the shift in silhouettes and colors that go with the times (khaki military-style jackets for hard times, embellished velvet blazers in jewel tones for when the economy is on the up-swing), and the difference that a new outfit can make in my sense of well-being. But after ten years, I was eager to care about a different kind of customer need. Fidelity gave me the opportunity to help customers who were saving for their retirement, or putting their kids through college, or just trying to make the most of their financial resources through wiser investing.

One of the projects at Fidelity that drove home the importance of sound process design as the foundation for competence and trust was the transfer of the assets of a deceased family member. This process was the brainchild of Fidelity's then chairman and CEO, Edward (Ned) Johnson III, who realized that the spouses of customers who had recently died needed unique types of support at a particularly fraught time in their lives. I blush to confess that inside Fidelity this process improvement project was dubbed the "Pearly Gate" or the "Death Gate." But once we dug into the details of managing the financial side of death, we realized we had an opportunity to make a really, really tough time in someone's life a little easier. We created a specialized team in one of our call centers to handle this work. While the team was trained to be sensitive, it was just as important that they were effective. The last thing a grieving spouse should have to deal with is a glitch in the system for handling financial assets. My personal aha from this experience was that sound process design is the foundation of building trust en masse. Ever since, processes have been dear to my heart.

Companies like Fidelity that become trusted for their technical competence reliably live up to the promises they make to their customers. They do what they are supposed to do extremely well, and can repeatedly produce the same result for customers over and over again.

Returning to Uber, let's take a moment to appreciate the magic of Uber's processes. Its technical competence enabled the creation of systems and processes that produced experiences that built its business. Understanding why Uber was able to gain an overwhelming position in the market requires knowing a bit of history, so we'll take a few steps back in time to discuss the ride-sharing apps that came before Uber, as told by Brad Stone in his book *The Upstarts.*

Stone tells the story of Tom DePasquale, who founded Taxi Magic in 2007. Taxi Magic was an app that worked with taxi companies to pair customers and drivers. It allowed customers to use their phones to choose a taxi company, book the taxi, and pay for the ride. However, the app partnered with taxi fleet owners, not drivers.

When a customer booked a cab through Taxi Magic, the dispatch system assigned drivers based on which ones had been waiting for passengers the longest, instead of which drivers were closest. The Taxi Magic app didn't have a map that showed passengers the location of the driver. Instead, customers received a status page with their driver's name and an estimate of how far away the driver was. Since drivers had no particular obligation to pick up a customer or to use Taxi Magic, a driver might abandon a Taxi Magic customer if he or she found another customer en route.[33] Meanwhile, as long as taxi drivers paid them rent, the fleet owners were satisfied and had no incentive to think about the level of service taxi drivers provided.

Taxi Magic was followed by Cabulous in 2009, a company that was developed in a Best Buy incubator program to find and nourish employee start-up ideas.[34] (Best Buy never took any equity in the company.) The app allowed customers to see cabs on a map, and customers could use the app or call the fleet to book a ride—and they could even hail their favorite driver. Cabulous ran into a few problems when it started because at first it relied on drivers to use their own phones, many of which did not work well so the app's performance was shaky. However, Cabulous faced a larger problem: it had no ability to influence supply and demand. On busy nights, drivers wouldn't turn on the app and customers were left to old-fashioned human ride-hailing: arm raised high in the air, urgent running to intercept an approaching taxi, and all the other pre-Uber delights of getting a cab.

Uber developed a host of new processes to improve the experience of ordering a ride. To begin with, Uber made sure there were enough drivers on the streets through the much reviled surge pricing. It earned plenty of bad press but solved an important problem, which was ensuring that Uber could actually influence supply and demand. If there was a huge demand for rides after a concert, by raising the price of a ride, Uber could motivate more drivers to get on the road, while decreasing customer demand. Surge pricing enabled Uber to manage the demand problems that Cabulous failed to address. Then there's everything from the work Uber did to make sure passengers and drivers can find each other by providing an interactive map and contact information, to transparent automatic billing, charging passengers a fee for no-shows, and finally the rating system where both customers and drivers rate each other, reinforcing good behavior from both parties.

In order to make all these customer-facing processes happen, Uber needed to create ambitious back-end processes. Uber collects a wealth of data on driver behavior—everything from speed to harsh braking[35]—and pairs them with processes to improve service.[36] On the front end, drivers receive messages urging them to take breaks and keep their smartphones mounted to the car's dashboard, as well as data on how their driving compares to other local drivers.[37] Uber's processes are definitely subpar when it comes to driver privacy concerns. But, solely from a customer perspective,

Uber's innovations have transformed the taxi experience from utterly painful to purely addictive. As one journalist wrote in *Fast Company*,

> Uber has made life dramatically easier on those who can't afford a Manhattan apartment or to live especially close to a subway stop. Back in the old days, if you wanted to take a taxi home...the city's iconic yellow cab drivers generally flat-out refused to take you to a borough. If you managed to get in the cab, they might simply drive around in circles, with the meter running, until you got out, miles away from your destination. And they also routinely racially profiled passengers and refused to take anyone to neighborhoods like Harlem that are predominantly African American.[38]

Love or hate Uber, their processes have transformed the taxi industry. Uber's processes are a continuation into the twenty-first century of the principles of process design and improvement that came from the thinkers and doers in the "hard" world of product manufacturing. The building blocks of these systems and processes are people, physical resources, and technology.

Technical competence is the science of combining people, resources, and technology into a process that reliably produces a product or customer experience. Hundreds of years of thinking have shaped process design, and the weight of this thought has gone on to influence how we think about processes today. It would take another book—or library—to catalog all the thinking on how to craft a good business process. The sensibilities and values companies think about as they design their processes will vary, as will the constraints they are dealing with, such as limited resources in a postpandemic economy or a start-up strapped for capital.

However, a good process is about reliability in delivering a product or service that is fit for use; that is, it does what it is supposed to do. Whatever industry you are in, many of the fundamentals are the same. Focus on the needs of customers. Think about your business as a series of processes that have the customer at one end, and at the other a web of functions, departments, suppliers, and organizations that need to be linked together as a smooth chain that connects your company to the experience the customer has. Involve the people who do the work in improving how it's done. Why? They know the most about it. Drive out waste—wait times, excess materials and scrap jobs that don't contribute to creating value for the customer. Waste is not just bad for costs; it's a sign of processes that could be improved. Collect data and study them to continuously improve the processes and the work that people do, so you get better and better at meeting customer needs.

Processes are not just reserved for creating products or technology: they can also be applied to human behavior. The Ritz-Carlton's "Gold Standards" are a good example of the idea that technical competence is the ability to create *any* of the necessary infrastructure to create a desired customer experience. They are the brainchild of Horst Schulze,[39] former president and chief operating officer, a smallish, dapper, charismatic figure who, after joining in 1984, created out of whole cloth The Ritz-Carlton management and human resource systems and the values that drove them, and championed the application of total quality management in the hotel chain. The Gold Standards are the foundation for delivering on the customer promise of The Ritz-Carlton.[40] The first standard comprises their Three Steps of Service:

1. A warm and sincere greeting.
2. Use the guest's name. Anticipation and fulfillment of each guest's needs.
3. Fond farewell. Give a warm good-bye and use the guest's name.[41]

This is a brilliant piece of behavior engineering—simple, clear, and memorable—that allows the thousands of people who work at The

Ritz-Carlton globally to consistently produce *customized personal experiences.*

Schulze then created the more detailed The Ritz-Carlton "Basics." There are twenty of them. One requires Ritz associates to use the Three Steps of Service in every interaction. Others provide concise principles to apply to more complex processes, such as handling guest complaints. That basic states, "Whoever receives a complaint will own it, resolve it to the guest's satisfaction, and record it."

Behind that statement is a detailed procedure for handling guest difficulties. It requires employees to break away from work—to stop doing whatever they are doing to take care of the guest. This involves using a process called LEAP when interacting with the unhappy customer: **l**isten, **e**mpathize, **a**sk for clarification, and **p**roduce a solution. Employees then follow up with the guest within twenty minutes to find out if the guest is satisfied with the solution. Finally, they record what happened on a form that includes a before and after spectrum of "guest temperature" on a scale of "livid" to "calm"[42] and whether the problem was resolved to the guest's satisfaction.[43] This form is distributed to all departments involved and reviewed the next morning at the hotel's daily lineup.

The daily lineup is a ten- to fifteen-minute meeting held by every department, every day, in every Ritz-Carlton around the world. In addition to discussing problems, the hotel's employees will also discuss their experience with The Ritz-Carlton's Basics. The corporate vice president of human resources explained why. "After cleaning 16 rooms to our standards, you are exhausted.... If I don't remind you that customers are important, that being nice to them is critical, that eliminating defects is paramount, that the genuine care of the customer is crucial, well, then you'll forget. You'll think that you just come to work to clean rooms."[44]

The Ritz-Carlton twice won the US Malcolm Baldridge National Quality Award, first in 1992, when it was the only hotel company to ever win the award. Examiners identified more than seventy specific areas in which they could improve. The Ritz worked on those and in 1999 became the first and only service company to win the award twice.[45] Since then, its various locations have racked up a long list of awards for quality, including the Forbes Travel Guide five-star hotel award each year from 2002 to 2020,[46] and multiple awards from J.D. Power and Condé Nast.[47]

Technical competence requires that companies engage in continuous process improvement. It is a never-ending battle to keep doing what you do extremely well.

Managerial Competence: The Art of Navigation

The Ritz-Carlton was one of the first companies I studied when I moved from Fidelity to begin a career in teaching and research at Harvard Business School. From the moment I entered The Ritz-Carlton in 2000, I knew I was dealing with a company that embodied excellence in customer service. In one especially striking instance, I got to walk down the stairs to the ballroom level of the hotel in the West End district of Washington, DC, with new employees who were about to start their training. It was one of those wide and gracious "grand" staircases. Lined up on both sides were the local DC managers as well as Ritz employees who had been flown in to help with the training. As I passed, each person said, "Welcome!" "I'm so glad you're here!" and "Thank you for joining us!" I must confess that in a life blessed with many, many happy moments (marrying a wonderful husband, parenting two kids I treasure, being lucky to work with Shalene), I felt a remarkable warmth and feeling of acceptance as I walked down those stairs. And I wasn't even an employee! Talk about an experience of excellence that was filled with warmth.

While companies can build their processes in-house and exercise unfettered control over them, they must also manage relationships with a number of different groups in order to navigate an uncertain environment. You need to understand what your customers want and how this varies from customer segment to customer segment. You must be able to work with suppliers and civil partners such as NGOs, media, and unions, as well as government officials and regulators to be able to bring your product or service to market. You must identify potential and existing competitors and know how to deal with them in order to survive and thrive. Above all, you must be able to motivate your employees so they will want to stay at the company and do the best work possible. In short, managerial competence is the art of managing internal and external relationships so the company can achieve its objectives and adapt to changing circumstances.

On the most fundamental level of managerial competence, to successfully deliver a product or a service you must understand your customers' needs in the present as well as the future. Understanding goes beyond listening to what customers say they want. You need to read the room and intuit what customers will want. Think Steve Jobs, who famously said, "Our job is to figure out what they're going to want before they do. I think Henry Ford once said, 'If I'd asked customers what they wanted, they would have told me, "A faster horse!"' People don't know what they want until you show it to them."[48]

Thanks to Apple's commitment to anticipating customer needs, we have the iPod, iPhone, iPad, and Apple Watch, and the company has surprised and delighted its customers for decades.

At heart, Jobs was discussing innovation. While we tend to think of innovation as inventing clever new products and processes that make life easier, that's only one part of innovating—the technical competence part. In order to convince customers to purchase something new that they don't understand—such as a car or an mp3 player—you have to be able to understand what customers can and can't absorb. (For those of you who are too young to remember, an mp3 player is a device that plays mp3s, which are digital audio files. People used them during the dark and dreary stone age when phones could not play songs.)

Steve Jobs did not earn his fame because he was the world's best engineer or computer programmer. Steve Jobs is celebrated because he understood how to create new products and turn them into essentials. When the iPod entered the market, there were about fifty other digital music players on the market. None of them were popular because there was no efficient way to load songs onto these players. Broadband internet wasn't widely available, which meant it could take hours to download multiple songs, and there wasn't a major retailer selling mp3s. First, the iPod used a FireWire instead of USB cables. At the time a USB could transfer about 1.5 megabytes per second, while a FireWire could transfer 25 megabytes per second, making it much faster to load music on an iPod.[49]

Second, Apple's iPod entered the market in 2001, three years after the first mp3 player was announced. However, by 2001, the number of homes with broadband internet was growing, and two years later, Apple created the iTunes Music Store where customers could purchase albums or songs piecemeal. The iPod became the best-selling mp3 player on the market.[50]

Jobs understood that a music player without music was pointless. Apple also couldn't directly change the prevalence of broadband internet. However, what Jobs could manage was adding a cable that was faster and timing the release of the iPod with an ecosystem that would set it up to become a product customers loved instead of an overpriced paperweight.

Companies that have made names for themselves for being innovators are not only excellent at producing a new product or service—they've done an extensive amount of work to create something that fills an existing customer need, as well as make it intuitive and easy to use.

Once a company understands what customers want and need, they also need to be able to take the product or service to market, and build an ecosystem filled with competitors and regulators, both of whom have the ability to stop a company in its tracks.

Here Uber is a complex case. It faced a highly regulated industry whose players did their best to shield themselves from newcomers. Around the time of Uber's conception, the taxi industry was highly fragmented and dominated by local operators.[51] In a savvy move, Uber started off in the black car service, which was less regulated than the taxi industry, and even then, entering that market had several challenges. As Brad Stone relates in *The Upstarts*, in 2003, Jason Finger, the cofounder of Seamless, an online food delivery service, wanted to enter the black car business in New York. Advisors warned him to be careful since rumor had it that the mafia was involved. When Finger received a threatening message on his office voicemail he exited the black car business. As Finger and his wife recall, the message went something like this:

> Jason, we understand you've been pitching a car service to large enterprises in the New York City area. We don't think that would be a good idea. You've got such a beautiful family. Why don't you spend more time with your beautiful baby daughter? You've got such a good thing going with your food business. Why would you want to broaden into other areas?[52]

When Uber started in San Francisco, its executive team didn't receive death threats, but Uber did—in a manner of speaking. In 2010, Uber received cease and desist notices from the California Public Utilities Commission, which regulated livery service, and the San Francisco Municipal Transportation Agency, which regulates taxis. Uber ignored these and continued to operate even in the face of fines and possible jail time. Travis Kalanick even humblebragged at a 2011 conference, "I think I've got 20,000 years of jail time in front of me."[53]

Uber was on tricky terrain that required clever maneuvering. It developed a strict process for entering new cities that included sending in two teams that worked over six weeks to ensure Uber was ready to operate,[54] and wooing local influencers by offering them free rides and hosting splashy launch parties. Its tactics were also aggressive. The guidelines for entering a new city included hiring lobbyists and lawyers to deal with anyone who protested the tactics Uber used, such as blithely running over regulations, in accordance with its modus operandi of expand, expand, expand.[55] Perhaps there was no other way for Uber to take on regulators, but Uber's tactics went far beyond aggressive and into brutal territory, and then went far past brutal into flat-out-wrong land.

On the brutal side, when New York City mayor Bill de Blasio proposed capping the growth of Ubers on the road in 2015 to 1 percent until September 2016 (at the time Uber was growing 3 percent a month),[56] Uber added a "de Blasio" tab to its app, which was available to about 2 million New York City customers, showing how much wait times would go up if the cap were approved by city council.[57] They coupled that with letters and ads depicting de Blasio as being an "obstacle" for working residents of the city.[58] The tab was an innovative way to illustrate to Uber's customers how a cap would impact their lives. Effective? Perhaps. De Blasio ultimately backed down.[59] However, it didn't win Uber any friends in the mayor's office, and the story has a sequel (stay tuned).

Apple was able to flatten the existing competition by sailing into the market with a well-designed product at the right time. Poor design and high prices hobbled the existing competition— for example, one existing player stored fifteen songs and sold for $200, while the first iPod cost $399 and held up to five gigs of music.[60] By 2004, Apple had 92 percent of the market.[61] Meanwhile, its competition finally got its act together and started to unroll new devices, but by then it was too late—Apple was deeply entrenched in the market.[62]

Uber was in a different situation. It had a competitor that offered a fairly similar service of booking rides through your phone: Lyft.[63] Apple's tactics wouldn't be as easy to apply here since Lyft offered a comparable service. So, what next?

Here, Uber's take-no-prisoners approach drove right into flat-out-wrong territory. In 2014, before Uber's campaign against the proposed NYC cap, news reports revealed Uber had developed a process called Operation SLOG (Supplying Long-Term Operations Growth) to stymie Lyft's growth. Uber gave contractors burner phones and credit cards. They booked rides with Lyft drivers and tried to recruit them for Uber and received up to $750 for each driver successfully recruited.[64] In true Uber form, the process was incredibly well thought out, and Uber contractors working for SLOG received a thorough briefing email that laid out exactly what to do, from the questions to ask during small talk, to how to respond depending on what the driver being recruited said.[65]

In addition, Uber employees booked rides with competitors Lyft and Gett and then canceled them in order to throw a wrench into their operations.[66] Lyft estimated Uber employees booked and canceled more than 5,000 rides in a period of almost a year, between 2013 and 2015.[67]

Uber's ruthlessness also manifested in its treatment of drivers. It used psychological tactics to manipulate drivers into working more. Typically, there are laws preventing employers from doing this, but since Uber drivers are contractors, they have fewer legal protections. Uber made merry with driver data and designed processes to "gamify" driving so it became addictive. When drivers reached the end of their shift, they received messages urging them to stay on. Furthermore, drivers can receive badges such as "Excellent Service" and "Entertaining Drive." Uber driver Josh Streeter reported receiving several messages like "Make it to $330. You're only $10 away from making $330 in net earnings. Are you sure you want to go offline?"[68] Meanwhile the app also displays the number of trips drivers have made during the week, how much money they've made, their overall ratings, and how much time they've spent driving. In addition, Uber (and Lyft) uses forward dispatching, which means that drivers are paired with the next client before their current ride ends. This is ostensibly good for drivers because idle time means they aren't getting paid, but it's also great for Uber and Lyft because it keeps drivers on the road, creating a steady supply. Meanwhile, drivers got to the point where they weren't even taking bathroom breaks, so Uber finally installed a pause button.[69] These tactics are clever, yes, but whom do they benefit? The drivers or Uber? As for customers—is it even a good idea to get into a car where your driver is tired and possibly needs to use the restroom?

Contrast this with how The Ritz-Carlton chose to motivate employees. When I was at the all-hands meeting of new hires, Horst Schulze led the new employees down the stairs then bounded to the stage to the familiar motivational pull of Queen's "We Will Rock You." He began his address by describing his philosophy of service:

> You are not servants. We are not servants. Our profession is service. You are Ladies and Gentlemen, just as the guests are, who we respect as Ladies and Gentlemen. We are Ladies and Gentlemen and should be respected as such.... If we do what we do right, we become as important as the [guests] are.[70]

The Ritz-Carlton's values of equality and respect for the work of service were married to a promotional system that encouraged and rewarded excellence with upward mobility. Schulze, after all, had started his career in Germany as a busboy. At the time I was conducting my research, 25 percent of The Ritz's managers had begun their careers in roles as housekeepers, restaurant servers, and hourly supervisors.

After the all-hands meeting, Schulze met separately with the new managers of the hotel, who he believed had deep obligations to the hotel's rank-and-file employees. "People have a right to come to work for a purpose. The chairs you are sitting on are doing work. If you don't give your employees a purpose, you make them chairs."

This is not to say that The Ritz-Carlton is solely focused on its employees' well-being. The Ritz's standards are high. In Schulze's address to new managers, he told them point-blank that The Ritz existed to make money, and employees had to perform to a high standard:

> We still only deliver 92% of customers who are satisfied. That gives us occupancy of 80%. Why not celebrate? Only 8% are not satisfied. Of those, 2% to 3% want things we cannot do, or things that, if we did them, would dissatisfy all of the other customers. But 5% represent satisfaction that we want. Those 5% are dissatisfied because of stupid, pathetic defects that are repeating—stupid, pathetic defects that you should have eliminated permanently. That 5% translates into 200,000 dissatisfied customers. That is an army—attacking us—saying that we are not good. If we satisfied this 5%, within three years we'd run at 88% occupancy. What does 88% mean in dollars? Three hundred million to the bottom line. We are leaving $300 million on the table because of 5% defects.[71]

When I teach this case study, I ask students for a show of hands of who would want to be a manager at The Ritz-Carlton. Given the harshness of Schulze's tone, I always expect that number to be low, but it's usually at least 30 percent or more of the class. When I ask them why they'd want to work as a manager at The Ritz, the students say that they'd love to work somewhere where the management is so clear and transparent about what they are trying to achieve. They get it that it's their job to improve how reliably and consistently the company proves its competence.

It's not just my students. Employees respond well too: When I studied The Ritz, the annual rate of employee turnover in the hotel industry for hotels that had been operating for at least a year was

100 percent. In 2019 it had dropped to 78.8 percent according to the Bureau of Labor Statistics. At The Ritz, it was 20 percent, an average it has maintained.[72] The Ritz was so intent on treating its employees well that it held a "Day 21" event, a process check three weeks after any new hire's start date to confirm that the company had lived up to the commitments it made during the employee's orientation and training.[73]

The Ritz's focus on excellence has three benefits. It benefits customers who expect a top-quality stay. It benefits employees by giving them a sense of equality and purpose to their jobs. And finally, it also benefits The Ritz's bottom line. Contrast this with Uber's tactics. While Uber was able to manage its relationships with regulators to enter new cities, drivers to get them to stay on the road longer, and competition to make them less of a threat, Uber's tactics only benefited Uber. In the long term this self-interest came with a high cost: an erosion of trust.

Competence Alone Does Not Beget Trust

Uber's aggressive, brutal, and flat-out-wrong approaches to the managerial dimension of business may have accomplished its objectives in the short term, but in the long term Uber paid a price. The sequel to the de Blasio story?

In 2018, in the wake of Uber's manifold scandals, New York City passed the first legislation in the United States limiting the number of app-ride cars on the road for a year.[74] In 2019, de Blasio moved to extend the cap permanently as well as cap the amount of time drivers can spend cruising the streets looking for new passengers.[75] A couple months before the cap was extended, de Blasio commented that he wanted the cap extended to prevent app companies from taking "advantage of hardworking drivers, choking our streets with congestion, and driving workers into poverty."[76] In February 2019, Uber sued to overturn the caps,[77] and in December of 2019 a New York state judge blocked the cruising cap.[78]

We can't know about the shadow life Uber would have led if it'd taken a slightly less aggressive stance—perhaps calling the de Blasio tab the wait tab instead. After all, the cap extension hurt both Uber and Lyft. However, what we can see is that Uber's actions have left a decidedly slimy residue on the public. We don't feel good about Uber as a company. What company would want the *New York Times* to write a think piece about how customers have angst about using their product or service titled "To Delete or Not to Delete: That's the Uber Question"? The article ended with a quote from one unhappy customer who commented, "There is a difference between being competitive and being dirty. It is bad-boy, jerk culture. And I can't celebrate that."[79]

Cynics might point out that while there's angst, and Uber's received its fair share of bad press, Uber hasn't had to deal with any serious consequences—after all, Uber still exists, and bookings grew 28 percent in 2019, while its revenues grew 37 percent.[80]

Yet what company would want to go through what Uber has gone through? Aside from being bloodied in the headlines during most of 2017 and former CEO Travis Kalanick's subsequent ousting in the same year, Uber failed to reach projections of 44 million users in 2017, only reaching 41 million.[81] Growth projections anticipate the slowdown will continue until 2021, and Uber has ceded market share to Lyft.[82] Meanwhile, from October 2017 to October 2018, Lyft's revenue grew twice as fast as Uber's.[83] What would those numbers look like if Uber hadn't been through a #DeleteUber movement, or if people felt good instead of slimy every time they booked an Uber?

It doesn't stop there. Two days before Uber's much anticipated IPO fell flat in 2019, Uber drivers around the world went on strike to protest their working conditions.[84] Uber's first earnings report for 2019 revealed that it had a net loss of more than $1 billion in its first quarter.[85]

While competence is the bedrock for trust, Uber illustrates that it's only the beginning of trust. A technically competent company will produce an excellent product or service. In order to get it to market, the company needs managerial competence. However, managerial competence is not enough. As we saw with Uber, a company that nails managerial competence may be effective in the short term, but in the long term if its tactics are purely self-interested, unfair, and don't create a positive impact for customers, drivers, employees, and investors, the company will pay a price.

THREE

MOTIVES

A Fine Balance

*It's motive alone which gives character to the
actions of men.*

—Jean de La Bruyère

WE ALL INSTINCTIVELY UNDERSTAND THAT COMPANIES
have to make a profit to survive. Yet, a tougher and subtler
issue raises its head. We want to know—as customers, employees,
investors, and members of the public—what are a company's motives beyond making money? That very question became front and
center for Tommy Adaptive, an initiative that seemed to be on the
side of the angels.

It all started with former Saks Fifth Avenue fashion stylist
Mindy Scheier. Scheier, who has a commanding voice and curly
red hair, is passionate about clothes: she believes they have a mag-
ical ability to transform people. Yet for years, Scheier's son Oliver had to dress in sweatpants. Oliver was born with a rare form
of muscular dystrophy. Oliver struggled to manage buttons and

zippers, and pants didn't fit over his leg braces. If Oliver wore jeans, Scheier had to accompany him to the bathroom.[1]

And then, Oliver came home one day during third grade and declared, "I'm going to wear jeans like everyone else gets to wear." Oliver, too, had a passion for fashion—but there was nothing he could wear that would allow him to express it.

"It was such a kick in the stomach moment," Scheier recalls. "Here I was in the fashion industry and literally thought about what I wear every day because I love to get dressed and I missed it with my own child. Clothing is critically important to who you are as a person and how you show up to the world."

Scheier spent an evening retrofitting Oliver's jeans so he could wear them. She removed the zipper and added an elastic band so he could pull them up and down, and cut up the legs and put Velcro in the sides so they would fit over his braces. "When I showed Oliver my arts and crafts project, he absolutely beamed. He went into school with his head held so high. Those jeans transformed him. He was able to get dressed on his own, he was able to go to the bathroom on his own; those jeans gave him confidence."[2]

And then Scheier took it a step further. She researched choices for Oliver and found that there wasn't much on the market, mostly hospital gear or clothes for the elderly. And Oliver wasn't alone. There are roughly 61 million people in the United States, or 25 percent of the population, who have a disability.[3] In 2013, Scheier started the nonprofit organization Runway of Dreams to educate the fashion industry on how it could better serve the disabled community. Scheier partnered with Maura Horton, a designer who had developed a magnet system to close shirts instead of using buttons. Horton's husband had Parkinson's disease, and she had created the system so he could independently open and close his dress shirts. Scheier and Horton approached several design labels with a plan for creating adaptive clothing. The labels all turned Scheier and Horton down, reasoning that if adaptive clothing was such a good idea, someone would have done it before. Finally, the duo struck gold with Tommy Hilfiger.

In 2016, the Tommy Hilfiger team launched a children's collection of adaptive clothing with Runway of Dreams. The following year, the team launched Tommy Adaptive, a line of clothing for people with disabilities. The clothes included T-shirts that had magnets sewn behind decorative buttons, so the shirts looked like standard polos but were easier to open and close, and pants with hook-and-loop closures instead of zippers. For the Tommy Hilfiger team, Tommy Adaptive became more than a new line of clothing: it became a passion project.

To roll out the line, the Tommy Hilfiger team conducted extensive focus groups with people who had disabilities to understand the products that would best serve their needs. They investigated the barriers to purchase, how to market the clothing to this audience, and offered their customer service associates sensitivity training, as well as training on the new products. Team members worked long weekends and looked into partnerships with different organizations outside the fashion industry. "We want to create a movement," said Gary Sheinbaum, the CEO of Tommy Hilfiger Americas.

Several members of the Tommy Hilfiger team explained that working on Tommy Adaptive gave them purpose. They felt that they were making a truly meaningful contribution to society. Employees were so passionate about the product and so moved by the stories Tommy Adaptive customers told them that one manager commented there was a long period of time when there was no meeting without crying.

While the line was priced similarly to Tommy Hilfiger's other products, it yielded lower profit margins, a result of the higher costs of adapting closure systems, fit, and other special features.

Overall, customers with disabilities loved the line. Usually customer service centers for retailers can expect at least some complaints, along with customer inquiries. However, the customer service team for Tommy Hilfiger had the opposite experience with Tommy Adaptive: people called to say thank you and share stories about how the product had helped them.

However, in a world where no good deed goes unpunished, Tommy Hilfiger's motives could be questioned by customers wanting to know if the brand was producing Tommy Adaptive for the "right reasons." According to management consulting firm McKinsey & Company, "getting woke" (that is, showing an awareness of social injustice) was one of the major trends for fashion companies in 2019: socially conscious customers had come down hard on fashion brands when they felt like the brands had failed to deliver inclusion and diversity in an authentic enough manner. For example, retailer Primark faced backlash in 2018 for releasing Pride T-shirts produced in Turkey, which has one of the lowest rankings in Europe for LGBTQ+ rights. Meanwhile, taking a stance on one issue doesn't mean a company is protected from other issues. Nike supported football player Colin Kaepernick when he chose to remain seated, and later decided to kneel, during the National Anthem to protest the oppression of black people and people of color.[4] However, Nike still got slammed for failing to pay fair wages in developing countries.[5]

The quality of Tommy Hilfiger's adaptive line was undeniable, and so was the benefit it created for people with disabilities, but an outsider could question Tommy Hilfiger's motives. Did the company really care about the people with disabilities, or was it just out to make a profit? Why was Tommy Hilfiger in the business of adaptive clothing anyway?

THERE ARE TWO SIGNIFICANT—AND VERY different—reasons why understanding the importance of your company's motives is so crucial. The first is practical. Companies have enormous power over us, and we need to know that their products and services will not harm us. For example, we depend on cars and planes to transport us. But if safety guidelines are abandoned, these cars and planes become killing machines. Consider Boeing's 737 Max 8 jet. On the morning of October 29, 2018, within minutes of takeoff, a Lion Air flight from Jakarta tumbled into the Java Sea, killing all 189 people on board. And only five months later, on March 10, 2019, a second Boeing 737 Max 8, flown this time by Ethiopian Airlines, crashed shortly after takeoff as well; all 157 on board were killed. The 737 Max 8 jets had a faulty software system. The jets came with a new automated system that pushed the nose of the aircraft down to prevent it from stalling. However, the system only relied on one sensor. If the sensor malfunctioned, the system continued to push the nose of the plane down, causing it to crash.[6] An investigation later revealed that Boeing had bypassed safety steps in order to protect its bottom line, putting profits ahead of customer safety.[7]

We expect when we buy a product or a service that it will live up to its promise and that the company that sold it to us will not actively try to harm us and will take a reasonable amount of care to ensure our well-being. We cannot police each and every thing a company does, so in order to engage with a company, we have to generally trust that they have good motives and do not intend to hurt us.

For example, we expect that Facebook will allow us to contact friends and family. We understand this may lead to occasional sticky situations when Grandma reads something that was meant for our best friend. We expect that Facebook will use our data if we give it permission to, and we may even expect that Facebook will not be very clear about how to opt out of giving it permission to use our data. However, we do not expect that Facebook will allow a third party to collect and use our data without our permission, as it did with Cambridge Analytica, the data firm hired by the Trump campaign for the 2016 presidential election, which gained access to private Facebook data on 87 million users and allegedly used these data to create targeted political ads.[8]

Businesses create situations ranging from building products that can be harmful (such as planes that weren't built with adequate safety measures) to taking actions that will impact the economy (like the risky mortgage lending that led to the Great Recession). Given the enormous powers businesses have, we want to know that we can trust a company to do right by us regardless of the circumstances they face.

The second reason is emotional. As human beings we instinctively crave morality: we want to know that people will do right by us simply because they believe it's the right thing to do. Aristotle called this disposition to do the right thing for its own sake moral virtue. In her essay "The Discernment of Perception: An Aristotelian Concept of Rationality," American philosopher Martha Nussbaum explains our craving for rightness using Aristotle's concept of virtue. She writes, "Even where correct choice is reached in the absence of feeling and emotional response, Aristotle will insist that it is less virtuous than choice that is emotional. If I help a friend unfeelingly, I am less praiseworthy than if I do so with appropriate love and sympathy.... Without feeling, a part of correct perception is missing."[9]

Even though Tommy Adaptive created products that filled unmet needs for a marginalized group, if it wanted to avoid the problems other fashion brands had run into, it would have to make its mission of inclusive fashion clear to the public.

We could argue that, logically, Tommy Hilfiger's reasons for selling adaptive clothing shouldn't have any bearing on the positive effects these products have and how they are perceived. We would, however, then miss several of the more intangible benefits that come with being motivated to do good. Because the Tommy Adaptive team was motivated to do right by people with disabilities, they conducted an exhaustive market research process including multiple focus groups. They pushed themselves to find ways to better serve customers with disabilities. These efforts ranged from ensuring their customer service and website offer best-in-class

ADA compliant processes to finding the most effective ways to create brand awareness. Without these motives, it's doubtful the team would have gone the extra mile for a product that had lower profit margins.

In fact, one of the challenges the team faced was how to advertise adaptive clothing to its target audience. There was no existing benchmark, so the team had to create a marketing campaign from the ground up. In focus groups and design sessions, people with disabilities stressed over and over again that they did not want to be seen as different. Using a very targeted message would be the obvious solution from a marketing standpoint, but it would also contradict the wishes of the community Tommy Hilfiger wanted to serve. As Sarah Horton, senior director of marketing, who was deeply involved in the creation of Tommy Adaptive, commented,

> When we embarked on our adaptive clothing journey, we knew we needed to speak to consumers with disabilities to ensure their needs were met.... While it is not easy to build awareness for a new product or idea, our goal has been to keep this conversation going, and to share our story with as many people as possible. We are proud that Tommy Adaptive was built by this community, for this community.

While Tommy Hilfiger's product was unique at the time (it has since been joined by Nike, Target, Zappos, American Eagle, UGG, and a growing list of other companies), its motive—a deep desire to help others—is hardwired into us as individuals. According to research by experimental psychologists and specialists in brain and cognitive science, we want to help each other so much we're willing to do it even when there's no reward and it may not be in our best interest.

David Rand, now a professor at MIT, and two Harvard professors, Martin Nowak and Joshua Greene, conducted and reviewed studies on human cooperation that were published in 2012. They aggregated data from ten experiments on a game where groups of four people were given money. Participants could choose how much money to put in a pool where it would then be multiplied and divided evenly among the four people.[10] Even though it was possible to make money by contributing nothing, most people contributed something.[11] There was no punishment if people didn't contribute, and no real reason to contribute, yet still the majority of people chose to help the group.

In 2016, Rand published a follow-up experiment and found an interesting wrinkle. He analyzed sixty-seven studies on economic cooperation games and found that when subjects were given more time to think about their decisions, they behaved more selfishly and gave less. This makes sense (even if it is somewhat dismaying). If you sit and really think about the economic game we described, why would you contribute money? You don't know anyone involved, and you can walk away with more money if you don't put anything into the pool. However, when people were given less time and forced to use their intuition, they contributed 17.3 percent more money to the group.[12] We have a strong desire to help each other, but as Rand found, we are also fully capable of overriding that desire if given enough time to think.

However, overriding these instincts may actually hurt us. In addition to our penchant for cooperation, we also tend to instinctively avoid people with selfish motivations. In 2018, Swiss-Austrian economist Ernst Fehr and then PhD student Ivo Schurtenberger published a review for the journal *Nature Human Behaviour* summing up the research on anonymous strangers playing one-shot social dilemma games for money.[13] One-shot games are when participants must choose between contributing to the group or keeping their money. Once the game is over, players don't play again, which means they have no incentive to worry about harming their reputation.

Fehr and Schurtenberger found that across studies about 30 percent of players are freeloaders who try to get something for nothing, and 50 percent of players are "conditional cooperators." That is, they will scale their cooperation to that of other players, increasing or decreasing it depending on how the other person treats them.

They also found that players have a strong desire to punish freeloaders. This desire is so strong that people prefer situations where there are opportunities to punish freeloaders, even if meting out punishment is temporarily detrimental to the punisher and to the group's overall welfare.

Motives are so important to us that if we know someone unintentionally caused harm, we see the harm as less severe. In a 2013 study, Daniel Ames, now a business professor at Columbia University, and Susan Fiske, a psychology professor at Princeton, had participants read about a CEO who owned a business where employee pay was partially based on company profits. The CEO made a bad investment, which meant employees earned less. Participants then rated the amount of harm caused from 0 to 100. Half the participants were told the CEO intentionally harmed his employees because he wanted them to work harder to increase profits. The other half were told the CEO genuinely thought the investment would make money and everyone would benefit. On average participants rated the scenario with intentional harm at 66, while the second scenario of unintentional harm earned an average score of 48—even though the result of less pay was *exactly the same*.[14]

In a subsequent study, Ames and Fiske found the converse to also be true. When people knew harm was intentional, they tended to overestimate the extent of harm. They had a more accurate assessment when they knew the harm was not intended. For example, Ames and Fiske gave participants a story about a nursing home employee who gave residents the wrong medicines. The cost of the actual harm was $4,433. Participants who thought the mistake was unintentional estimated that the harm was $4,557. However, participants who thought the mistake was intentional estimated the damage as $5,224. Moreover, in a follow-up experiment where participants could solicit signatures for a petition for the employee to be investigated, participants who thought the employee intentionally created harm worked four times as hard to get signatures as participants who thought the mistake was unintentional.[15]

So, what's the bottom line? Businesses would do well to act in the interests of others, because we feel good about people who cooperate to further our collective interests. We want to work with them and reward them. When they cause us harm unintentionally, we will be more forgiving, but if we believe they harmed us on purpose, we will magnify the extent of the impact. We abhor those who are only interested in their own benefit, and if there are opportunities to punish them, such as not do business with them or go after them legally, we will.

This does not mean that we expect businesses to be completely altruistic. Businesses and in fact humans require some level of self-interest to survive, and a business that manages to stay open and profitable can do more good (e.g., employ people, produce needed goods and services) than one that goes bankrupt. Rather, we expect businesses to do what they need to do in order to function while at the same time minimizing the amount of harm they cause their stakeholders. Even in cases where businesses might have a reason to do harm—say to stay abreast of the competition, we have a limited tolerance for what is acceptable. When news stories broke that Uber was deliberately booking and canceling rides from its competitor Lyft, as well as creating a team to recruit drivers away from Lyft,[16] this was not celebrated as a clever technique. Instead, we thought Uber was a bully.

The Quakers, also known as the Society of Friends, are a sect of Christianity devoted to peaceful principles. They are a striking example of how being trusted for motives can lead to business success. The Quakers were banned in England from attending universities and going into politics until 1828,[17] so most of them turned to business.[18] During the days of the Industrial Revolution, between the mid-1700s and mid-1800s, the Quakers made a name for themselves as entrepreneurs because people trusted their motives. People knew their business practices were faith-based and that Quakers would keep their promises even if it wasn't in their best financial interest to do so.[19] For example, the Darby family who founded the British iron industry refused to follow the lead of their competitors and make cannons, a clear statement that their business principles were based on more than just profits. Instead the Darbys focused on domestic iron goods.[20]

Quaker business practices were also set up to ensure that the community benefited from businesses. During Quaker meetings, everyone's business activities were reviewed by peers. This served two purposes: first, ensuring that the business plans were solid, and second, ensuring that the Quakers' interests as well as those of the broader community outside the Quakers were protected.[21] During meetings, members were warned against speculation, reminded about the importance of paying bills on time while avoiding large debts, and urged not to do business beyond their means,[22] so the Quakers ended up building solid cash reserves.[23] There were also stiff penalties for bankruptcy—usually expulsion from the group—which also helped cement the importance of good business practices.[24] Moreover, Quakers were known for being honest and fair,[25] especially with weights, measures, and their pricing.[26] In an economy where bartering was the norm, Quakers were the first to set prices, providing a degree of certainty in what was otherwise a highly variable deal-by-deal market. Their factories had better work conditions than was common at the time, and Quakers employed doctors and dentists to take care of their workers. Customers believed the Quakers weren't out to make a profit at their expense or at the expense of their employees.[27]

Trust became a competitive advantage for the Quakers. In the 1850s Quakers made up just over 0.5 percent of the British population,[28] yet they started several business empires including Barclays Bank, Clarks shoes, Cadbury chocolates (a gift to us all), and Carr's Crackers, all of which are still in business today.[29] The combination of business know-how plus community-mindedness led a group of forty-five Quakers to each set aside 10,700 pounds to create a life insurance fund in 1832.[30] This grew into the English life insurance firm Friends Provident, which endured over the years until it was sold to insurance group Aviva in 2015.[31] And although it pains us to recognize it, one of Harvard Business School's competitors—University of Pennsylvania's Wharton—the world's first collegiate business school, was founded by a Quaker entrepreneur, Joseph Wharton, who wanted to prepare graduates to become "pillars of the State, whether in private or in public life."[32]

Quaker management principles are alive and well in some corporations, but not, to be sure, in most. Since the mid-nineteenth century, there have been two main schools of thought in America about the role of businesses in society: whether businesses should focus on making a profit or whether they should serve a larger social purpose.

William T. Allen unpacked this duality in his famous article "Our Schizophrenic Conception of the Business Corporation." Allen was particularly well positioned to comment since at the time he was the chancellor of the Delaware Court of Chancery, a US court that is famous for being the definitive voice for settling law cases between corporations and other parties. Allen explained that there have always been tensions between these two views of the firm in the United States. These views are known by many names. Allen preferred the property and social entity views,[33] while others use the label of classical versus managerialism.[34] However, the gist is shareholder/property theorists believe the role of the company is mainly economic. A company exists to create wealth and its first responsibility is to its stockholders who "own" the firm, hence the term "property" view. Employment, innovation, and other social goods are beneficial side effects of business, but not its main purpose.[35] Stakeholder/social entity theorists, on the other hand, believe that companies have a social and moral purpose.

They are responsible for creating quality products and services at a reasonable cost, providing long-term employment, and benefiting society.[36]

Corporations have had dual purposes—the schizophrenia that Allen writes about—pulling them toward duties to shareholders on the one hand and toward stakeholders on the other. The corporation was born in the nineteenth century in the US, and the initial legal conception was that a firm is more or less like a limited partnership, established so individuals could pool capital, invest it, and create returns for its individual investor-owners.[37] At the same time, nineteenth-century companies were also state-chartered institutions, and the earliest charters were quite specific, generally granted to fund the building of something like a bridge—a public service investment beyond the financial reach of individuals.

In the 1930s, the publication of *The Modern Corporation and Private Property* by Adolf A. Berle Jr. and Gardiner C. Means codified the beliefs of stakeholder corporations. The hallmarks were support for labor unions, the creation of employee pension programs, and actions to enhance the stability and prosperity of the communities that housed the companies. The post-WWII cushy economic environment of prosperity, low competition, and lack of powerful shareholders nourished the growth of stakeholder corporations.[38]

However, the 1970s marked the return of the property/shareholder view. Milton Friedman, a University of Chicago economist, spearheaded this movement. He wrote, "There is one and only one social responsibility of business—to use its resources and engage in activities designed to increase its profits so long as it stays within the rules of the game, which is to say, engages in open and free competition without deception or fraud."[39]

By the 1980s, the economy had changed. Companies were facing growing global competition, capital market innovation, and the growth of a newly powerful class of institutional investors.[40]

Friedman's ideas took root and ushered in the return of the share-holder. Companies focused on shareholders' needs, squeezing their budgets to wring out every last cent of profit. Around the same time layoffs increased, research and development budgets were cut, and companies focused on short-term profits for share-holder gain rather than the long-term interests of the firm.[41]

However, all of that came with a cost: the loss of trust in com-panies. In 1974, 31 percent of Americans said they trusted major corporations—which is low and alarming if you think about the fact that that was trust's heyday—but by the 1990s this had dropped to 20 percent according to the University of Chicago's General So-cial Survey. (Unsurprisingly, trust hit an all-time low during 2010, right around the Great Recession, when it was 13 percent).[42] The relentless pursuit of wealth had consequences.

The Rise of Purpose-Driven Companies

Today, we're seeing a backlash against the supremacy of share-holder interests. Increasingly, people want companies to have pos-itive social motives. According to a survey conducted by American Express, 81 percent of the US millennials surveyed said a success-ful company needs to have a genuine purpose, while 78 percent said their employers' values should match their own.[43]

As a side note, a company's purpose is different than its mo-tives. Purpose defines the goal a company wants to achieve, while motives refer to the company's reasons for choosing that goal. A company's purpose may change over time and under different market conditions. For example, in the 1890s William Hesketh Lever founded Lever Brothers with the purpose of making "clean-liness commonplace; to lessen work for women; to foster health and contribute to personal attractiveness, that life may be more enjoyable and rewarding for the people who use our products."[44] Lever Brothers ultimately became Unilever in 1930.[45] Today Uni-lever has made it a point to bake social and environmental goals into its corporate purpose. Its Lipton tea brand aims to produce tea sustainably, while Dove, which sells soaps and shampoos, aims "to make beauty a source of confidence, not anxiety."[46] Unilever CEO Alan Jope recently said that if its brands don't have a clear environmental or social purpose, they could be cut from the Unilever product line.[47] Meanwhile Unilever's overarching corporate purpose is to be the leader in sustainable business and prove that brands with purpose grow.[48] The purpose-driven corporation grew out of stakeholder thinking, adding to it clear and simple statements of intent to shape company actions and set expectations of what the company can be held accountable for.

Some CEOs are getting the message that focusing purely on investors has hurt business, and they are rethinking the role of the company and moving back to a more stakeholder-centered philosophy. In 2018, Laurence D. Fink, chairman and CEO of Black-Rock, the largest investment manager in the world, wrote a letter to major company CEOs asking them to pay attention to social, environmental, and legal concerns. The letter generated a fierce debate.[49] Real estate mogul Sam Zell commented, "I didn't know Larry Fink had been made God," and called the letter hypocritical.[50] Warren Buffett commented that he did not think investors should mix politics and business: "I don't believe in imposing my political opinions on the activities of my business," he said.[51]

However, CEOs paid attention. In August 2019, the Business Roundtable, a group of about 200 CEOs from America's largest companies including giants like Apple and Walmart,[52] issued a statement defining the purpose of a company. The statement declared, "While each of our individual companies serves its own corporate purpose, we share a fundamental commitment to all of our stakeholders." The Business Roundtable broke down corporate purpose into five elements: delivering value to customers, investing in employees, dealing fairly and ethically with suppliers, supporting the communities in which we work, and generating long-term value for shareholders.[53]

While the members of the Business Roundtable were ostensibly speaking about purpose, they hit upon the main complexity behind motives when they broke down a company's purpose into commitments to meeting the needs and expectations of different groups. There are times when stakeholders' needs will conflict and companies have to make tough choices about whose needs to prioritize. Yet, if a company wants to remain trusted for its motives, it cannot actively harm its stakeholders either. Companies are tasked with determining whether their motives are trustworthy from the perspectives of multiple stakeholders by asking three questions:

- Who are our stakeholders?
- What do we owe our stakeholders?
- How can we balance competing stakeholder interests?

WHO ARE OUR STAKEHOLDERS? Determining whether you're successfully doing right by stakeholders starts with a good understanding of who they are. They include the usual suspects: customers, employees, investors, and the communities where you do business. Companies, however, have far-reaching impacts, and stakeholders also encompass a larger ecosystem including suppliers, regulators and government officials, and society. In the case of Tommy Adaptive, for example, the subgroup of customers with disabilities was an important stakeholder. This meant Tommy Hilfiger had to think through its marketing campaign as well as its distribution processes and customer service in order to best serve customers with disabilities.

HDFC Ltd. (Housing Development Finance Corporation Limited), an Indian financial services company, has accomplished astounding results by keeping in mind that one of its most important stakeholders was Indian society at large, something that has been fundamental to the company since its founding.

During India's first years of independence, in the 1950s, Indians invested about 3 percent of the GDP in houses. By the 1970s this had fallen to 1.5 percent, and there was a pressing need for more houses.[54] At the time there was little infrastructure for home loans, while the existing banks, mostly state owned, had little ability to enforce payments or foreclose on defaulters.[55]

In 1977, H. T. Parekh launched HDFC to provide loans to people who wanted to buy a house.[56] In 1978, HDFC's first borrower, D. B. Remedios, took out a modest Rs. 30,000 loan at a fixed interest rate of 10.5 percent to build an Rs. 70,000 house in Mumbai.[57] At the time, the typical borrower was middle-aged and accustomed to using savings to purchase a house since it was difficult to get a loan, and loans were also not part of the culture.[58] (It's a testament to HDFC's success that today home loans have become an essential part of Indian life. Borrowers are in their early thirties and tend to seek out loans that are about 65–80 percent of their house's purchase price.)[59]

Soon, HDFC earned a reputation for high integrity and customer care. At the time, the banks had a reputation for acting as if they were doing customers a favor by serving them. Parekh instructed employees to "make [the customer] feel that you need him more than he needs you."[60] HDFC trained employees not to accept bribes, though bribery was a widespread practice in India at the time. If customers offered a bribe, HDFC rejected their application, while employees who accepted bribes were fired. And while nationalized banks took six months to a year to approve a loan, HDFC made approvals within six weeks.[61]

HDFC was a massive success, and until the 1980s it held 100 percent of India's market for housing loans. Parekh could have decided it was better to have a monopoly, but he believed that India needed a much larger industry to meet its vast housing needs. In a highly unusual move, HDFC worked with public sector–owned banks to invest up to 20 percent in three other companies to create a home lending industry.[62] It also supplied the companies with management and employee training, even though it would end up competing with these three entities for business.

HDFC did in fact take a hit from investing in a home lending industry. Its market share fell to about 75–80 percent, but its growth remained the same: about 30–40 percent per year.[63] However, the investments in competitors created so much trust in HDFC as a company that was actively seeking to benefit society that the government regularly consulted it as an advisor for various policies including extending tax benefits to borrowers for home loans. HDFC had earned so much trust that the government believed its recommendations would benefit the whole industry.[64] Today HDFC has gone on to create several other subsidiaries including HDFC Bank, India's largest private sector bank.

As a side note, HDFC's current chairman, Deepak Parekh (H. T. Parekh's nephew), is highly regarded and seen as the government's unofficial "crisis consultant." Among other crises, in 2009, Deepak Parekh was brought in as an advisor for the "Enron of India," the Satyam Computer Services scandal. Satyam Computer Services had a fictional $1 billion on its books,[65] and Parekh led the effort to sell it and rebrand it, in order to help protect India's reputation as a technology hub.[66]

WHAT DO OUR STAKEHOLDERS EXPECT? A company has three major responsibilities: economic, legal, and ethical. *Economically*, we count on companies to create value. *Legally*, we expect them to follow the law. And *ethically*, we want them to have a positive impact and use fair means to achieve their ends and govern their interactions with stakeholders.

How this works in practice varies, depending on the stakeholder. Providing economic value for customers means the company creates goods and services that add value to their lives. Employees, on the other hand, see economic value as a livelihood, as do suppliers on a much larger scale. Investors look for returns, regulators expect companies to abide by the law, and society expects companies to add to the economic development of the regions they work in. Companies can't build trust unless they understand the implicit promises widely different stakeholders expect them to keep.

STAKEHOLDER	ECONOMIC PROMISE	LEGAL PROMISE	ETHICAL PROMISE
Customers	• To provide products and services that enhance their lives	• To follow consumer protection laws and industry regulations	• To make good on commitments • To disclose risks • To remediate mistakes made or harm done
Employees	• To provide a livelihood (pay, benefits, training, opportunity)	• To follow labor, antidiscrimination, and workplace safety laws	• To provide safe work conditions and to disclose risks • To be transparent about job security • To treat everyone fairly
Suppliers	• To be paid in a timely manner	• To honor all contracts	• To prevent harm • To honor commitments • To provide accurate information
Investors	• To provide returns • To manage risk	• To fulfill fiduciary duties • To disclose material information • To abstain from insider trading and self-dealing	• To exercise diligent oversight • To oversee leadership and company conduct

continues

continued

STAKEHOLDER	ECONOMIC PROMISE	LEGAL PROMISE	ETHICAL PROMISE
Government	• To pay taxes and relevant fees and fines • To provide accurate information • To support open and fair markets	• To comply with existing regulations • To contribute to legislation and rule-making that advance social priorities	• To follow the spirit of the law even if there are loopholes • To cooperate with regulators and officials in addressing problems
Society	• To offer employment and economic development • To fulfill important needs	• To follow local and federal laws protecting the public and the environment	• To minimize harm and protect public health, the environment, and the local community • To set industry standards

If it seems surprising to see government as a stakeholder that companies need to build trust with, consider the consequences when trust with government regulators breaks down. At a recent transportation conference we attended, a European government official told us about the fallout after the Volkswagen diesel emissions scandal, where the German car company installed software in the cars to help them cheat on emissions tests. "We felt betrayed by Volkswagen," the official said. He continued by pointing out that regulators don't write the laws expecting them to be broken. But once a scandal happens, regulators tighten laws, limiting companies' powers and making it more difficult for everyone to do business, even those with the best of intentions. The Volkswagen emissions scandal broke in September 2015, and by January 2016, the European Union was already working to tighten regulations to ensure that the cheating could not be repeated.[67] Lest it seem that

Volkswagen did not suffer consequences (by 2018, it was growing again in the United States),[68] we'd like to point out that in the aftermath, Volkswagen's profits tumbled by 20 percent during the first quarter of 2016,[69] it had to trim its workforce by 30,000 in 2016,[70] and it had to pay $35 billion in settlements and fines in 2019.[71] Ex-CEO Martin Winterkorn was charged with fraud,[72] while as of 2020, German authorities have filed charges against six Volkswagen executives.[73] Meanwhile, Volkswagen has stiffened its internal conduct rules. In 2019, the company fired 204 employees for infractions like unexcused absences or ignoring drug and alcohol bans.[74] While Volkswagen's sales may be climbing back, it is still dealing with the reputational stains from the scandal.

HOW CAN WE BALANCE COMPETING stakeholder interests? Motives will continually be tested over time. There's no one-and-done test in the eyes of stakeholders. And, for many, the moment of truth comes when competing stakeholder interests have to be balanced. Since the needs of all stakeholders can't be met at every moment, and stakeholder expectations may conflict, companies have to figure out how to balance expectations. What this balance looks like varies from company to company, and may change depending on the situation. It may be necessary to let a stakeholder's needs go unmet for the moment, or just aim for the bare minimum, but there's a difference between temporarily putting a group's needs on the back burner versus actively harming them. The challenge companies face, particularly when they are in difficult situations or strapped for resources, is figuring out whom to prioritize while paying sufficient attention to other groups of valued stakeholders.

A prime example of elegant and effective balancing is the global manufacturer Honeywell during the Great Recession of 2007–2009. Dave Cote, Honeywell's CEO at the time, was one of very few leaders who recognized the damage layoffs caused and minimized their use, relying instead much more heavily on furloughs. At the same time, he knew he had to balance the needs of employees with investors, who were expecting the company to produce returns. Cote is proof that doing the right thing can make sound business sense. Tall and imposing, Cote is a clear, confident speaker who tells great stories while communicating complex ideas. During his tenure at Honeywell, particularly during the recession, his leadership style demonstrated prioritizing doing right by each stakeholder in order to ensure Honeywell's survival.

First, some background. Cote stepped into his position at Honeywell in 2002 and inherited a mess. Honeywell had gone through three CEOs in four years. It had billions in environmental, pension, and asbestos liabilities that weren't resolved; cultural warfare from a messy merger; and "unhealthy" accounting practices.[75] Cote was an unlikely candidate for CEO. He grew up in small-town New Hampshire. He dropped out of college as a junior to become a commercial fisherman. After that, he worked night shifts as a factory worker at General Electric. However, when his wife got pregnant, and he realized he couldn't support a family as an hourly employee at GE, he went back to school. "I didn't know what success was, because it was hard to find anyone in town you'd describe as successful," he said.[76]

He returned to GE as an internal auditor and worked his way up the ladder, attracting the attention of CEO Jack Welch, who promoted him three levels. Cote even made the list of contenders to succeed Welch; however, he wasn't a finalist and ultimately left GE.[77]

After Cote joined Honeywell as CEO in February 2002 (and chairman in July of that year) he realized that he'd have to reduce Honeywell's earnings estimate. In fact he ended up reducing the estimate two times—swiftly losing the trust of investors, who already knew he hadn't been a finalist to run GE and was not the first choice to run Honeywell.[78]

One of Cote's first tasks was to turn around a company that had divided into factions. Honeywell had merged with AlliedSignal and Pittway, but the three were at war with each other because of vastly different cultures. A manager who had left AlliedSignal and then returned after the merger commented, "When I left, there was a huge energy in the place. When I came back the building was almost empty and a lot of people in it seemed beaten up."[79]

As Cote described it, the Honeywell culture focused on "customer delight—new technology and creating the next great thing." However, this meant that Honeywell would make commitments to create new products regardless of whether they could reasonably keep them. AlliedSignal focused on productivity and making the quarterly numbers, prioritizing the short term while neglecting to create a product pipeline. Pittway focused on capturing market share through creating new products while maintaining a healthy profit. However, they were fiercely independent and acted as if they hadn't merged with the two other companies.[80]

Cote's solution was to build a company culture where everyone focused on the customer and decisions were based on what would be best for the customer. As part of this he created the Honeywell Operating System (HOS), which was based on Toyota's lean manufacturing system, with the aim of standardizing the manufacturing process across the company. He also focused on developing talent within the company and instituted disciplined hiring practices to break Honeywell of the practice of over-hiring and then resorting to layoffs during downturns.[81]

He also took on two highly fraught issues. First, he reformed Honeywell's "unhealthy" accounting and management practices. This included discontinuing the practice of loading end-of-quarter sales that had been used to enhance reported earnings. Cote also moved to a more aggressive position on expense recognition, consistent with Generally Accepted Accounting Principles (GAAP), to more accurately match revenues with cash outflows and give Honeywell better information for making decisions.

Second, Cote created a new process for settling environmental claims brought against AlliedSignal, which had a long history of harm stemming from its decades in the chemical business. He increased the budget for environmental remediation, and instead of adopting AlliedSignal's strategy of challenging claims, he took a cooperative approach, spending $3.5 billion over fifteen years to resolve claims. He also worked with regulators to come up with solutions for the environmental damage, which went above and beyond Honeywell's legal responsibilities. "When we engaged with affected communities, we wanted to see if we could find solutions that got the job done right, but did so in innovative, cost-effective ways. We wanted everyone to win—the environment, local communities, *and* our shareholders," the ever-practical Cote later wrote in his memoir.[82]

As part of this, Honeywell cleaned up polluted sites and developed them into neighborhoods that had small businesses and created jobs. Among other projects, Honeywell invested $100 million in cleaning up hazardous waste in Baltimore's inner harbor, in a project that earned praise from local politicians. One community leader commented, "Throughout all the years that we've known Honeywell, we've developed trust and friendship. Honeywell has done everything they said they were going to do and more."[83] Making sure everyone was winning made Honeywell flourish: by the time the Great Recession rolled in, Honeywell's sales had increased about 10 percent each year and cash flow had doubled.

When the Great Recession hit, Honeywell, like most other companies, had to reduce costs as revenues fell. Again, Cote focused on how everyone could win: customers, investors, *and* employees.

Cote prioritized customers' interests during the downturn. "Our first priority is customers. We need to make sure we can still deliver, that it's quality product, and that if we've committed to a project that it will get done on time, if there's a new project that we've promised that it'll come out on time."[84] However, Cote realized that surviving the recession didn't mean ignoring the needs of investors and employees; it meant balancing them. "We have to balance the pain.... Investors need to know they can count on the company, that we're going to be doing the right things for the long term," Cote said.

> After all, they're the owners of the company and we work for them.... But at the same time we need to be recognizing that the employee base is the base for success in the future... and we need to be thoughtful about how we treat them. And I think if you get the balance right between these two... investors might not be as happy in the short term if you could have generated more earnings, but they're definitely going to be happier in the longer term. Employees might not be as happy in the short term because they might have preferred that you just say to heck with all investors. But in the long term they're going to benefit also because you're going to have a much more robust company.[85]

During the Great Recession, companies laid off 8.7 million Americans.[86] Layoffs, it almost goes without saying, are a trust killer for employees. A 2007 study of employees laid off during the 1982 recession found two decades later they were still earning 20 percent less than their peers.[87]

Honeywell took a different route. It furloughed employees. Furloughed employees do not report for work and receive varying amounts of pay from their employer depending on their country that can range from no pay at all, as in the US and Canada, to partial payment, common in many countries in Europe and Asia. Furloughed workers are eligible for government assistance in the form of unemployment benefits or compensation based on some portion of their normal pay.[88] At Honeywell, the furlough's length varied depending on the business unit and how well it was weathering the recession. None of the furloughs lasted more than five weeks. Painful certainly, but better by far than being out of a job altogether.

To minimize the scale of the furloughs, Cote also used a number of other cost-cutting measures, such as freezing hiring and eliminating salary increases, and cutting the company's retirement matching program from 100 percent to 50 percent. Meanwhile Honeywell distributed a reduced bonus pool as restricted stock so employees could benefit as the stock price rebounded during the recovery. Cote and his leadership team also refused their 2009 bonuses. He didn't share this with his employees until six months into the recession because he didn't want to look like he was preempting the board, which set his bonus. Cote later wrote in his memoir that this was a mistake and he should have let the team know early on, because the assumption that he would get a bonus created resentment.[89] (If the perception that Cote had a bonus created resentment, imagine what would have happened to trust at Honeywell if he had actually taken a bonus while issuing furloughs.) Honeywell also placed advance orders with suppliers that Honeywell could activate as soon as sales picked up. Suppliers were happy with the guaranteed production, and Honeywell stole a march on its competitors by filling customer orders faster as the recovery began.

Cote's balancing act paid off. During the recovery from 2009 to 2012, Honeywell's stock price shot up by over 75 percent, Honeywell outperformed the total stock returns of its closest competitor by over twenty points, and investors reaped the value of these benefits. Cote, who had entered Honeywell mistrusted by investors, no longer had a trust problem. In 2012, Morgan Stanley named Honeywell a star performer, noting there was no debate, it had definitely changed.[90] A year later, Morgan Stanley analysts called the furloughs a "smart decision" during a 2013 five-year review of Honeywell.[91] In the same year, *Chief Executive* magazine named him CEO of the Year based on nominations from a peer group.[92] In addition, Barron's declared Cote one of the world's top thirty CEOs for five years running, from 2013 to 2017.[93]

It is important to note that throughout his tenure at Honeywell, Cote was always balancing stakeholder needs. The cultural merger he orchestrated when he first arrived set employees on a new path and aligned their efforts toward a common goal. At the same time, he implemented policies that were good for his investors so that when the time came to put their needs on the backburner, he had built up enough trust with them to be able to do so. Alex Ismail, then Honeywell's president and CEO of transportation systems, commented, "Dave told us we would continue to do the right things in good and in bad times and that was critical."[94]

Trust is the currency of business, and companies need to build trust with multiple parties. We want to use the products and services we value from companies, to work for them, to do business with them, and to let them continue to exist. To allow any company to continue exercising the staggering amount of power it has over us, all of these parties need to trust in its motives. However, even if a company has the best of intentions, these intentions do not matter if a company cannot execute fairly on its decision-making—something we'll discuss more in our next chapter.

FOUR

MEANS

When All Is Fair

Being good is easy, what is difficult is being just.

—Victor Hugo

On September 8, 1999, Michelin, the French tire-maker, had good news and bad news, or good news and disastrous news depending on whom you were asking. The good news: it announced a 17 percent growth in profits for the first half of the year. The bad news: it would cut 7,500 jobs across Europe as part of its plan to improve profitability by 20 percent over the next three years.[1]

Earlier that year, Édouard Michelin had become co-CEO, inheriting the position from his father. Throughout the 1980s, sales in Europe had been falling, while Michelin faced pressure from low-cost Asian competitors. In addition, Michelin had been steadily losing market share to its main competitor, Bridgestone-Firestone.[2] So, even though Michelin was profitable, the new CEO knew that if the company was going to successfully compete in the new business landscape, something had to give.

Unsurprisingly, the news did not go down well. In fact, Michelin's announcement was a disaster. Two weeks after the announcement, 3,500 of Michelin's 15,000 employees in Clermont-Ferrand, Michelin's headquarters, took to the streets to protest the layoffs. They shut down shop in five factories to march in front of the headquarters building. On Michelin Avenue, employees ripped down street signs and replaced them with signs that read "Avenue of Full Employment." Protests erupted across France.

With all the union organizing actions and subsequent media attention, politicians became involved. France's prime minister, Lionel Jospin, stepped in to comment that there was very little the government could do to stop Michelin from restructuring. This generated so much outrage that Jospin's government revolted against his perceived weakness. The resulting hullaballoo became known as l'affaire Michelin.

Forced to respond, Jospin took action not just against Michelin, but against business in general. He vowed to deny subsidies to any company taking layoffs that wasn't struggling financially and to limit the use of part-time and temporary working contracts.

This would be a blow for any company, but it was particularly wounding to Michelin, a company that had historically gone to great lengths to make sure it was not just a good but an excellent employer. After its founding in 1889, Michelin built infrastructure in the surrounding communities around Clermont-Ferrand to support its new employees, including housing, schools, health clinics, and even swimming pools. For Michelin, employees were people first who deserved to be cared for, and not "natural" resources that could be used until they were depleted, or discarded like machines that were made obsolete by cheaper and more efficient models.

Michelin even made it a point to use the rather old-fashioned term "personnel" rather than human resources. Remi de Verdilhac, who worked in Michelin's personnel management for three decades, explained, "A human being is not a resource.... People have the potential to develop." As such, employees were hired for their cultural fit and values rather than for any particular role. They were assigned a career manager who worked to match them to jobs that would fit their talents and stretch them so they were always on a path to grow their skills and capabilities.

However, Michelin was also notoriously anti-union, and François Michelin (Édouard Michelin's father) strongly believed in the pro-employee management philosophy that became known as *paternalisme* (paternalism).[3] "Unions," he said, "aren't at all necessary for the existence of the company. They are only the expression of the inadequacy of company owners."[4] Consistent with this logic, François Michelin was also the CEO responsible for developing Michelin's career management system.

Yet this time Michelin had failed spectacularly in its goal to treat employees as "personnel." With the announcement of impending layoffs, Michelin seemed to be moving toward the philosophy of workers as an expendable resource it had criticized and proudly stood apart from for more than a century.

Michelin's actions had angered its employees to the point of inspiring a new federal law—a reality check like no other. What had gone wrong? At the heart of the matter was Michelin's employees and their judgment of the company's actions. Michelin had profited from their labor; why should they be punished by losing their jobs? The layoffs simply weren't fair.

To Be Trusted, Be Fair

Our sense of fairness runs deep and shows up nearly from the time we are born. In a 2017 *Scientific American* article, researchers summarized the "mountain of evidence" of how fairness is imbedded in child development.

Infants as young as 12 months expect resources to be divided equally between two characters in a scene [that was playacted in front of them]. By preschool, children will protest getting less than peers, even paying to prevent a peer from getting more. As children get older, they are willing to punish those who have been unfair both when they are the victims of unfairness as well as when they witness someone else being treated unfairly. Older still, children show…they would rather receive nothing than receive more than a peer.[5]

(How, you might wonder, do researchers divine what children as young as twelve months are thinking? By measuring what they look at, and for how long. It turns out that multiple studies have shown that infants and toddlers reliably spend more time looking at things that defy their expectations and surprise them, which they do when they see someone being treated unfairly.)[6]

Organizations that are trusted for their means, by which we mean the way they do things, have processes for making fair decisions on behalf of all their stakeholders. This is more difficult than it sounds. Business leaders are often biased in favor of shareholders, which leads to prioritizing financial returns over, say, employee well-being. Part of this is because of CEOs' compensation structure.

Over time, a larger and larger share of CEO compensation has been given as stock awards. In 2010, stock awards made up about 32 percent of CEO compensation for S&P 500 companies. By 2016 this had jumped to 47.4 percent.[7] Meanwhile, the consulting firm McKinsey analyzed how a change in stock prices affected CEO compensation. They found that a 50 percent increase in stock price (hefty, to be sure) translated to a *six-fold* pay raise for CEOs.[8] In other words, CEOs' incentives strongly favor just one of their stakeholders: investors.

And if you really want to get into unfairness, consider the discrepancy between CEO pay and worker pay. In 2018, the average CEO earned 278 times more than the average worker.[9] This point-in-time statistic shows vast inequities between what CEOs are paid compared to their workers. Supposedly CEOs "get the big bucks" because they have hard jobs (and really, they are hard: see Chapter 7 on leaders and trust). And there's no simple yardstick to use to determine just how much more in pay they should receive for that harder work. But the real story of unfairness is revealed in the *rate of growth* that each group has seen in its earnings, since that statistic shows the trend in how the economic pie has been divided over time. The average employee's compensation in the United States has increased by 11.9 percent in the forty years between 1978 and 2018, while the average CEO's pay has increased by 1,007.5 percent over those same forty years. Even though I've been an executive, I can't imagine a rationale that would explain how the contribution of CEOs warrants a rate of growth that is 100 times that of the employees whose innovation and productivity create the increased value and earnings that benefit companies and CEOs.

Meanwhile, companies do receive feedback if they are unfair to their customers and can see a direct hit in sales. Netflix found this out the hard way in 2011 when it decided to raise prices. At the time, customers paid $9.99 for unlimited streaming and DVD rental services. Then, Netflix decided to unbundle its services: customers could pay $7.99 for unlimited streaming or unlimited DVD rentals. If they wanted both, they were charged $15.98, a 63 percent price hike.[10] Customers quickly voted with their feet: Netflix lost 800,000 customers in the months following the decision.[11] As a side note, in 2014 when Netflix next decided to raise prices for streaming from $7.99 to $8.99, it tiptoed carefully. The price hike only applied to new customers, while old customers were allowed to stay at $7.99 for two more years. Netflix had learned its lesson about fairness the hard way.[12]

Fairness to employees is trickier to manage than fairness to customers because often the effects are indirect and emerge over time. To learn more about the hidden impacts of unfairness to employees, in 2017, European researchers conducted a field experiment by setting up a call center where they hired 195 people. They then laid some of them off to see whether this would impact the productivity of those who remained.[13] While real-life "experiments" of this kind go on all the time in companies, in this case, the researchers were trying to get a more precise understanding of how unfairness in the conduct of layoffs would affect the productivity of staff who were not laid off.

The researchers randomly selected 20 percent of the workers to be laid off, and told the group the layoffs had been random and were needed to cut costs. Productivity among layoff *survivors* (i.e., employees who were not laid off while others were) immediately decreased by 12 percent. This may not sound too bad, but imagine a drop of over 10 percent in the productivity of employees and the hit in profits if that occurred. When the researchers followed up, survivors were most unhappy about the random selection of workers to be laid off. To them, it was completely unfair.[14] While this was just a research study (and one hopes that participants were properly debriefed so it had no lasting emotional effects), layoffs like this are all too common in real life.

Leaders would be wise to take note of this study's results. A drop-off in productivity will affect the company and its profitability, but since it is not as visible and identifiable as plunging stock prices or lost sales, unfairness to employees is easier to downplay or ignore—until, as in the case of Michelin, employees make it clear they won't tolerate it anymore. The call center employees who were not laid off also expressed their displeasure but in ways that show how difficult it can be to connect the dots. In response to the layoffs they believed were unfair, they took longer breaks at the start of their second shift and began to leave work early.[15]

On a societal level, it can be even easier for companies to ignore or downplay the impact they have on the public and the communities they work in. For example, since 1988, just 100 companies have been responsible for 71 percent of global emissions.[16] To be sure, some industries are more likely to pollute than others by virtue of the business they are in. And these companies may very well have taken steps to lessen their environmental impact. But we might expect that aggressive and concerted action would lead to one or even a few of them dropping off the list. That they are all still responsible for the majority of global emissions indicates that whatever actions they've taken have not been sufficient, and they continue to create emissions that damage the environment.

This is a good example of how patterns of trust betrayal may be even harder to recognize than individual incidents, because you need to pull all the data together—over time—to get the real picture. My Harvard Business School colleague Steve Kaufman has wisely referred to this as "the tyranny of incrementalism." Take this as a warning to see whether there are trust breaches that have gone on for so long in your company that you are routinely acting unfairly, even if less so than in the past. This is a sign of a "satisficing" mindset, a kind of blindness where modest (and even hard-won) improvement becomes sufficient, rather than the larger changes that may be needed to transform how fairly your company acts.

When unfairness reaches a tipping point and communities rebel, companies can find themselves in hot water. For example, consider our discomfort with Uber. Much of it is rooted in how Uber treats its stakeholders. Among other harrowing details, Susan Fowler described how HR gave her a choice between staying with a manager who allegedly sexually harassed her and probably receiving a bad performance review, or transferring to a new team since they weren't "comfortable punishing" the manager, who was a high performer.[17] Unsurprisingly, according to Fowler's blog post, the number of women at Uber during her time there dropped from 25 percent to less than 6 percent of the workforce.[18] Even when unfairness is directed at employees, where the costs can be hidden for longer, companies will still see an impact.

This predisposition to fairness is why means—how we go about achieving our goals—are so important to being trusted. When we trust companies on the basis of means, we are trusting them to set rules of engagement that treat us fairly. But what should guide these rules? What do we mean when we expect a business to be fair?

There are many types of fairness, depending on the context, and the ideas they represent are as complex as the situations we humans create. For example, medical ethics is grounded in the principle of doing no harm, but it also encompasses other types of fairness. The first is beneficence—purposefully aiming to do good; the second is respect for patient autonomy, which underscores the importance of the patient's right to make their own healthcare decisions; and the third is distributive fairness—how to determine who in a society has access to medical care and at what cost. The principle of distributive fairness is useful to challenge what might otherwise be biased or "automatic" assumptions about how to ration the use of scarce resources, such as intensive care unit (ICU) space during a pandemic, to ensure that the needs of whole populations are taken into account. Respect for patient autonomy, on the other hand, inspires doctors and other caregivers to provide more rather than less information if wanted by the patient, and requires that decisions about treatment are being made by the patient or her medical proxies, with medical staff providing input, rather than the other way around.[19]

The same is true of fairness in business: fairness is not just one thing. For decades the field of organizational justice, which studies questions of fair treatment by organizations and their members, was riven by debates about the definition of fairness in business and how many types of fairness there might be.

This is not just a theoretical concern for academics. If you want to know whether a certain type of performance appraisal is perceived as fair or unfair by employees, you need to understand how they think about what is fair. Consider the "rank and yank" appraisal system, popularized in the 1980s by Jack Welch, GE's former CEO, which advised stack-ranking employees by performance and removing the bottom 10 percent every year. By the mid-2000s GE had abandoned the system,[20] but that was after it had become standard operating procedure at hundreds of companies whose leaders wanted to match GE's long record of increased earnings. But is the system really fair? What happens if every employee performs really well: Is it fair to penalize someone whose performance would be great in a different division, but who has the bad luck of being with a whole team of star performers? Is losing your job as a result of being at the bottom unfair or the reasonable consequence of less-than-average performance?

In 2001, Jason Colquitt, a management researcher who is interested in the benefits of managing employees fairly, broke new ground by creating and validating a four-dimensional measure of fairness that has since become the most widely used measure of fairness in the field of organizational justice.[21] Colquitt's model divides fairness in organizations into four categories. Colquitt uses the term "justice," but we've taken the liberty of using "fairness" for the sake of discussing trust in a business context.

The first category is *procedural fairness*, which is fairness in decision-making: consistency, accuracy, and a voice for those impacted by the decision. When The Ritz-Carlton's managers invite, indeed expect, employees to participate in continuous improvement, they are not just giving the people who work in their hotels a voice, they are also ensuring that the company has realistic data, informed by employee experience, to help them make sound business decisions.

Second is *informational fairness*: how clearly leaders describe the rationale for their actions and how truthful they are when they communicate. Dave Cote strongly believed in using furloughs instead of layoffs to help Honeywell recover quickly from the Great Recession, and described his rationale to customers, employees, shareholders, and suppliers. But be warned: candor that challenges conventional wisdom is not always appreciated. In a 2015 interview he recalled ruefully, "It was in the beginning of 2010 or thereabouts that it became pretty clear that the recovery was real, that there was the potential for a V-shaped recovery...(which I had said could happen but nobody ever thought it was possible), but once it started happening then I looked pretty good. But for that 15-month interregnum there were a lot of questions about my sanity."[22]

Third is *distributive fairness*: an assessment of how fair the outcomes of decisions and actions are. This is what so enraged the participants in the layoff research study—that a decision about something as important as who would keep or lose their job was based on chance. If a company lumps good performers and bad performers together, or better trained employees and just-off-the-street novices, they create an environment where effort and achievement are not rewarded, eliminating any reason for employees to work hard.

Fourth is *interpersonal fairness*: how individuals and groups are treated in personal interactions with a company and its members. The Ritz-Carlton treats even the employees they don't hire to a respectful interviewing experience, a box of miniature chocolates, and a fond farewell when they leave. As the chief human resources officer explained, "If someone is not hired and we just disregard them, what does that accomplish? You create someone in the community who looks at you and says, 'Those guys are morons. They are arrogant imbeciles who don't understand who I am, who don't value me as a person.' We don't want that."[23]

So, what does it look like to bake fairness into your company's processes?

After its disastrous 1999 layoffs, Michelin realized it would have to continue cutting jobs in Europe to remain competitive. Michelin's restructuring was driven by two factors. First, Michelin's production footprint in Europe was dominated by small and inefficient plants, which needed to be converted to larger and more productive facilities. The second factor was the location of Michelin's European factories. Michelin had expanded over the years into small towns where they could be a dominant employer with close ties to the community, and where they had a better chance of avoiding the waves of unionization that had been sweeping France and other countries.[24] Those small and isolated factories were now dragging down Michelin's profitability. Édouard Michelin knew he needed to transform the patchwork he had into an efficient production footprint. Moreover, he was determined to create what he called an "all-terrain capability" that would enable the company to anticipate market shifts and changing economic conditions in order to manage through good times and bad.

The question was how to do all of this without incurring further wrath from their employees, the public, and the government. Thus began a ten-year quest to find a way to restructure fairly as Michelin embarked on fifteen separate layoffs that would affect nearly half of its 35,000 employees working in Europe.[25]

Procedural Fairness

Michelin began its quest for a fair layoff by developing a process in 2003 for planning restructuring projects. Patrick Lepercq, the former head of public affairs for Michelin, along with other key senior managers, created this process to ensure that the company had a defensible business case for each restructuring project, starting with the creation of an internal team for each one. Instead of

automatically jumping to the conclusion that a layoff or plant closure was the best solution, the task force asked themselves four
questions:

1. What is the business problem to be solved?
2. What are the root causes of the problem?
3. Why is downsizing the only or best alternative?
4. What *could* be accepted by the various stakeholders?

The team included all of the departments involved in the restructuring: typically representatives of the business lines, social
relations (unions), public affairs, territory (country) development,
economic development, and corporate development in the event
of a potential spin-off. The team was in charge of the total project, from the anticipation phase through implementation. One
of their major goals, in addition to providing internal guidance,
was to ensure external parties Michelin had close relationships
with would understand the business rationale for the restructuring project and have accurate information about Michelin's
actions.

This approach was called the Ramp Down and Up Model.
Ramping down meant eliminating product lines or closing a plant,
while ramping up involved transferring production and employees to other expanding plants. Fifteen restructuring programs were
implemented over a decade using these approaches, in actions like
the three-region plan for production in Spain, Italy, and France.
That plan required closing six car tire plants while investing heavily in four other plants in the three-country region.

As Michelin continued to work on restructuring, it developed
a second model, the Turnaround Model. This model allowed local
management, unions, and employees to generate a plan to *turn
around* a plant. For the turnaround, the plant would change its
mission and produce a different product or set of products. The
turnaround process was based on answering the four questions

listed above and encouraging an open and detailed examination of the way that plant operated and how it could be improved.

Michelin wasn't just being collaborative for the sake of being collaborative. Its instincts were excellent. It turns out that involving people in a process of making a decision gives them a greater sense of fairness even if they have no control over the decision itself. In 1975, two professors, John Thibaut and Laurens Walker, introduced us to this idea in their groundbreaking (and aptly titled) book *Procedural Justice*. Thibaut and Walker studied legal conflicts settled by a third party.[26] They found, surprisingly, that people believed a process was fair if they had control over how their case was presented and for how long, even if they had no control over the actual decision.[27] In organizational justice research this became known as the fair process effect and also the voice effect, and it is one of the field's most replicated findings.[28] As Michelin and countless other organizations have found, Thibaut and Walker's findings aren't limited to the legal field.

In 2013, Michelin began the first public test case of its new turnaround approach. Its French Roanne factory, located between Clermont-Ferrand and Lyons, produced 16- to 17-inch tires and was struggling. Instead of shutting it down and moving the production to a more efficient factory, Michelin asked the plant's managers and employees if they could come up with solutions for keeping the factory open profitably. Remi de Verdilhac, the director of the territory of France for Michelin, recalls several discussions with managers and employees and union officials facilitated by an outside consultant. The discussions included everything from new quality standards, to production costs, the working environment, and safety standards. De Verdilhac noted, "We worked all together, so it wasn't just a union diagnostic, or a worker diagnostic, or a management diagnostic. We worked all together, with a mediator, just to trust each other."

After the discussions came the planning. From October 2014 to March 2015, six working groups involving over seventy people from Michelin's headquarters, the local company, and its plant in Roanne worked to develop a full turnaround plan. The plan involved changing the type of tire the plant manufactured. However, the plan had to be approved by the executive in charge of that product line for Michelin, as well as by Michelin's executive committee.

Finally, on May 21, 2015, the local company and unions signed a Pacte d'Avenir 2019 (Future Pact 2019) with the approval of 95 percent of the factory's employees. In the agreement Michelin committed to invest at least €80 million to create a new production line of premium tires from 19 to 21 inches for luxury vehicles, replacing the inefficient 16- to 17-inch tire production line.

Under the plan, the total headcount at the factory fell from 850 to 720 through natural attrition. The plant reorganized into five teams, which worked around the clock, seven days a week, compared with the previous structure of four teams that worked Monday to mid-day Saturday. The employees also agreed to work up to six additional days per year. These changes gave Roanne the flexibility to increase or decrease its annual production volume by 12 percent and respond rapidly to shifts in customer demand. It created a real competitive advantage for the site against other Michelin factories as well as the factories of competitors.[29] As part of the investment, Michelin agreed to €2 million to improve the quality of life at work.[30]

The final victory came in the form of an endorsement from the head of one of the unions, whose comment underscores how perspectives of stakeholders can differ: "We maintained our level of wages and operating of 35 hours: it is a rather good agreement."[31]

Instead of closing down Roanne, Michelin got everyone involved to come up with a solution that allowed the factory to continue to operate without resorting to a single layoff and improved Michelin's competitiveness, a win for everyone.

So, how do you design a fair process? Researcher Gerald Leventhal and colleagues brought greater precision to the idea of a fair process by developing six criteria for judging what makes a process fair.[32] In their model, a fair process is consistent, free from bias, accurate, correctable, and ethical, and allows for different voices.[33] This model provides a useful diagnostic to determine whether a process you are using would be perceived as fair, using questions like the following.

 » *Are we being consistent?*

Are we applying our process consistently across people and time?

In Michelin's case this meant that every site that was going through a layoff analysis had an internal task force that asked the same questions to determine its future.

 » *Is our process free from bias?*

Have we ensured that our processes aren't being driven by parties with vested interests in a particular outcome?

Michelin made sure several different parties from managers to union members were involved in the decision-making process and used outside consultants to facilitate the discussions.

 » *Is our process accurate?*

Have we collected and used accurate information in making decisions in this process?

Michelin's internal task force held multiple discussions in Roanne to gather the information from a broad range of perspectives, and spoke to enough people to ensure that the information was correct.

 » *Is our process correctable?*

Do we have a mechanism to correct flawed or inaccurate decisions?

Michelin's process was to use an internal task force to study the best business solution for a factory and investigate and discuss ideas that came from factory employees. This allowed Michelin to self-correct its strategic decisions rather than have a few executives far removed from the situation make decisions.

» *Is our process ethical?*

Does our process conform to personal, organizational, or prevailing standards of ethics and morality?

Michelin's relentless focus on making sure employees could come up with a way to keep their livelihoods while also ensuring Michelin was able to sustain a profit is just about as fair as business gets.

» *Does our process allow for different voices to be heard?*

Does our process ensure that we take into account the opinions of individuals and groups affected by our decisions?

We can't stress it enough, but think about all of the people who were given a chance to speak up at Roanne and the seventy people were involved in developing the turnaround plan.

Informational Fairness

When I left my job at Fidelity Investments to join the Harvard Business School faculty, I knew I owed both my husband and children a conversation. I used different approaches (key to maintaining a happy family): full-on dialogue with my husband about pros and cons before making the decision, and then a straightforward and low-key description of the change for the kids. I knew I owed everyone similar content: an explanation of why I'd made the decision, how I foresaw it impacting them, and answers to whatever questions they had. Whether consciously or unconsciously, I was practicing informational fairness. Informational fairness is the art of communicating clearly and truthfully how a decision was made and why it was made to the people the decision impacts—in this case both my husband and children. (Note: My kids were strangely relieved. "At last," they said, "we can finally describe what you do for a living.")

Informational fairness is the crux of the promise organizations make to their customers. After all, customers make purchases under the assumption that they can trust what a company says about its products.

Consider Alibaba's redemption story. In 2011 the news broke that Alibaba, the massive and highly successful Chinese e-commerce company, had been accepting kickbacks and allowing fraudulent sellers to skip its verification process and set up accounts while still being certified as a "Gold Supplier." Although only 100 of Alibaba's 5,000 or so sales team members were responsible, they allowed 2,326 fraudulent merchants on the Alibaba platform, who set up accounts with the intent of defrauding customers.[34]

This was particularly damaging because Alibaba's promise to customers was that its Gold Suppliers had gone through a certification process that meant they could be trusted. The fraudulent sellers threatened the entire credibility of Alibaba's platform, and a slew of news articles followed questioning whether Alibaba would be able to survive the scandal. After all, if Alibaba's sales team was telling customers that fraudulent merchants were trustworthy, why would customers shop at Alibaba at all?

Jack Ma, Alibaba's founder, knew he had to act quickly to prevent Alibaba from losing its customers. He fired all the employees who had knowingly set up the fraudulent accounts as well as any employee who had known what was going on but not done anything. Alibaba's CEO and COO were also forced to resign even though they were not personally implicated in the scandal.[35]

Ma's vigilance was rewarded: in 2016 Alibaba briefly became the world's largest retailer, surpassing Walmart,[36] though Walmart later took back the crown.[37] However, had Ma not acted so swiftly and decisively, it's doubtful Alibaba could have achieved so much growth.

Informational fairness is just as important for employees within an organization. Jason Colquitt and a colleague conducted a field study to understand how the four dimensions of fairness (informational, distributive, procedural, and interpersonal) relate to trust.[38] They found informational fairness was the most important dimension for nurturing employee trust.

This bears thinking about. Understanding why a decision was made and how it was made was actually more important for employee trust than distributive fairness, which refers to how resources and pain points are allocated.[39] This is not to say that if a company is being completely unfair and senior leadership is raising its salaries while lowering everyone else's, employees will cheerfully swallow this news if there's an explanation. Rather, the point is that if a company is acting in good faith and makes a difficult decision, they will have a good explanation. Helping employees understand why a difficult decision was made and why this was the best way to go, can help employees accept it.

Yet companies don't tend to make use of this wisdom. Transparency during a layoff can be hard to come by. Frequently senior management will delay announcing layoffs until the last possible moment. Employees will lurk in the hallways speaking in hushed voices, forced to exchange information that is more rumor and gossip than fact. This situation is good for no one. It only adds to fear in an already unstable situation, and misinformation spreads.

Michelin went to extremes to make informational fairness a core part of its new restructuring process. It developed a communication strategy that took into account the needs and potential reactions of each of its different stakeholders, ranging from investors and government officials to unions and employees.

As a starting point, each of Michelin's task forces had to build a business case for restructuring. The task force documented the full history of the plant, commitments Michelin was expected to meet, and its past history of meeting those commitments.

In the case of a plant that it had to shut down, Michelin took special care to develop a strategy for discussing the closure with employees. Bruno Jacob was asked to develop the communication strategy for restructuring in Europe. He noted the first step was to communicate the why of the restructuring project. This entailed laying out all the facts for employees so they could understand the economic and competitive conditions that Michelin was responding to, rather than leaving employees to conclude that Michelin's decision was arbitrary or made because it prioritized profits over people. Jacob commented, "It is important to make understood not only what is happening in the closure, but also what is driving it—the external reasons coming from the market and from competitors—to understand the whole picture."[40]

For a plant that was going to be shut down, Michelin made sure that each shift of employees all heard the message together. Then, managers would deliver the message again to employees in their areas, so employees could ask questions or simply react. Michelin wanted to make sure people had enough time to absorb the news emotionally, process it, and then have another opportunity to come back with questions and reactions.

Michelin also supplied managers with presentations of the restructuring strategy and its rationale, complete with special guidance for how to respond to questions of the employees, and built similar communication materials for staff who dealt with other stakeholder groups like unions, the press (of course), and members of the government. At first Michelin focused its communication strategy on factory closures, but this evolved to include any kind of major change. "We have gone from communication about factory closures, to communication on changes in the company... to communication about the global organization—that's a key change," Jacob said.

In addition, Michelin extended its commitment to informational fairness to its investors. Prior to 2001, Michelin had shrouded itself in secrecy. Its particular form of incorporation meant that shareholders had limited influence over the company's management. Starting in 2001, Michelin instituted regular lunches and meetings with analysts and fund managers to help create more transparency and accountability with investors.

Michelin's communication process is novel and thorough, but how can you determine if your company's communication is fair? The first step is understanding that your audience members will have different reactions to news. Some will be positive, others negative, and the amount of time and ability of each person to absorb what they are hearing will vary widely. A fair communication process should expect a range of reactions as well as time and space for people who absorb information at different speeds to react.

Anticipating how others might respond to news is especially important when the information strikes you as both reasonable and right. This is an understatement, based on personal experience. Speeches about organizational change—at least in the near past—lent themselves with numbing regularity to a two-column chart, with one side labeled "before" and the other "after." The before list was a description of all the stupid, or poorly thought through, or inefficient, or somehow misguided actions that created the sorry state of the business prior to the change. The after column was usually a reversal of those critiques (say, "open" for "closed," or "fast" for "slow") that depicted the new world that would unfold, brought about by the new leader and leadership team.

The problem, of course, is that a good number (probably even most) of the people in the room were part of that before time, so the kind of frontal critique that makes so much sense to you as the new leader is an assault on all the people from the before regime. What sounds objective to you may come across as deliberate shading and exaggeration, leading those from before to doubt not just your ability to say what is true but even to see it.

Communication is more likely to be perceived as fair if it is managed as a two-way process, enabling people an opportunity to respond—to ask as well as be told. Technology can be used to either help or hurt this process. On the upside, technology can allow leaders to easily communicate with lots of people at once. However, beware of the downsides. Town hall formats and senior leader video communications aren't great for two-way dialogue. This can be managed to a certain extent with some thought: at HBS, when we have a celebrity speaker, we allow students to submit questions in advance. That way questions can be curated for quality and relevance, and similar ones can be condensed. However, leaders delivering unpleasant news should be aware that when there are curated questions, employees may become suspicious that difficult questions are being suppressed.

Michelin's low-tech solution of delivering news twice had a simple brilliance. It allowed employees time to process the information and come up with questions. The second round, where the information was delivered in small groups with a familiar manager, gave employees space to ask questions without the pressure of speaking up in a large group or to someone whom they may very well never have spoken with before.

Information fairness is rooted in respect for people. Above all, this means showing that you understand that you are communicating with lots and lots of *individuals*, who together make up a group. Some helpful questions to consider when trying to create an informationally fair process include the following:

- What information and evidence are we basing our decision on?
- With whom has this information been shared?
- What has been shared?
  - How relevant is the information to the individuals who are told?

- How well does it answer questions that the person in that role would be thinking about?
- What has not been shared? Why?
  - Is the withheld information relevant and material to the individuals impacted?
  - What is the justification for withholding it?
- When has it been shared?
  - How timely is the disclosure in relation to the action that is taken?
  - How much reaction time is provided to individuals impacted by the action?
- Have we put in place a process to receive, respond to, and act on feedback?

Distributive Fairness

While the evidence is that informational fairness is a key factor for being perceived as trustworthy, that doesn't mean that transparency is enough. Companies are still on the hook for how they make decisions about the allocation of benefits such as opportunities, harms such as layoffs, or resources such as pay. In other words, people still care about distributive fairness. When companies get this wrong, their relationships with stakeholders erode. Just as the babies in the earlier studies we described judged whether the distributions they were watching were fair, resource allocation decisions are similarly judged by the way the pie gets divided. Take, for example, the uproar over equal pay that BBC News dealt with beginning in 2017.

In 2013, Scottish journalist Carrie Gracie decided to take a newly created position as a China editor with the BBC. Gracie was, to use the technical term, a rock star. She had spent nearly three decades with the BBC, was fluent in Mandarin, and had won a Peabody Award for her ten-year reporting project on a rural Chinese community.

The new BBC post came with hardship. It required living 5,000 miles away from her teenage children, and it was very likely that Gracie would be subject to intimidation, surveillance, and police harassment from the Chinese government. She accepted the offer on the condition that she be paid the same salary as the BBC's male foreign editors. The BBC agreed and paid her a salary of £135,000.

In the summer of 2017, the BBC published a list of the pay of all of its employees earning over 150,000 pounds, including its highest paid journalists. The list comprised sixty-two men and thirty-four women. Gracie didn't make the list—nor did several other female stars. "I can only describe the feeling of being kept on much lower pay than male colleagues doing the same jobs for years," Samira Ahmed, the BBC journalist wrote, "as feeling as though bosses had naked pictures of you in their office and laughed every time they saw you. It is the humiliation and shame of feeling that they regarded you as second class, because that is what the pay gap means."[41]

Middle East editor Jeremy Bowen earned between £150,000 and £199,999, and Jon Sopel, North America editor, was paid between £200,000 and £249,999. Gracie was making 50 percent less than her male counterparts. Gracie was furious and heartbroken: "It's such a deep blow that your body kind of goes into a profound stop," she told the *New Yorker*.[42]

Gracie, however, did not stop. She and a group of colleagues sent a letter to Tony Hall, BBC's then director general. After the BBC responded by offering Gracie a 33 percent pay raise, Gracie posted an open letter of resignation. She wrote,

> But for far too long, a secretive and illegal BBC pay culture has inflicted dishonourable choices on those who enforce it. This must change.
>
> …It is painful to leave my China post abruptly and to say goodbye to the team in the BBC's Beijing bureau. But most of them are brilliant young women. I don't want their generation

to have to fight this battle in the future because my generation failed to win it now.[43]

Her letter launched a national movement encapsulated by the #IStandWithCarrie hashtag.[44] On January 31, 2018, Carrie testified in Parliament, which had demanded a hearing on the BBC's pay practices. In March, a group of BBC colleagues protested by visiting Tony Hall, the corporation's director general, with badges identifying each executive's salary.[45]

However, when we reached out to the BBC for comment, they maintained that at the time that Gracie was appointed she was paid the same as the editors for North America and Europe, and it did not commit to maintaining parity of pay. Rather, it tried to pay reporters according to their skills, experience, and the demands of the role.

The question of what it means to be fair can be tricky. Does fairness mean everyone receives the same salary? But shouldn't a star performer receive more than an employee who isn't pulling the same weight? What about a layoff—who gets to stay, and who has to go? What happens when you have an average performer who has been at your company for over a decade, versus a new hire with highly sought-after credentials? Do things change if one of these two employees has a family to support or is a student or has medical debt? These questions don't have easy answers. In fact, entire empires have started and ended because people have had different answers to these questions.

In the field of distributive justice (yes, it's a field of study— so don't feel too bad if you didn't have immediate answers to our questions), philosophers have come up with different types of principles that are used by groups to distribute benefits, resources, and harms fairly:[46]

- Strict egalitarianism, or total equality. Everyone receives the same thing regardless of who they are and what they need or want. This gets tricky because some resources are easy to measure and distribute equally (money, time off), while others aren't (authority to make decisions, social capital). Moreover, people value resources differently.

- The difference principle, associated with the philosopher John Rawls. He established his difference principle after stating two even more fundamental principles of fairness or justice: First, each person has a justified claim to the same basic human rights as any other person. Second, there must be fair equality of opportunity, in which everyone has the same ability to compete for ways to better themselves. Rawls's difference principle then allows for inequities in distribution as long as the distribution makes all people better off, and especially those who are the least fortunate in society. In other words, a distribution is fair in which wealthy people are richer, as long as the poorest people are also the best off that they could be, compared to any other distribution scheme.[47]
- Equality of opportunity/resource egalitarianism. Everyone has the same access to resources, but they can choose which resources they want. Philosopher Ronald Dworkin used the metaphor of a fair auction to illustrate this. Everyone is given the same amount to spend at the auction, but they can choose what to buy, and will end up leaving the auction with different resources depending on what they want and their ability to bid strategically.
- Welfare-based, or distributing resources in order to maximize the overall well-being of the group. This does not take into account individual differences and needs but rather prioritizes the larger picture.
- Just deserts. Under this principle, people deserve rewards because of their contribution to the group through their actions or character. The challenges with this are who measures the contribution and how. This can also perpetuate inequalities

because those who can give the most are often the ones with the most resources, best education, and so forth.

- Libertarian. Any distribution of resources is fair as long as the resources are acquired through a legitimate process or transferred to them through a legitimate process.
- Critical theories. There are a number of theorists who argue that due to the injustices of the past, certain groups deserve remuneration, or should be given extra consideration in the principles outlined above.

None of these principles provide *the* right answer for how a company should practice distributive fairness. Rather, they present a menu of options that can be taken into consideration in making decisions. A company could practice distributive fairness by choosing among one or some of these norms. However, what is important—as we just discussed in procedural fairness—is that there is a process for establishing distributive fairness and it is applied consistently instead of on a case-by-case basis.

First, it's important to select a philosophy and understand which distributive norms it will apply. For example, in the US government, pay is driven by egalitarianism. The General Schedule lays out different pay grades. Jobs are assigned a pay grade, and everyone in the pay grade receives the same pay. The BBC's pay, on the other hand, was theoretically driven by just-deserts fairness— those who contributed more should receive more. And Gracie was given assurances that her pay would be the equal of other foreign editors, yet the BBC failed to deliver on just-deserts fairness, not to mention its own word.

Second, it's important to understand the criteria you use to allocate benefits, resources, and harms, and the ways that these criteria will be perceived. The government doesn't have a reputation for hiring competitive alpha types, but in many countries, it does have a reputation for paying equitably. Meanwhile, while the BBC appeared to be rewarding merit, it was actually rewarding gender: men earned more than women in comparable jobs.

Third is the need to understand the context. What is the world you are operating in? How will specific benefits, rewards, and harms actually be perceived? This may feel straightforward, but leaders get this wrong all the time—to the point that Jack Welch, the former CEO of General Electric, devoted a few pages of his memoir to reminding business leaders that rewards for employees should not be punishments. (It turns out Welch wasn't wrong about everything related to employee morale.) He waded into the details and point-blank told managers to avoid "stilted, company-orchestrated parties that everyone hates," and think about something that employees would actually enjoy: an all-expenses paid trip with their families, or tickets to a show, or the latest tech gadget.[48] Meanwhile, the BBC rewarded gender, perhaps without even being aware of the bias in its decisions, leading to the Carrie Gracie story in 2017.

Fourth is the need to get stakeholder agreement. The distribution of benefits, harms, and resources is one of the powers that companies have, and it has a huge impact on people's lives. One of the key steps to ensuring that stakeholders are on board and feel they are being treated fairly, is to check in with them and ask what they think. When Dave Cote made the decision to furlough employees at Honeywell, Honeywell held periodic town halls and had a company hotline where employees could submit anonymous feedback on how the furloughs were going.

When you do this, understand that employees (and managers, and executives) rarely feel they are being treated entirely fairly when it comes to distribution outcomes like pay. This conclusion is generally drawn in a vacuum or with incomplete information, since distribution outcomes are rarely made public.

I learned the power of seeing the whole picture myself when I served for a while as a human resources vice president. One of my responsibilities was to make recommendations to our president on increases in pay and other financial incentives for our senior team. I began my career as a female executive in the mid-1970s and believed I was simply being realistic in assuming that I was being paid less than men in comparable roles given how few female executives there were. When I finally opened the files with everyone's pay history, I was surprised—pleasantly so—to see how appropriately I felt the members of our team were being paid. I must confess I felt lighter after I had this realization. I had not realized the hard rock of never-expressed resentment I had been lugging around, but it's true: it was only after I saw what my peers were paid that I finally believed I was being treated fairly in my own compensation.

But my intuition that I might be underpaid because of my gender didn't come from nowhere. I was a lucky exception rather than the rule. Getting lower pay was, and continues to be, an unfortunate and unfair reality for many women, certainly then, and frustratingly, still now. Based on 2018 census data, on average, US women of all races earned 82 cents for every $1 paid to men of all races. When you compound racial bias with gender bias, the spread gets much larger: Black women earn a median wage of 62 cents; Native American and Alaska Native women earn 57 cents, and Hispanic or Latina women earn 54 cents. Asian women as a whole are closer to the wage for white, non-Hispanic men, earning 90 cents, but subgroups such Nepali women earn just 50 cents.[49]

Since 2017, the UK (home to Carrie Gracie and the BBC) has required companies and public institutions with more than 250 employees to report their gender wage gaps, but this additional sunshine (or name-and-shame) strategy has yet to pay off, since their median gender wage gap numbers were stubbornly stuck at 17.3 percent in 2019, down marginally from 17.8 percent in 2018.[50] The *Financial Times* summed up the situation: "There are still no sectors of the UK economy where women are paid the same as men."[51] Nonetheless, you have to give the Brits their due. At least they are moving the gender gap in both private and public institutions directly into the broader court of public opinion where pressure for change can mount as the yearly reporting goes on and the numbers don't budge.

Many companies adopt practices that are transparent around pay, such as publishing pay bands for specific positions and for a given level of performance. Even then, it is worth asking questions like the following to understand how the members of your organization understand and evaluate the fairness of the distribution decisions you make.

- How do you understand our company's philosophy for making decisions around pay and promotions?
- Do you believe we are making decisions using the best (i.e., fairest) criteria?
- How do you assess the outcomes we achieve through our pay and promotions processes—are they fair?

Distribution is fundamentally an interaction, a decision made by one party about the allocation of benefits, resources, and harms that creates an outcome for another. Interactions are the give and take that trust is built upon, so knowing whether you are succeeding at being perceived as fair is worth finding out, especially if you're not.

The Carrie Gracie story does have a happy ending: Eventually, after nearly a year, Carrie Gracie and Tony Hall reached an agreement and issued a joint statement on June 29, 2018. Carrie Gracie received 280,000 pounds in back pay, which she donated to a charity established in 1866—the Fawcett Society—which campaigns for gender equality in pay and women's rights. At her request, Gracie took an unpaid leave from the BBC to speak and write about her work in China and about equal pay, and she wrote a book about her experiences. In 2020, Gracie left the BBC.[52]

Meanwhile, the BBC continued its efforts to both report on and reduce its pay gap, which declined from 9.3 to 7.6 percent in one year. Today it is 6.2 percent, substantially lower than the UK's national average of 17.3 percent. The July 2018 report on highest earners also showed more women than in 2017, though none were among the top dozen earners.[53]

It took the BBC several missteps to correct its error. By contrast, Michelin's approach to divesting its rubber plantation in Bahía, Brazil, exemplifies what thinking about distributive justice on several dimensions looks like.

In 2004, Michelin owned rubber plantations in Nigeria and Brazil. The Brazilian plantations were under assault by the South American leaf blight fungus, and Michelin wanted out of the plantation business in general. Exiting, however, was not so simple.

Michelin was the largest employer within a radius of 150 kilometers. The plantation's 600 employees had few prospects of finding new employment. Bahía was one of the least developed areas of Brazil and home to an important hotspot of biodiversity and many endangered species. The Bahía region was also dealing with deforestation by the local agriculture industry.

Rubber is an environmentally sustainable crop, since once rubber trees are planted, they have a productive life of between thirty and forty years. Any other industrial activity that replaced the plantation would likely have a negative environmental impact. Already, in its examination of the problem, Michelin scores points for thinking about the distributive norms of equity and needs of multiple groups at once—what did it owe its employees as well as the surrounding community where it had worked for decades?

Michelin considered several options. The first was to transfer the plantation to the government to be redistributed through the national land reform program. This option posed environmental and social risks if the people who received the land didn't receive adequate sustainability training. The committee also considered transferring the plantation to a conservation NGO or selling it to another business. If they transferred it to a conservation group, they would have allowed the plantation to revert to forest, eliminating any employment. However, a new company might not commit to environmental sustainability.

Michelin took a novel approach and decided to break up the land into twelve smaller parcels, which it turned over to its employees. The owners of these small-scale plantations would then be able to sell the rubber to Michelin or to other buyers. Twelve owners would be selected using a rigorous process (check mark for distributive fairness through just deserts), each to manage one of the small plantations.

Michelin gave the selected candidates loans to purchase their plantations and provided seeds and seedlings at cost as well as technical assistance. Rubber trees take between five and seven years to reach maturity, at which point they can be tapped for their sap. Michelin developed a rotation system with other crops including bananas and cocoa that would allow the farmers to earn income throughout the year while they waited for the rubber trees to mature.

Approximately 95 percent of the Michelin employees were absorbed into the new plantations. All employees were offered severance packages in accordance with Brazilian labor law—check mark for distributive fairness through equality. As a condition of the transfer of ownership, the new owners had to apply the same labor rights to the workers that Michelin provided, including the right to organize and to collectively bargain over wages, hours, and working conditions.

No one would have blamed Michelin if they had chosen any of the options they initially considered for the Bahía plantation. Instead, they embarked on a journey into the unknown. In 2015, ten years after the project began, the plantations were still operational.

All the loans to the plantation owners had been reimbursed. Michelin had 200 employees still on site working in an R&D center and rubber processing plant. The small plantations employed 350 more people than they did when Michelin owned the plantation. And more than 1,000 farmers in Bahía had also benefited from participating in the agriculture training programs Michelin started. Both Michelin's employees and the surrounding community benefited from Michelin's distributive fairness. Not only did Michelin manage to distribute the pie fairly to multiple stakeholders, they also managed to do it so well that they made more pie for everyone.

Interpersonal Fairness

The dynamic of interpersonal fairness—the respect and consideration we are shown by others—is a concern for all of us. It colors our feelings about people, based on how they treat us. And in the context of business, we are quick to assess how we as individuals or as members of a group are treated in personal interactions with companies and their members.

When a company has to restructure and can offer—as Michelin did—the opportunity to move to another division or production site it engages in interpersonal fairness. But an action that sounds so straightforward and logical is in reality anything but. Imagine, just for a minute, what you would have to give up if you were to move to another place. When you think about how deeply you are imbedded in your home community, it's hard to seriously consider moving. (Relax. It's not just you. According to the Holmes and Rahe scale of the most stressful life events, moving is a solid 20 points, the same as a major change in working hours.)

Michelin was dealing with a large population of blue-collar workers who needed to be relocated. Thierry Chiche, Michelin's former head of industry for the European car and light truck business, described the scale of a restructuring in human terms. "When you have to deal with 1,000 people, which might be a collective of five different groups of people, that's five different sets of emotions at five different times, and also 1,000 individuals with their problems, their families, their specific cases, with their mindset—we have to manage that and we have to be prepared for that."[54]

To facilitate relocations, Michelin built processes to help their workers learn about the new town they would be moving to. These included having employees spend one or two weeks at the new plant, and giving them time to visit the region to look for schools and housing and to get used to the new environment. In addition, Michelin organized forums where people already working at the plant would describe their region, factory, and jobs. Franz Bléhaut, former head of the personnel department in France, commented, "That's useful to decrease employees' fears of relocation. Since people are talking together, things change. You have a personal relationship with someone and it's very helpful."[55]

Interpersonal fairness is judged by the respect and consideration we show to others. But that raises an important question: How do we learn what someone else would regard as respect and consideration? Please note that I am using the word "learn" rather than "understand" deliberately.

Understanding is passive, especially when it comes to apprehending the perspectives of others. Learning looks more like the expression "Walk a mile in another person's shoes." One form of learning is to try to imaginatively replicate someone else's experience in order to understand it. Or, as a particularly insightful MBA student pointed out in class, while you can't always replicate the *experience* of someone who is different from you, you can identify the *feelings* that person is having, recall a time when you felt like that, and learn where they are coming from through your shared feelings.

From Michelin it would appear that there is yet another path, and that is the path of learning through an active search for understanding. We see a common approach in the stories recounted by the Michelin managers. Whether it's learning how much empowerment can strengthen workers' resilience by being involved in turning around a plant, or what it takes to motivate an employee to move from one factory town to another, Michelin's managers treat their goal of interpersonal fairness as an object of study. They assume that what works will never be readily apparent, will always need to be tried, and can always be done better.

Of course, Michelin's approaches won't necessarily work for other companies, since they were specifically tailored to solve Michelin's problems. However, they serve as an excellent guidepost to show us what is possible. In order to design our own processes that are interpersonally fair, you can start with the list of questions below:

- Have we tried to imagine how we would feel if we were in the situation of the other person or group?
- Have we asked any questions to find out how the other person feels about the situation?
- Do we treat people with the respect we would want others to show to us if our roles were reversed?
- Do our words and actions show consideration? How well do we take others' situations and needs into account?
- Do our words and actions show respect? Do we treat people as having value because they are people—individuals who are worthy of respect simply by virtue of being another human being?
- Do we assume that individuals and groups are different, and that we will need to learn each time what allows them to feel understood and valued?

Overall, Michelin implemented fifteen restructuring programs in Europe between 2003 and 2013 and has conducted others since, improving its process along the way. About half of the 35,000 people working in European industrial facilities were involved in the changes, as workers in sites that were closed or downsized, or in sites that were expanded through the transfer of production volumes from other facilities. The true measure of their success? Michelin stayed out of the papers, and as far as we know, is still famous for their tires, their really cute logo, and the Michelin star rating for restaurants instead of a slew of horrific layoffs. In other words, the second time around, Michelin made a smashing success of being fair and took it to an entirely different level, unlocking new avenues most people would have never thought possible.

FIVE

IMPACT

Our Actions Speak

It is not only what we do, but also what we do
not do, for which we are accountable.
—Molière

W E CAN OFTEN FOOL OURSELVES INTO THINKING THAT
good intentions—taking actions we believe are for the good
of others—are all that matter. The actual truth—the result of your
good intentions—can be difficult to foresee, something we've all
experienced in our personal lives if we think deeply about the past
and are honest with ourselves. What people actually care about,
and what history will remember you for, is the impact you create. Your intentions matter, but your impact matters even more, as
Mao Zedong discovered with his disastrous Four Pests campaign.

The year was 1958, the country China, and our protagonist,
Chairman Mao, had an ambitious plan to improve public health.
The Communists had been in power for nine years,[1] and China was
in the midst of launching the Great Leap Forward, a movement
to industrialize and catch up with the West. Strategies included

switching to a communal lifestyle where everyone turned into an industrialist:[2] people dropped everything to make steel in their backyards. Even pots and pans were sacrificed to the goal of making more steel, while farmwork stopped.[3]

The Chinese were also grappling with a wave of deadly diseases that had swept through the country: tuberculosis, plague, cholera, polio, malaria, to name a few. The infant mortality rate was 300/1,000.[4] Mao's government had taken the first steps of creating a public health system, which included vaccinating nearly 300 million people and building water sanitation systems.[5] Still, death and disease lingered in the air. Something had to be done.

To address this, Mao's government came up with the Four Pests campaign. The campaign aimed to eradicate flies, mosquitos, rats, and sparrows. Flies spread diseases like typhoid and cholera; mosquitos, malaria; and rats, the plague. (Scientists now argue that human parasites spread the plague, and rats have unfairly taken the rap.)[6] Meanwhile, sparrows, while cuter than rats, mosquitos, and flies, nibbled the grain peasants worked so hard to plant and harvest. At the time, scientists estimated that each sparrow was responsible for stealing and eating 4.5 kg (roughly 10 lbs.) of grain a year.[7] Mao was determined: the sparrows had to go.

Mao's government put up colorful illustrated posters urging the public to fight these four public enemies. Everyone from the elderly to the very young got involved. Businesses, schools, and government agencies held contests for cleanliness and handed out rewards to people who collected the most flies, mosquitos, rat tails, or sparrow carcasses.[8] Children would bang pots and pans so sparrows wouldn't be able to rest and would tumble from the sky, exhausted.[9] Overall, people collected 100 million kg of flies (220 million lbs.), 11 million kg of mosquitos (24 million lbs.), 1.5 billion rats, and 1 billion sparrows.[10] The campaign was a massive success.

Sort of. It turns out that sparrows are an integral part of a healthy ecosystem: they eat insects, including locusts. Without sparrows to keep the locust population under control, the locust population ballooned. Locusts swarmed the land, gobbling up crops. Meanwhile, government officials—either out of devotion to the cause or fear—exaggerated the amount of grain they'd produced and even exported some.[11] Combined together, these actions triggered the Great Chinese Famine, which killed up to an estimated 45 million people.[12]

Journalist Yang Jisheng lived through the famine and spent over ten years working undercover to collect evidence about it, which he later wrote about in a book (which is banned in China). He recalls returning to his hometown after being told that his uncle was dying of starvation and finding a ghost town: the fields were bare,[13] there were no dogs or chickens, and the trees had no bark because it had all been stripped off and eaten.[14] "Documents report several thousand cases where people ate other people.... Parents ate their own kids. Kids ate their own parents," Yang told NPR in 2012.[15]

Officials tried to blame the famine on natural disasters like floods, but Yang found documents from the head of the statistics bureau written in 1958 that admitted "we give whatever figures the upper-level wants" and evidence that reports of the incidents of natural disasters during the famine years had been inflated to perpetuate the official narrative.[16]

What officials were trying to hide was the enormous failure of Mao's policies, including the Four Pests campaign. The campaign exemplifies good intentions and terrible impact—the annihilation of millions. The campaign was incredibly effective: Chairman Mao was able to mobilize the population to collect millions of pounds of dead insects, rats, and birds. If that isn't competence, we don't know what is. Companies and governments wish they could change people's behavior on such a grand scale. The campaign was well intentioned—the goal was to improve public health, which can hardly be argued with. On the other hand, it unleashed wildly destructive unintended consequences, and for that reason alone, the Four Pests campaign is remembered as a spectacular failure, never mind Mao's good intentions or the excellent execution. It turns out, impact matters a great deal. At times, it is the difference between life and death.

Judged by Our Actions

We certainly judge people on why they do what they do and find many reasons, as we saw in Chapter 3, that convince us on the basis of intentions alone that some people can't be trusted. Yet the impacts of people's actions are deeply important to us. In fact, I had a student observe that her post-millennial generation was even more sensitive to impact than to purpose, the result of knowing it was up to them to fix the inequities and rapidly escalating climate changes of the world they've inherited. While trust is built from the inside out and starts with a company's motives, for customers, employees, investors, and the public, impact is motives brought to life. When people experience negative impacts from a company's actions, they begin a process of unraveling trust, asking how competent the company could be, and what, after all, were its motives—why did it act as it did?

As we mentioned in Chapter 3, as human beings, we crave virtue. We long to know that people are acting with good intentions, and when we believe in their good intentions, we are willing to forgive them much. However, if virtue is sufficient to have a positive view of someone's actions, we would be satisfied with Chairman Mao's campaign to eradicate the sparrows. Instead we are horrified, because we are practical and judge by results and not just the aspiration or the journey. We may crave virtue, but we are also deeply interested in the fruits of virtue, and at times conflate the two, imagining that good intentions are enough to lead to good impacts, when this is by no means always the case.

Craving virtue for virtue's sake is woven into the history of philosophy. Aristotle wrote about it, and humanist philosophers such as the Dutch scholar Erasmus and English statesman Thomas More built their reputations and work in the 1500s on their belief in the power of human virtue. In fact, they were good friends, and both attempted to educate leaders in the virtue of virtue: Erasmus wrote *The Education of a Christian Prince* in 1516,[17] the same year that Thomas More's "Utopia" was published. "Utopia" is a thought experiment that describes a fictional world where no one owns property and money does not exist but everyone has access to all of the natural resources they need.[18] Erasmus believed that education could eradicate human evil by bringing out the best in people,[19] while More believed in the power of human reason to mitigate human evil.[20]

As human beings, we love that belief, even though it may not be realistic for a world that's filled with plenty of vice. We have a history of canonizing people who believe in virtue for virtue's sake. We admire Thomas More because he was such a staunch believer in his ideals and his religion that he died for them. As the story goes, King Henry VIII wanted the pope to annul his marriage to Catherine of Aragon (she had not been able to bear a healthy male heir) so he could marry Anne Boleyn. When the pope would not annul the marriage, Henry VIII rejected the pope and demanded that More, his lord chancellor who oversaw the legal system, do it instead.[21] Eventually, after a five-year standoff, More refused, on the grounds that it went against his religious convictions, and Henry VIII had him put to death. Today, we remember him as a martyr.

Whenever I teach Thomas More in my Moral Leader class—complete with students' viewing the 1967 Academy Award–winning film *A Man for All Seasons*—some students are inspired, and others are furious. It's painful to see a compelling character like Thomas More, especially Thomas More as depicted by the British playwright Robert Bolt, die for what seems like no good reason. Thomas More might actually be immoral, some students argue, because what about the impact of his moral beliefs on his family? (You have not truly lived until you've seen a classroom full of smart and passionate students arguing that Thomas More is *immoral*.)

My students are getting to an important point, however, which is that we care deeply about impact, and we may care even more about it than we'd like to admit. It's a concept that Machiavelli, a contemporary of More and Erasmus, was quick to recognize and point out. Machiavelli's *The Prince*, written in 1513, led the British philosopher Isaiah Berlin to conclude (in an essay aptly titled "The Originality of Machiavelli"[22]) that Machiavelli's real argument—the reason his book is so unsettling and continues to be debated 500 years later—is that "princes" must have a different kind of morality than that which governs other people. They are, according to Machiavelli, under a special obligation to ensure the survival of the state. Rather than cultivating virtue through education or moral reason as Erasmus and More suggest, Machiavelli believed that leaders should cultivate the *appearance* of virtue. Machiavelli advised, "It is unnecessary for a prince to have all the good qualities I have enumerated, but it is very necessary to appear to have them."[23] In other words, Machiavelli would have figured out a way for More to live while maintaining a reputation for virtue. Ironically, Machiavelli's blunt and practical take did not help his own appearance of virtue. Instead, his name has become synonymous with connivance and deceit. There is even a psychological metric named after him, the Mach scale, which, according to the American Psychological Association's *Dictionary of Psychology*, is "a measurement of the degree to which individuals condone, tolerate, or condemn the use of manipulation and deceit in pursuit of material or other aims."[24]

When we combine the additional insights provided by Machiavelli with views of the humanists, we have a more complete view of how we trust. We may crave virtue, but that does not mean we are blind to the impact of someone's actions no matter how well intentioned. Machiavelli warns that leaders earn hatred when they take away their followers' land or women (we prefer the term "loved ones").[25] In other words, we start to hate and mistrust a leader when the impact of their actions hurts us.

We made the point in Chapter 3 that we want to know companies operate from well-intentioned motives. However, that doesn't mean that companies are necessarily off the hook if they cause harm. In that chapter we described an experiment designed to understand how people assess harm based on whether it was committed inadvertently or out of bad intent. In the study, a fictional CEO ran a company where salary was partially based on profit-sharing and the CEO made a bad investment. When participants were told that the CEO intentionally made a bad investment, hoping that if employees earned less, they would work harder, to improve future profits, they rated the harm of his actions from 0 (no harm) to 100 at an average of 66. When participants were told the CEO made the investment because he thought the gains from it could be spent in ways that would allow his employees to earn more, participants rated the harm he created at an average of 48.

Although it's impossible to say what 66 points of harm means to each person, if you compare 66 to 48, on average, good intentions did not entirely wipe away the CEO's impact.

While this finding comes from an experimental lab where participants are given a limited scenario to assess, it holds true in the world outside. We can see how it plays out in companies and industries from the 2019 Michelin Movin' On transportation conference. It was held in Montreal, and business and government leaders and researchers and scientists who work on transportation came together to discuss ideas. Amid a colorful backdrop of circus performers putting on impromptu performances in the hallways, and panels interspersed with local singers and dancers giving mini shows, we attended a panel on the future of environmental sustainability.

There, a senior leader from a major oil and gas company discussed his company's plan for environmental sustainability. He sounded great! He was well versed in the vocabulary and actions of the fight to save the environment, using terms like "clean energy" and "going green," and discussed how his company was committed to sustainability goals. We nodded along happily because he sounded reasonable and we agreed with the goals his company had set. Yet at the same time, it was hard to know how seriously to take him and his company's plans. After all, according to the Carbon Majors database, ninety companies have been responsible for over 63 percent of all carbon dioxide and methane emissions since 1751, while the top twenty polluters have been responsible for 29.5 percent of emissions.[26]

After he spoke, there was silence. Someone asked a polite question about how he planned to implement the environmental sustainability goals, and he responded with an even more encouraging reply. Then someone from the audience went for the money: "Given the amount of damage your company and companies in your industry [have] created, why should anyone believe a word you're saying?"

To the leader's credit (and neither of us would have liked to be in his shoes), he answered a difficult question deftly by pointing out that because his industry had had such a large impact, it was in a prime position to lead the charge for reversing the damage. A good answer, but neither the audience member nor we were entirely satisfied. Good intentions could not erase the impact of past damage in our minds. In part, this is why some industries are judged more harshly than others—it's hard to trust someone from an oil and gas company when they talk about saving the environment, or someone from a tobacco company when they talk about health, given how dangerous their products are to public and personal health.

However, most people don't have a clear view into the internal motivations of a company. Instead our relationship with a company is based primarily on how a company's actions impact us and those around us. A company's impact will be used to assess its good intentions, as Boeing learned.

Prior to the 737 Max 8 disasters, the public in general didn't have any questions about Boeing's trustworthiness as a company. After two of its 737 Max 8 jets crashed in October 2018 and March 2019, killing nearly 350 people, countries all over the world grounded the Boeing 737 Max 8 jets. The consequences didn't stop there. Next came the questions. In the space of two crashes, Boeing had lost the trust of the public, airlines, governments, and regulators because of the horrific and unquestionable impact of its planes. The 737 Max 8 jet had killed people. Boeing came under scrutiny. What had happened, why, and who was responsible?

First, there was a competence problem. The jets had a flawed design. Their new automated system relied on only one sensor. If it malfunctioned, a crash could be triggered. This was "not a good engineering system," an aeronautical engineer told the *New York Times*, labeling the design a royal screwup.[27]

But Boeing is one of the largest airplane manufacturers in the world. It wouldn't have gotten where it was if it was in the habit of designing faulty planes and had a serious competence problem. What went wrong with the 737 Max 8 jet?

This question inspired a full-on investigation of what happened, comparable to cleaning out the Augean stables. The resulting muck included 117 pages of internal communications showcasing a fractured culture at Boeing[28] and a decade-old Dutch study that criticized Boeing but was never published at the time.[29]

In the internal communications, a Boeing employee called the 737 Max 8 jet a joke as early as 2016, while others expressed concerns about the safety of the planes and said they wouldn't put their families on them.[30] Boeing executives had seemed to view the Federal Aviation Administration's regulations as a roadblock and made significant efforts to get the FAA to drop requirements like requiring pilot simulator training for the 737 Max 8, which also benefited Boeing's bottom line. (Boeing used the absence of pilot training as a negotiations carrot to increase their profits. For example, Boeing promised Southwest Airlines a $1 million rebate on each plane if the FAA ended up requiring that Southwest invest in simulator training.)[31] When an employee suggested adding more information in the pilot manual for how to handle the 737 Max 8 during emergencies, the idea was quashed because the extra information might make regulators require Boeing to provide more training to pilots, an expense Boeing wanted to avoid. "We need to sell this as a very intuitive basic pilot skill," the employee was told.[32] In designing the 737 Max 8 jet, Boeing had thrown both motives and means out the window. It worked to bypass rules set up for customer safety because it wanted to increase its bottom line and win its never-ending war with Airbus, its sole competitor.

Meanwhile the decade-old Dutch study suggested that this wasn't actually the first time Boeing had a problem.[33] The study was commissioned after a Boeing 737 crashed in Amsterdam in 2009 killing nine people, and it revealed patterns similar to the 737 Max 8 crashes.[34] However, the report acknowledges a series of pilot errors, and Boeing tried to deflect blame by drawing attention to those errors. That plane was also designed with no backup for its single sensor. Boeing knew of the design flaw and hadn't included any information in the pilot manual to help in case the single sensor malfunctioned.[35] The Boeing crashes led to an investigation that unearthed good reasons to distrust Boeing for both its fairness and its motives.

Alongside the negative consequences of losing impact-based trust, there's a growing push for companies to create a positive impact. The Business Roundtable's statement defining the purpose of a company in 2019 didn't come out of nowhere: It was a reaction to forces that had been gaining momentum in the business ecosystem for years. These forces are fueled by a growing awareness of the danger increasingly posed by climate change, and in part by the need to attract and retain millennial employees, who differ from the prior generation of workers in their desire to work for companies with a clear social mission and a culture that promotes authenticity and personal growth.[36] According to *Fortune*, in 2019 only 7 percent of Fortune 500 CEOs reported believing that companies should "mainly focus on making a profit and not be distracted by social goals."[37] In a 2019 survey of over 1,000 employees, the consulting firm McKinsey found that employees' top two priorities were contributing to society and creating meaningful work.[38] It's not just employees: according to McKinsey, 47 percent of customers who are disappointed with a company's stance on a social issue will stop buying its products, and 17 percent will never return.[39]

Meanwhile, investors who have traditionally had a reputation for thinking with their wallets instead of their hearts are becoming increasingly interested in the impact companies have on the world. In response, investment companies have created funds that seek to marry social or environmental goals with financial opportunity. The funds, generally known as "sustainable" or "ESG" investments (for environmental, social, and governance) in 2018 captured $30.7 trillion in assets under management.[40] Sustainable investing refers to investments that take into account companies' performance on environmental impact such as carbon emissions, social impact such as human rights, and corporate governance practices such as executive compensation. The economic logic behind these investments is that these factors, coupled with a company's financial performance, present a more complete picture of a company's potential for delivering long-term returns, rather than just looking at financial performance alone. BlackRock has funds like this, designed to further different types of goals ranging from reducing companies' carbon footprint to achieving the UN's Sustainable Development Goals.

In addition, there is the much smaller segment of impact investment funds, which invest in companies whose business model includes achieving specific social goals. Goldman Sachs has committed $7 billion since 2001 to impact investments that have helped revitalize New Orleans, created affordable housing in New York, and prepared students in Camden, New Jersey, for college.[41] In 2018, the impact investing segment as measured by the Global Impact Investing Network was $715 billion.[42]

As much as 40 percent of the $76.9 trillion in global assets under management take sustainability data into account in their investment strategies.[43] It's clear that we're moving more and more toward a model where investors factor in companies' behavior and impact on the world at large into their decision-making, instead of just looking at financial performance.

But how does one go about creating a positive impact? To understand impact, we will examine the three actions that make it possible for this to be a realistic strategy for business. First you must define and commit to the impact you want to create—and commit means that you are willing to see the impact through and put it before profits or short-term gain. Second, you must measure the impact you are creating to see if you are actually making a difference. Third, you must actually check to see if your impact really is beneficial, or if it is neutral or even creating unintended harm. Just because one person with power thinks it's a good idea to kill all the sparrows, doesn't actually mean that it's a good idea.

Define and Commit: Discovering the Boundaries of Impact

While being a purpose-driven company is becoming more and more accepted, there's a gap between saying you want to do something and actually doing it. In McKinsey's 2019 survey of 1,000 employees, 62 percent said that their company had a purpose statement, yet only 42 percent said that their company's purpose statement actually resulted in creating a positive impact.[44] Companies might be doing a great job of saying they want to have a positive impact, but they are doing a mediocre job of following through.

Closing this gap means companies have to make good on their commitments. This might mean trading off some short-term profitability for the long-term goal of creating a positive impact. Creating a positive impact means companies and leaders have to be committed to rewarding employees for creating the desired impact, instead of just paying it lip service. Consider the difference between Volkswagen and Patagonia, the American outdoor apparel company whose mission statement is "We're in business to save our home planet."[45]

Volkswagen promised to make cars that met some of the most stringent emissions standards in the world. Instead, VW ended up creating software that cheated on emissions tests since it could not at the same time invest in emissions reduction and achieve their promised growth targets.

Volkswagen's goal in 2013, two years prior to its emission scandal, was to "offer attractive, safe, and environmentally sound vehicles which can compete in an increasingly tough market and set world standards in their respective class."[46] Crystal clear and socially conscious. Then, Volkswagen completely failed to follow through in the worst way possible. Not only did Volkswagen fail to produce emissions-friendly cars, its employees used considerable energy and ingenuity to create cars that actually cheated on emissions tests. Rather than reduce emissions, Volkswagen made cars that continued to pollute, adding tons of damaging emissions to the environment the more cars they sold.

How did things go wrong? To begin with, Volkswagen was driven by ambitious but potentially conflicting goals. Former CEO Martin Winterkorn announced in 2015, "We want to be volume number one but we also want 8 percent in operating profit."[47]

Volkswagen wanted to sell the most cars without sacrificing profit, and at the same time, it wanted to meet some of the most stringent emissions standards in the world.[48] Executives described how the targets turned Volkswagen into a pressure cooker. "If you didn't like it, you moved of your own accord or you were performance managed out of the business," one said.[49] Others spoke about how Winterkorn was a perfectionist who took bad news poorly.[50] The combination of exacting standards and an environment where people were afraid to deliver bad news and failure was punished, was a ripe breeding ground for falsifying results rather than creating environmentally sustainable cars.

In 2014, three West Virginia University graduate students, Hemanth Kappanna, Marc Besch, and Arvind Thiruvengadam were doing research on car emissions.[51] When they tested two Volkswagen cars they found both cars were far over the legal requirement for emissions.[52] Spurred by these results, further investigation revealed that Volkswagen had installed software that helped it cheat on emissions in 11 million cars globally,[53] and the cars emitted up to forty times more pollution than the legal limit in the United States.[54] For Volkswagen to install software that helped it cheat on such a large scale meant that corruption must have been entrenched throughout the organization on multiple levels. Volkswagen's goal to offer "environmentally sound" vehicles was about lip service rather than saving the environment. The company was committed to a different type of goal: working to further profits no matter what the cost to customers, the public in every country where the cars were sold, regulators, and governments around the world that were already struggling with goals to reduce emissions.

By contrast, consider Patagonia, founded in the 1970s by Yvon Chouinard, a California rock climber. Chouinard got his start by selling climbing pitons. As demand grew, he started selling clothing and recruited others to help. His plan was to give the money he earned to environmental causes. However, a consultant advised him against this and told him to sell Patagonia and start an environmental foundation instead. Chouinard decided to go in a completely different direction. He decided to mirror the values of an environmental foundation: he wanted Patagonia to be a company that created products in an environmentally friendly way.[55]

Unlike Volkswagen, Patagonia's track record shows a commitment to this mission—despite some missteps along the way, which we'll touch upon later in the chapter. Since 1985, Patagonia has donated 1 percent of its sales revenue to environmental conservation groups and given over $89 million to these groups.[56] In 2016 it donated 100 percent of its Black Friday sales to environmental nonprofits: about $10 million. In 2013, it created a venture capital firm that invests in start-ups with an environmentally friendly mission such as Bureo, which makes sunglasses out of old fishing nets.[57] Meanwhile, Patagonia hasn't been afraid to take a political stand to defend its values. In 2017, Patagonia sued President Trump after he issued a proclamation decreasing Utah's Bears Ears National Monument by 85 percent and its Grand Staircase–Escalante National Monument by 50 percent.[58] (As of this writing, the case is still under way.)

Inside the business, Patagonia's commitment to the environment can be seen in its processes and business model. In 1993, Patagonia was the first company to create synthetic fabric to make fleece out of recycled plastic bottles.[59] Three years later, Patagonia decided to switch to organic cotton to reduce its environmental footprint. This increased the cost of production, since organic cotton fabric was triple the cost of regular cotton, while the limited supply of organic cotton meant that Patagonia had to cut its product line from ninety-one styles to sixty-six styles. In the short term, these actions cut into Patagonia's profits.[60] In 2005, it created an initiative where employees teach the public how to repair their gear, even though this might mean customers would purchase fewer new products.[61] In 2012 it created a Worn Wear program where customers could trade some of their gently used Patagonia pieces for store credit, and the used clothing was resold at a lower price. This had the bonus of making Patagonia accessible to customers who would not otherwise be able to afford its products.[62]

In 2011, Patagonia ran an ad campaign with the slogan "Don't Buy This Jacket," which openly encouraged customers not to buy their products given the environmental impact of producing new clothes. Cynics might point out that Patagonia has built a billion-dollar company out of environmental sustainability and the campaign was nothing more than an attention-getting ploy. We'd argue that given a choice between having outdoors enthusiasts buy from a retailer with no proven commitment to any social cause—environmental or otherwise—and having them buy from Patagonia, which donates to environmentally friendly groups, is willing to cut into profits to reduce its environmental footprint, and encourages customers to repair and re-wear their goods, we'd vote for Patagonia any day of the week. And so, it would appear, do a number of customers: in 2012, after the "Don't Buy This Jacket" campaign, Patagonia's sales increased by 30 percent to $540 million.[63]

Creating an impact doesn't mean only sticking to a defined vision. More broadly, it means assessing the current situation and recognizing you have the power to do something about it, even if it's "just" making policy changes that can impact the lives of the public.

For example, Walmart has become an unlikely advocate for gun control. Walmart has had an on and off relationship with gun sales. In 2006, Walmart stopped selling guns at a third of its stores. However, it started selling guns again during the recession to bolster flagging sales.[64] In 2015, Walmart, the top gun and ammunition vendor in America,[65] announced it would stop selling some semiautomatic rifles, which has been the weapon of choice for 115 mass shootings since 1999.[66] Used in mass shootings from Connecticut to Las Vegas, they have long been on the list of weapons that gun-control advocates have wanted to ban.[67] Walmart claimed the ban was because of declining demand. Analysts were, however, skeptical given that gun sales in America were holding steady[68] and background checks for gun sales actually increased the summer Walmart made its decision.[69] Then in 2018, Walmart spoke again through its policy. After a nineteen-year-old shot and killed seventeen people at his former high school in Parkland, Florida,[70] Walmart raised its minimum age for purchasing guns throughout the US from eighteen to twenty-one.[71]

A year later, on August 3, 2019, an armed man shot and killed twenty-two people and injured twenty-six more at a Walmart in El Paso, Texas.[72] Three days later, Thomas Marshall, an e-commerce specialist for Walmart, pushed the company to do something about tragic situations such as this. He sent an email and message through the company's messaging system to the company's entire e-commerce team pushing for a strike to "protest Walmart's profit from the sale of guns." He wrote that "as associates, we have the power, ability and opportunity to change this company for the better."[73] Walmart reported no changes in employee attendance, and so it is unclear whether the call to go on strike had an impact.[74] What we do know is that Marshall wasn't alone in his call for action. In September following a petition signed by 128,000 people urging Walmart to stop selling guns,[75] Walmart announced it would cease the sale of handgun ammunition and short-barrel rifle ammunition. It also stopped selling handguns in Alaska, the only state where it still did so. In the short term it wasn't a winning proposition for Walmart's profits. The changes were expected to decrease its market share for ammunition to between 6 and 9 percent, down from 20 percent.[76]

Walmart's response might seem tepid—after all, with the relentless frequency and large number of shootings in the United States, why not just stop selling guns altogether?[77] On the other hand, when you consider that Walmart was making a solid profit from selling guns and ammunition, and that 28 percent of Americans don't think gun laws should be tougher,[78] its policy changes are a fairly loud statement for a major corporation. The changes have a nontrivial impact on how easy it is to get a gun, which in turn can impact the number of shootings in America. Shortly before the new changes were announced, a *Business Insider* reporter tried to buy a gun at Walmart to find out just how easy it was. It took her an hour and a half of phone calls to find a store that sold guns. When she arrived, she was told to come back the next day because none of the employees who were authorized to sell a gun were working. When the reporter came back two days later, she failed the background check because her home address didn't match the address on her license. She left the store empty-handed and gave up.[79] We can't know how many shootings Walmart stopped in making it that much harder to buy guns, but at least it's a start.

Measure

"What gets measured gets done." The truth of this adage is obvious to anyone who has worked in any kind of an organization. After all, how do you know if something has (or has not) occurred if you don't measure it? Measurement is a powerful tool for creating behavior change. If you know the kind of impact you want to create and how much of it has already taken place, then half the battle is knowing what further changes need to be made.

You can achieve powerful results when you collect data and use them to highlight a problem. At Siemens, the German manufacturing conglomerate, new CEO Peter Löscher made one small change in measurement that effectively got his senior leadership team to become more customer focused.

When Löscher entered Siemens in 2007 he had a giant mess to clean up: bribery was endemic at every level of the global company.[80] From the late 1990s until 2007, Siemens made it a practice to bribe government officials all over the world to win contracts.[81] Ultimately, in 2008, the US Securities and Exchange Commission charged Siemens with allegedly spending $1.4 billion in bribes between 2001 and 2007 across six continents.[82]

Löscher was the first outsider to become a CEO at Siemens. To understand what was going on at Siemens and what changes he would need to make to eradicate the culture of bribery, Löscher made it a practice to travel to Siemens locations across the globe and talk to people. In the mornings he had breakfast with customers, followed by meetings with more customers and politicians. At lunch he met with rising-star employees; after lunch he conducted business reviews with local teams and town halls. This was followed by dinner with local senior leaders, and after dinner, Löscher would catch a plane and do it all over again the next day in a different city.[83] Phew. Grueling.

One of the many changes Löscher decided Siemens needed was in its approach with customers. Historically, Siemens cultivated customer relationships through the local Siemens organization. Löscher favored a more hands-on approach from the top, and instead made specific managing board members responsible for individual customer accounts. However, he was unsatisfied with how much time managing board members were spending with customers. Traditionally at Siemens, the top 600 to 700 managers gather in Berlin for a leadership conference. Before Löscher's first one in 2008, he collected Outlook calendars from all of the division CEOs and board members, graphed how much time everyone had spent with customers, and ranked them. At the conference, he projected a giant graphic with everyone's rankings on a screen for all to see. Löscher had debated with his team whether to use names, since that could be embarrassing, but ultimately decided that to make the point clearly, and inspire individual action, it would be most effective to use the executives' names.

Using names proved to be the right move. The first year Löscher did the exercise, he was at the top of the rankings: he'd spent 50 percent of his time with customers—a first-place ranking he found unacceptable. If his senior leaders were in charge of specific accounts, he reasoned, they should actually be spending more time than he had with their customers. When he repeated the exercise in 2009, 2010, and 2011, most leaders had either surpassed Löscher or spent about as much time as he did with customers.[84] No one wanted their name to be ranked last. In Löscher's case, a very simple measurement was able to drive enormous behavioral changes.

Löscher nailed both of two main questions a company needs to figure out: what to measure, and how to measure it. Moreover his simple ranking exercise displayed all the hallmarks of a good system of measurement. According to HBS professor Robert Simons, who wrote an excellent book on this topic, there are three lynchpins of an effective system of measurement: it is objective, complete, and responsive.

An objective system of measurement enables different people to measure the same thing and get consistent results. A complete system of measurement is one that accounts for all the different aspects of what you want to measure. Finally, a responsive system of measurement is one that is able to gauge changes in what is being measured.

The right metric is a compass point guiding a company toward carrying out the impacts it wants to have. Creative and thoughtful metrics can fold in a company's values while also improving its business performance. However, without a system of measurement, it's impossible to say what impact companies are making. Skeptics can easily argue that there's no impact at all. Worse, no one in the company (or outside it) has the satisfaction of knowing the kind of impact that is being made over time.

A visible and external system of measurement can demonstrate how much a company cares about its impact. In 2007,

Patagonia launched "The Footprint Chronicles" to provide transparency about its supply chain and the amount of resources it consumed in making products.[85] The early version of the report explained how Patagonia measured its energy consumption, carbon dioxide emissions, waste generation, and water use (a later addition) as well as listing the numbers.[86] It also included seventeen of its products on the website, and customers could read about the environmental impacts of each of these products.[87] The Footprint Chronicles has since gone through several evolutions. The latest gives a comprehensive list of Patagonia's programs for sustainability, has a map that identifies each of their suppliers by name and address, and reports the number of workers they employ and the amounts of the goods they produce.[88]

Robert Eccles, at the Saïd Business School at Oxford University, a passionate evangelist for integrated reporting and a leader on how companies and investors can create sustainable strategies, champions combining traditional financial reporting with sustainability reporting, so investors and the public can see the full extent of a company's impact.

George Serafeim of Harvard Business School has taken the idea of reporting environmental sustainability one step further, by proposing that companies use "impact-weighted accounts"—line items added to a financial statement that translate a company's impact into a dollar value.[89] For example, to describe the impact of its efforts to eliminate waste production and reduce water consumption and emissions, Vodafone translated these impacts into a financial value. It lists how much waste it has created, explains its methodology for translating this into a financial amount, and lists the final amount in dollars (well, euros).[90]

It's a view we fully agree with. Companies have a much larger impact on society than their financials. This includes companies that work hard to have a positive impact like Patagonia, as well as actors on the other side of the ledger, like Volkswagen and the ninety companies that account for most of the world's pollution. If you want to have a positive impact on the world, you need to look to other measures beyond financials, such as environmental impact—what kind of an environmental footprint does your company have? How much wastewater do you use? What steps are you taking to reduce your footprint? Then, you report these metrics, hopefully in concert with your financial reporting. Finally, there is the new promise of impact-weighted accounts, which allow companies to measure the dollar impact of their activities and hold themselves, and be held, accountable for them.

Check: Not All Impacts Are Created Equal

The third step is to check that your impact actually benefits the people you claim to serve. It's easy to declare that a company wants to make a difference, but the proof is in how employees, customers, suppliers, investors, regulators, and the public experience a company's actions. This is a startlingly simple concept, but the discrepancy between what companies say they want to do and what they actually do can be shockingly large.

Take, for example, Wells Fargo. Wells Fargo's vision statement is "to satisfy our customers' financial needs and help them succeed financially."[91] Wonderful! Except, how to explain Wells Fargo's now notorious fake account scandal? From 2002 to 2016 (yes, that is a period of fourteen years), employees opened some 3.5 million accounts that were not authorized by their customers.[92] Employees reported that they felt they had no other option except to cheat, if they wanted to keep their jobs.[93] At one Wells Fargo branch employees reported they'd been told to hit the targets or risk getting transferred to a store "where someone had been shot and killed."[94] A former war veteran wrote to the then CEO, John Stumpf, saying a war zone was actually less stressful than Wells Fargo: and indeed between 2011 and 2016, Wells Fargo fired over 8,000 people for "subpar" sales.[95] It's no surprise that fake new accounts kept getting opened by the remaining employees who were desperate to keep their jobs.

The fake accounts had devastating ripple effects on customers. In some cases, the new account had annual fees, but since customers didn't know about the accounts, they didn't pay them and their credit scores took a hit. In other cases, Wells Fargo employees transferred money from existing customer accounts to cover the fees associated with the new account, which resulted in insufficient funds notices that resulted in further fees. Credit scores are scanned by landlords, and someone with several overdraft fees from unauthorized accounts could have trouble moving to the apartment of their choice.[96] To make matters worse (and in violation of their fiduciary duties), investors were fed false information about the company, because the fake accounts made its performance appear to be far stronger than it really was. And once the company's sales practices came under scrutiny, executives tried to hide the fraud by changing the description of what sales associates were being asked to do.[97]

Like Volkswagen, Wells Fargo did the opposite of what it claimed. Nick Hanna, the US attorney for the Central District of California, called the company's fraud "a complete failure of leadership at multiple levels within the bank."[98] (And in a rare note of poetic justice, CEO John Stumpf was fined $17.5 million and banned from the banking industry, while five other executives were also slammed with fines.)[99]

Now, Wells Fargo is an extreme example. It was practicing out and out fraud that was baked into its entire system. There are also cases where companies don't practice fraud, but the "good impact" they imagine they are creating may not actually be all that great in the eyes of their community, as we saw with Chairman Mao's sparrows.

In 2011, Patagonia conducted internal audits of their supply chain and found evidence of human trafficking, forced labor, and other forms of worker exploitation. A quarter of Patagonia's mills for producing fabric were based in Taiwan, and the majority of them relied on brokers to hire workers. These brokers often charged migrant workers enormous fees for jobs, while suppliers also confiscated worker passports, essentially eliminating their freedom of movement. Labor brokers are legal in Taiwan; there is, however, a cap on the fee they are allowed to charge, and Patagonia found during their audits that brokers were exceeding this fee by up to $7,000.

The audits were the result of an initiative that started in 2007, when Patagonia began to ramp up its internal investigations after coming under fire for labor problems in its factories. Patagonia cut its suppliers from 108 to 75, which helped ensure it was working with factories that treated workers well. Concerned that there may be more infringements of human rights further down in its supply chain, Patagonia investigated the mills and suppliers who work with raw materials and send them to factories to be turned into clothing. (Do not imagine this is standard behavior. The urge to look under the hood [as it were] on this problem is not universal: in 2013, Patagonia invited forty other companies to discuss suppliers' using forced labor, but only seven companies attended.)[100]

Once Patagonia received the audit results, it created a new set of employment standards and asked suppliers to reimburse workers for illegal fees. Beginning in June 2015, Patagonia required all of its suppliers to eliminate job fees. Patagonia also partnered with Verité, an NGO with supply chain expertise, to get help understanding hiring processes and the laws surrounding them, training suppliers, and auditing them.[101] Patagonia also began working with the Taiwan Ministry of Labor Workforce Development Agency, which helps employers hire migrant workers without using labor brokers. Patagonia has also applied its standard and approach for workers to the rest of its global supply chain, and published its standards so other companies could adopt them as well.[102]

A reasonable person might consider Patagonia a hypocrite: How can it claim to be about impact and then use forced labor? We would argue surely we should be glad that a company like Patagonia goes one step further into its supply chain to root out worker exploitation at the level of the manufacturers of the raw materials that go into its products—a second level down in its supply chain. Patagonia did not intentionally use forced labor, and it took the extra step of conducting internal checks two levels down in their supply chain to find the problem and make sure to root it out. According to a 2020 Cornell study that examined 40,458 supply chain audits from apparel brands, 45 percent of them contained inaccurate information. The inaccurate audits painted a rosier picture of working conditions, suggesting shorter workweeks and higher compliance with labor laws than in actuality.[103] However, these inaccuracies mean it is hard for apparel companies to understand problems with working conditions and address them. The fact that Patagonia conducted a thorough internal audit, found problems, and investigated them is a sign that they are doing more, not less, than the typical clothing brand.

However, internal checks are only half of the equation. There are times when companies act with the best of intentions but fundamentally misunderstand how others will perceive their actions. To make sure you understand how your company's impact is being judged, it helps to develop the skill of perspective-taking to develop insight into how others might think about the impacts you are trying to create. Otherwise, you are in a hermetically sealed echo chamber. It takes a curious (or worried, or caring) mindset to want to learn about how others think, and deliberate action to create practices that help you see the world as someone from outside your world might see it.

I learned this the hard way when I joined Fidelity in December 1986, where I was the head of quality for our three call centers. We had a far-sighted head of marketing who pointed out that the bull market would soon end. In January 1987, in order to get our customers to think more about the future, I asked our quality team to give additional points for service quality to any representative who closed their call by asking the client, "Have you invested in your IRA this year?" (And sure enough, the Dow Jones Industrial Average [DJIA] dropped 508 points in October 1987.)[104]

What I didn't consider was that in our pre-computerized world, lots of our mutual fund investors would call several times a week, some even daily, to ask whether their mutual funds had increased in value. (Remember, this was a bull market.) I was so bent on helping the company increase assets under management that it never occurred to me that I was in essence tormenting our clients with the same question, repeated call after call, about whether they had invested in an IRA. Customer complaints took a few weeks to mount, and I then learned that as hard as it was to get behavior in a group to start, it was even harder to convince the phone representatives that we really, really wanted them to STOP asking that question about investing in IRAs. I may very well be the worst quality professional the world has ever seen. And, at the same time, I also know what it's like to be caught up in a way of thinking that was blind to the effect of my/our actions on others.

Why, you might ask, did no one speak up? There are several answers to that question. One might be that we had a culture at Fidelity that discouraged candor in bringing problems to the attention of managers. As someone whose sole function was to encourage our managers and employees to do just that, I would rule out that cause, although we shouldn't underestimate it. We saw at both Volkswagen and Wells Fargo how long toxic, truth-shutting-down, psychologically unsafe cultures can survive.

Instead, let's turn to a helpful concept for people who work with others and who care about impact. It's called the Abilene paradox. This is the phenomenon where a group decides on something no one is very enthusiastic about but everyone believes everyone else wants to do.[105] The creator, Jerry Harvey, a professor of management science at George Washington University, introduced the Abilene paradox to the world in 1974 with this hilarious, but alas, too often true, story. On a hot July day in Texas (and by hot, Harvey states, it was 104 degrees), Harvey's father-in-law suggests driving fifty-three miles to the town of Abilene in a car with no air conditioning for dinner. Harvey's wife thinks it's a stupendous idea, and her mother-in-law agrees. Everyone piles in the car, drives to Abilene, and enjoys a subpar dinner.

Upon their return, the group collapses around a fan, exhausted. Harvey asks if everyone enjoyed the trip. Finally, his mother-in-law confesses: she never actually wanted to go, but just agreed because everyone else seemed enthusiastic. Harvey's wife admits she thought it was a crazy idea, but she wanted to keep everyone happy. Everyone turns to Harvey's father-in-law, who suggested the idea—and he admits he would have rather stayed at home, but he brought up Abilene just in case anyone wanted to go.[106] The Abilene effect for a family trip is painful, yes, but multiply it across an organization, Harvey notes, and it can cause an enormous amount of "human misery and economic loss."[107]

So, how do you engage in good perspective-taking while avoiding the Abilene paradox? There are many different answers, but global mining company Anglo American developed a tool in 2003 to help them understand the impact they had on the communities they operated in, which required extensive communication with local communities.[108] Mining companies know they are in the business of extracting local resources and that their presence has both immediate and far-reaching impacts on the communities they operate in that need to be managed. Concerned executives at Anglo American created an award-winning impact assessment tool with the acronym SEAT (Socio-Economic Assessment Toolbox), which laid out a detailed process for understanding the communities they were working with. SEAT aimed to minimize or avoid adverse social impacts, and to build better long-term relationships with stakeholders.

Managers were required to complete SEAT assessments for their operations every three years, regardless of whether they were just getting started or had been working there for years. SEAT had a seven-stage process that included the following:

- profiling the Anglo American site, assessing its socioeconomic impacts and social investments;
- profiling the local area and developing a stakeholder engagement plan;
- assessing issues and impacts;
- managing critical social performance topics including complaints and grievances, emergency planning, conflict management, resettlement, mine closure contractor management, indigenous peoples, and the voluntary principles on security and human rights;
- supporting socioeconomic benefit delivery including creating a process for increasing local procurement as well as processes for improving everything from microcredit, local infrastructure development, low-cost housing, and sustainable energy, as well as community health;
- developing a comprehensive social management plan; and
- creating a SEAT report to share results from the process with stakeholders.

If there was one critique that could be leveled at SEAT, it's that it was *too* detailed.

The Business for Social Responsibility, an independent NGO, found that trust had increased in 80 percent of the stakeholder sites where Anglo had used SEAT.[109] Anglo American executives knew the company had to rethink how it did business to make sure it could have a positive impact on the communities it worked in. In January 2020 Anglo American updated SEAT, creating the Social Way 3.0, which has processes that are more specific to Anglo

American. However, SEAT is still available on Anglo American's website for other companies to use.

Making sure perspective-taking happens requires baking it into the company processes. Some thoughtful companies put stakeholder maps right into their annual reports to show their understanding of who their stakeholders are and their importance to the company's performance. For example, BMW has made a practice of holding stakeholder dialogues, where they meet with different interest groups including scientists, members of NGOs, politicians, sustainability experts, and investors.[110]

BMW has a separate sustainable value report, where they review the outcomes of these meetings. They also describe their sustainability strategy in detail and have created metrics to mea-sure its progress: the report covers BMW's progress on the en-vironment, employee welfare, and social issues such as product safety, human rights, and combating corruption and bribery.[111]

In its 2018 sustainability report, for example, BMW discussed how during their meetings with stakeholders they received feed-back advising that they concentrate on fewer but more relevant sustainability issues.[112] The groups suggested that BMW con-tinue its focus on urban mobility, including the challenges pre-sented by traffic jams and poor air quality, as well as automated, connected, and electric cars. In particular, stakeholders wanted BMW to focus on producing emission-free cars.[113] As a piece of feedback, this is gold. It allows BMW to dig deeper into under-standing the sustainability issues that matter to its stakeholders, while giving it permission to narrow its focus and actions to ones that will really make the kind of difference they are in the best position to make as a car manufacturer. This is the kind of feed-back that can only come from respectful and candid exchange, where the parties are working hard to learn about the perspectives of the others.

Unintended Impacts

When actions create harm, despite the very best intentions, it's essential to take responsibility rather than have senior leadership wringing its hands and shifting the blame, or retreating into a stony silence. In 2015, PETA, the animal rights activist group, published a video of a Patagonia wool supplier abusing a sheep. Patagonia announced it would stop doing business with the supplier. It created the "Patagonia Wool Standard," a set of principles around their expectations for wool suppliers regarding animal treatment, land use, and sustainability.[114] However, not every company does this.

Consider how Facebook handled its fake news problem. Some history first. In 2011, Facebook's CEO Mark Zuckerberg crafted a strategy for Facebook to become the top platform for spreading news, in response to Twitter's growing popularity.[115] It involved adjusting Facebook's news feed (usually filled with cat pictures and various friends and family members humble-bragging) to give hard news stories more visibility.[116]

However, Facebook hadn't given all that much thought to what it means to be a news distribution site: How should stories be presented compared to op-eds or satire? It decided the best option was to be neutral and allow all posts. A hard-hitting news story and Grandma's garden pictures would be presented in the same way. This opened the door for fake news sites to spread their content: after all, how was the average reader supposed to tell if a story from the *Washington Post* was any different from the *Denver Guardian* (a fake news site)?[117]

Then, in early 2016, John Thune, a South Dakota Republican senator and chairman of the Committee on Commerce, Science, and Transportation, wrote Facebook a letter. He was worried that Facebook's Trending Topics section, which was moderated by twenty-five individuals with backgrounds in journalism, was politically biased against conservatives. Facebook responded by inviting a group of seventeen Republican media stars and analysts, including a Trump campaign advisor, to its headquarters for a feedback session.[118]

During the summer of 2016, the Trump presidential campaign did a much better job of connecting with voters than Hillary Clinton's campaign. The Trump campaign used data it had on potential voters to match them to their Facebook accounts and then used a tool to group voters according to their traits and sent out targeted messages to each group, and also tested its ads, making sure to kill ones that weren't working and spread the ones that were.[119]

At the same time, scammers started pushing fake news stories on Facebook that went viral—for example, a website told readers the pope had endorsed Donald Trump, and the story got nearly a million reactions on Facebook. Overall, fake news stories got more engagement than real ones. When Donald Trump won the election, blame was heaped at Facebook's door.

Meanwhile, don't forget the Cambridge Analytica scandal. This data firm was hired by the Trump campaign and had obtained access to private Facebook data on over 87 million users.[120] Cambridge Analytica used an app that paid users to take a personality quiz to siphon personal data from the quiz takers, *and* all of the quiz takers' friends—even though none of them had consented to having their data collected.[121] Cambridge Analytica then allegedly used the data to build psychological profiles of voters, and would have been able to target the voters with specific messages to swing votes. For example, someone who cares about gun rights would theoretically get ads about gun rights, while someone who cares more about religion might get more pro-life ads.[122] (This wasn't just an American problem. In India, there were reports of voter manipulation during the 2018 legislative election via WhatsApp, a messaging platform owned by Facebook.) While multiple platforms helped spread fake news including Google, Twitter, and Reddit, Facebook received the lion's share of the blame.[123]

Zuckerberg was slow to react. "The idea that fake news is on Facebook—of which, you know, it's a very small amount of the content—influenced the election in any way, I think, is a pretty crazy idea," he said.[124] Still, Facebook tried to take some steps. In December 2016 it introduced a system where users could flag a story they thought was fake. Stories with enough flags were sent to experts who would fact-check it.[125]

In 2018, Zuckerberg declared that fixing Facebook would be his personal project. He had limited success. In January, Facebook hired Nathaniel Gleicher, the former director of cybersecurity policy for President Obama, to staunch the flow of fake news. That summer Facebook removed hundreds of accounts with ties to Russia or Iran that were spreading misinformation.[126] In April 2018, Mark Zuckerberg was asked to testify before Congress, where he was grilled for two days and asked 600 questions on topics including Facebook's ability to protect users' data and control the spread of misinformation.[127] The overriding theme was that Facebook needed regulation, something Zuckerberg concurred with as long as it was the "right regulation."[128] (In 2020, Facebook called on governments to regulate it and provided a list of proposed regulations—most of which it already complied with.)[129] However, Zuckerberg's success at "fixing" Facebook is debatable. The same year Zuckerberg declared he'd fix Facebook, *Wired* counted twenty-one major Facebook scandals involving data privacy, fake accounts, fake news, and hacking.[130]

As of 2020, Facebook still has a major fake news problem—this time about COVID-19. Avaaz, a nonprofit that organizes community campaigns, found that over 40 percent of the misinformation about coronavirus on Facebook—that was debunked by fact checkers—stayed on Facebook and continued to be shared—an overwhelming 1.7 million times.[131] Facebook announced it would take steps like pinning government public health warnings to the top of people's news feeds, which led to 350 million people being redirected to reliable information, but experts think Facebook can do more.[132] While Facebook now reviews content for fake news, fake news continues to spread. Despite the massive extent of its problems, Facebook still hasn't learned its lesson.

Contrast Facebook's fake news problem with Pinterest, the popular social media platform where users share pictures of hobbies. In early 2018, Pinterest emerged as an unlikely hero in the battle against fake news. When anti-vaxxers started using Pinterest to spread misleading information about how vaccines are harmful, Pinterest took action. Since it was unable to completely remove the anti-vaccination content on the platform, it blocked vaccination searches.[133] It made a similar decision to block searches for bogus cancer treatments, and blocked accounts that promoted such treatments or linked to websites that did.[134] Users are still allowed to post content, but the content no longer appears in searches.[135] Similarly, Pinterest took action for COVID-19. When users search for COVID-19 or related terms, they can only see Pinterest boards owned by leading public health organizations such as the Centers for Disease Control, the World Health Organization, and the American Academy of Pediatrics. "There's nothing inspiring about harmful misinformation that might affect your health or your family's health or your community's health," said Sarah Bromma, Pinterest's head of policy.[136]

Pinterest has a team of human reviewers who determine whether a post violates its misinformation guidelines, and training material for the reviewers is updated every six months to keep up with the ever-evolving underworld of fake news.[137] In addition, its guidelines for what is and isn't appropriate content for the platform are detailed and thorough. The guidelines are divided into categories covering content safety, paid advertising, spam, and more. Under each category Pinterest elucidates what is and is not acceptable.[138] At one point they even had examples of what pictures were not permissible on the site.

While Facebook knowingly exposed its users' data, it probably never intended to swing an election, or spread massive amounts of false information (we hope). Yet when the time came for Facebook to do something, it stood still and issued a denial. Finally, when it acted, its actions were tepid, especially compared to Pinterest's swift and decisive action. Out of fairness to Facebook, it did try similar tactics, and for example tried to block nudity and then ran into trouble for blocking pictures of breastfeeding.[139] However, experts point out that Facebook's policy simply isn't nuanced enough.[140]

Given Facebook's enormous amount of power, its slow and ineffective response is deeply worrying: it's still dealing with a fake news problem four years after the presidential election, and it's no surprise that Facebook is struggling to retain users' trust.

After news of the Cambridge Analytica scandal broke, trust in Facebook dropped 66 percent according to the Ponemon Institute, a research firm that specializes in data privacy and protection.[141] After Zuckerberg's testimony, only 28 percent of Facebook's users believed Facebook was committed to privacy, a steep drop from 79 percent the year before.[142] This doesn't seem to be a blip. News site *The Verge* found that Facebook was the least trusted tech company: only 41 percent of those surveyed trusted Facebook, and 72 percent thought it had too much power.[143]

To get a sense of how much Facebook has blown it, compare Facebook and Google. When a *New York Times* journalist downloaded the data Google and Facebook kept on him, he found Google had an unnerving 8 gigabytes (eighty-three days of music) compared to Facebook, which had 650 megabytes of data (think six days of music).[144] Yet, in a 2019 NBC News/*Wall Street Journal* poll, 60 percent of Americans said they don't trust Facebook with their personal data compared to 37 percent of Americans who lack trust with how Google handles their data.[145] This is high, but given how much data Google has on us, the wonder is that we actually trust it as much as we do. Even though Facebook has a fraction of our data, it is much less trusted.

All is not lost for Facebook if it can get its act together. The actual work of repairing trust once a company has caused harm is long and complicated, but it can be done. In our next chapter we'll cover what recovering from a trust breach looks like: everything from how to apologize to long-term trust repair. However, when damage is done, the very first step a company needs to take is to acknowledge that yes, their actions made an impact for better or for worse and that impact is their responsibility. Our relationship with a company is defined by its actions and how we feel about them. That's why it matters so much that companies think about the multiple relationships they have with customers, employees, investors, and the public and hold themselves accountable for the impacts they have on each of these groups. It's essential that a company does everything it can to manage its impact, or it will soon find that no one wants to interact with them at all.

SIX

RECOVERY

Regaining Lost Trust

Betrayal is the only truth that sticks.
—ARTHUR MILLER

I N 1988, A CORPORATE SCANDAL SO LARGE ROCKED JAPAN that the prime minister resigned and a suicide followed. A reasonable person might think this would spell certain death for the company involved, but the scandal-plagued company, advertising and media conglomerate Recruit Holdings, is flourishing.

Today, you can find Recruit's headquarters a few steps away from Tokyo's bustling Tokyo station. The company is housed in a skyscraper where a steady stream of employees and customers flows through the doors and up through glass-paned elevators that provide a dazzling panorama of the city.

Recruit is the quiet tech giant most Westerners have never heard of: It specializes in platform businesses that connect sellers to buyers, such as websites for making restaurant reservations or hair salon appointments. It also owns the job search site Indeed and job review and recruiting company Glassdoor.[1] All in all, it provides information and services through 264 magazines that are mostly digital, over 200 websites, and about 350 mobile apps. In 2019, its revenue was north of $22 billion.[2] It is loved both by customers, for its quality services, and by employees, who know that sporting the Recruit brand on one's resume is a mark of distinction.

This makes sense. Recruit was created to be loved. Recruit was founded in 1960 by Hiromasa Ezoe with inspiring intentions: its company mission was to add value to society. True to form, its very first product solved an inequity in Japanese society. At the time, major companies such as Mitsubishi and Matsushita (now Panasonic)[3] recruited new talent by hosting exams at top universities. Candidates who were lucky enough to land a job could expect to work from nine a.m. to midnight. A few times a week, they'd go out drinking with their bosses for another couple of hours, finally returning home at about three or four a.m.[4] In return, the so-called salarymen could expect lifetime employment, with a steadily increasing salary, a hefty pension, and company-subsidized housing. When students sat to take these exams, they understood they were choosing a "company not a career."[5]

The process locked out smaller companies that could not afford to host exams and students at less prestigious universities. Ezoe started a job advertisement magazine for small and medium-sized companies so they could post their job openings at a much lower cost than hosting exams, reaching students at a wide swath of colleges and universities. The magazine was so successful that by the 1970s, Recruit launched several other magazines to solve other (in tech speak) "matching" problems of connecting individuals with needs to companies that could satisfy them. They included a first-ever job magazine for Japanese women so they could broaden their career options, and a magazine for buying and selling used cars. Recruit trained its salesmen to listen to customers and brainstorm creative solutions to industry-wide problems, which gave it a competitive edge.

Then disaster. The charismatic Ezoe sold 2.8 million shares of a Recruit subsidiary before it went public in 1986 to 159 members of Japan's political, business, and media elite, in exchange for insider information, beneficial business relationships, and appointments to four government committees. When the subsidiary was listed, the investors made between $165,000 and $350,000.[6] The debacle, known as the Recruit Scandal, forced the prime minister, Noboru Takeshita, and his entire cabinet to resign.[7] Takeshita's secretary, Ihei Aoki, committed suicide.[8] Ezoe was arrested.

On the heels of the scandal, Recruit's senior leaders discovered it was mired in debt worth roughly $14 billion. Ezoe had invested heavily in real estate, and one of Recruit's subsidiaries had failed. They had not realized how extensive Ezoe's investments were. The company now owed annual interest payments of roughly $637 million, but its operating income was only $607 million. Disheartened employees gave Recruit six months to live.

Given the extent of the problems, it would be natural to assume Recruit's employees were right and that the company went out of business in short order. Yet during the nineties, Recruit clawed its way back to solvency through tight budgeting and prescient decision-making about which new businesses to build and grow.

What Recruit pulled off sounds impossible: it regained the trust of the public and is still going strong despite its legendary mistakes of the past. We tend to believe that trust, once broken, cannot be regained, when actually the truth is somewhat more complex. Trust, once broken, cannot *easily* be regained. We fall into this fallacy for two reasons. First, trust is so hard to regain that so few do it, making us think that broken trust is truly lost forever. Second, because trust is so hard to regain, it makes more sense to focus on protecting your reputation and avoiding losing trust in the first place. However, consider Boeing, Volkswagen, Wells Fargo, and Uber. All of these companies are battered but still in business. A trust betrayal does not necessarily mean game over.

Still, be warned: trust regained looks different than trust that was never betrayed. Boeing, Volkswagen, Wells Fargo, and Uber are still in business, but they were condemned for very good reasons and dragged through the mud because of their wrongdoing. Their cleanup jobs were massive, and they are still dealing with the fallout of their actions. In particular, Boeing and Wells Fargo are struggling to shake off the shadows of the past and find their way forward. Meanwhile, the Recruit scandal was such a watershed event for the country that it makes an appearance in history books for elementary school students.[9] If you ask someone in Japan about Recruit, their reply will probably be, "Scandal?" Companies can be forgiven for their sins, continue to operate, and even cultivate a reputation for excellence as Recruit did, but it does not mean that those sins will be entirely forgotten.

A breach of trust involves much more than the risk of bad publicity. It can be an open invitation for customers to switch to another brand, employees to leave, investors to pull their funds, and governments to slap down sanctions, and it can lead to your company's demise. Death may not be immediate or happen at all, especially for large, well-capitalized firms. For example, British Petroleum is still around despite the explosion of the Deepwater Horizon oil rig in 2010 that spilled millions of gallons of oil into the Gulf of Mexico.[10] However, BP has had to suffer the consequences. In the months following the oil spill, BP's share price dropped 54 percent,[11] and it had to sell $60 billion in assets to cover its liabilities.[12] And it is still dealing with costs from the cleanup almost a decade later.[13] According to a study by *The Economist*, which compared the financial impact of scandals on eight major companies (including BP, VW, Wells Fargo, and United Airlines) to the performance of peer companies without one, a scandal cost the median company 30 percent of its market value.[14]

Trust breaches can also be an opportunity to rebuild for the better. When I was at Fidelity Investments, we conducted a study to find out how customers felt about the company after we had made a mistake in their account, such as a funds transfer that went to the wrong institution, name or address errors in opening a new account, and other problems that can be common to financial services institutions. We were amazed to discover that customers were *more loyal* to Fidelity if we had made a mistake and then fixed it to the customers' satisfaction than a control group of customers who had never experienced a problem with the company at all. This was immensely reassuring, because we learned that it was not the mistake that's the problem (or, at least, that it's not fatal)—it's how the company managed the mistake that mattered.

This finding initially sparked brief and silly speculations of the kind that managers indulge in when faced with a problem that almost looks like an opportunity: "Does this mean we should try to *create problems* to *increase customer loyalty*?" Instead, the response to the loyalty data was a company-wide initiative to identify where we were making the most mistakes, and where errors had the most severe consequences, and then to systematically improve the processes that created so many problems for our customers—and us. Granted, what was going wrong at Fidelity were mistakes due to poor process design and execution, and while individual customers were mightily ticked off at times, there was never a sense that the mistakes added up to something customers viewed as a scandal. But they were a serious blow to Fidelity's generally high ratings for competence, a core dimension of trust. So, the point still stands. Trust repair can be an opportunity to find redemption and rebuild for the better, whether it's at the level of scandal or more garden-variety mistakes.

Rebuilding trust has two dimensions. There's the short term, which involves addressing and remedying the incident that caused the problem, typically with an apology. Then there's the long term, which requires addressing the underlying causes of the problem to prevent a mistake of that kind from being made again. In this chapter we'll first address how to diagnose a trust breach and the type of solution that's needed. Then we'll cover the nuts and bolts of apologies: when to apologize, when not to apologize, as well as how to deliver an effective apology. Finally, we'll move on to rebuilding trust for the long term.

The Anatomy of Betrayal

While trust can be regained, what we often see is companies fall flat on their face (if companies had faces) because they do such a poor job of recouping the public's trust. They default to assuming all is lost, or worse, botch repair attempts by waiting until the problem has been fully tried in the court of public opinion before they communicate and act, as was the case with Takata, a Japanese airbag and seatbelt manufacturer.

In 2004, after a Takata airbag exploded, injuring an Alabama driver, the company performed internal tests that showed that its bags were faulty and could explode upon impact.[15] Engineers prepared for a recall, but executives instead ordered them to delete the data from the tests and continue to sell the bags.[16] The first Takata airbag recalls occurred at a glacial pace: four years after the initial findings from the test, and it was tiny—only about 4,000 cars were recalled.[17] In 2011 Honda expanded this recall to include over a million cars,[18] but Takata continued to drag its heels and obfuscate. It finally filed a defect report in 2013 with the National Highway Traffic Safety Administration (NHTSA),[19] nine years after the first airbag explosion. In 2015, under intense pressure from the NHTSA, Takata admitted there were defects in its airbags, leading to nationwide recalls of 22 million cars.[20] In 2017, Takata filed for bankruptcy, unable to keep up with the court fees, fines, and recall costs it had to pay.[21] At the time of its bankruptcy, its airbags had been linked to 16 deaths and 180 injuries.[22] A year later, nearly 42 million cars had been recalled.[23]

Yet, picture what would have happened if Takata had acted the moment it discovered the problem. Certainly recalling 42 million cars and admitting the problem would have been a long and difficult journey, but Takata might have had a fighting chance for survival. However, Takata turned away from that road, probably because it would be so unusual to imagine admitting fault and making plans to remediate the problem at anything near the eventual scale that was required. Companies try to slow-walk their way through these situations for many reasons. There are serious reputation costs to being known as a producer of a dangerous product. They want to avoid setting aside large reserves for potential lawsuits, which would come right out of their profits. They try to minimize the number of times they are exposed to the expenses of repair or recall. And they refuse to admit harm out of fear that the admission will be used against them by plaintiffs' lawyers to win more cases and exact higher awards than they might otherwise have to pay.

But it seemed as if there might be something else at work in how the leaders of companies respond, time after time, to situations that end up costing them far more than they might have if they had taken a different approach at the beginning. So, we looked to the research on cognitive biases to see if there is some way that we systematically depart from rational thought in responding to situations of this kind, when something really big and really bad could happen to us and we nonetheless refuse to accept and acknowledge the danger we are in.

It turns out that there is something called the normalcy bias, which has come out of the research into how people respond in the face of disasters—imminent catastrophic dangers like being caught at the World Trade Center as the planes flew into it on 9/11, or being stuck in a shipwreck, or in a plane that catches fire while still on the runway. Roughly 70 percent of people in these situations respond like the proverbial deer caught in a car's headlights; in fact, one of the articles about this bias was called "The Frozen Calm of the Normalcy Bias." The most common reaction is disbelief, leading to an inability to respond to the situation at hand, and to hope, instead, for reassurance that what you think is happening really isn't. As a woman caught in the World Trade Center on 9/11 recalled, after yelling, "What's happening?" "What I really wanted was for someone to scream back, 'Everything is OK! Don't worry. It's in your head.'"[24]

It's called "normalcy" out of our strong desire to believe that the normal world we live in is still intact, and it's a "bias" because it leads us to deny the new reality that exists. Our next reaction is to seek out information about the situation, and it has to be a lot to convince us that what seems to be happening really is happening. Research finds that people acting with a normalcy bias seek out four or more sources of information before they feel ready to act.[25] Some people who escape the normalcy bias may have had prior experiences with dangerous situations, giving them the advantage of pattern recognition to see what others don't. What seems to help is good information that people take the time to focus on and believe, which is really, really hard to do; ask anyone who works for an airline and has to deliver the potentially lifesaving information of where the exits are in a plane.

So, if you are in a company that is facing an imminent catastrophic disaster, like exploding airbags on millions of cars, try to watch for signs that you and others are trapped in a corporate version of the normalcy bias. Red flags will include a narrative of denial that the situation is even occurring, accompanied perhaps by demonizing those who present confirming information about it. Especially worrisome will be the tendency to minimize the potential scale of the harm, since this will lead to stalling, minimal levels of response, and the inability to act big that is so characteristic of company-created disasters that destroy trust. What you can do is to seek out information that would shed light on the potential size of the disaster and the resulting scale of the trust betrayal. We imagine all kinds of things in companies, from how a new product might work, to the impact of a really smart move on the part of a competitor, or even how to respond to a novel coronavirus. Armed with the defense of understanding the normalcy bias, you might be able to extend your imagination to areas that matter at least as much, since they affect your impact on others and, fundamentally, whether you will be trusted.

GIVEN ALL OF THIS, REPAIR is complicated and doesn't happen overnight. The organization has to prove over and over again that it's made lasting changes. In addition, different types of people trust differently. A group of business professors dove deep into the mechanics of how we trust and how we forgive by observing how MBA students behaved during a negotiation.[26]

They found that people tend to fall into two groups. The first, those with a fixed mindset, have difficulty changing their mind. They need a lot of information. On the other hand, those with a growth mindset change their minds quickly as soon as they get new information. It comes as no surprise that the two groups react differently to a trust breach.

It tends to be harder to lose the trust of people with a fixed mindset: they will give others the benefit of the doubt and come up with reasons to explain away the trust violation. For example, if they heard about an airbag exploding, they might assume it's a one-off incident. Companies might know these people as loyal customers and employees. However, if trust violations keep happening, such as if airbags keep exploding, they will eventually change their minds, and winning them back will be a long and slow process.

Conversely, it's easy to lose the trust of people with a growth mindset. Given information about an airbag exploding, they'll check their car to see if they have a faulty airbag. However, it is easier to regain their trust. If the company were to come out and say they had identified what had caused the airbags to explode, and that they had data (available to all) that showed that a new and improved production method had eliminated the reason why the airbags had exploded, this group would be likely to buy cars with airbags from the same company again. People with a fixed mind-set, however, might avoid the company for life.

Corporations looking to regain trust should keep in mind that they are dealing with both groups of people. They shouldn't assume that if they continue to make mistakes, loyal customers will stick with them. Moreover, once they've started to regain some trust, they cannot assume that the battle is over: they must maintain a consistent enough record to regain the trust of people with a fixed mindset.

The path to regaining lost trust is made all the harder by the fact that people tend to place more weight on negative events than positive ones (except, as we have seen in the discussion of the normalcy bias, if the events challenge their assumptions about what is normal to occur). But in general, it is much harder for positive trust-building stories to get the attention we pay to stories of trust betrayal—it's built into our psychology. And little wonder: think about how important it would have been for the evolution and survival of humans to learn to pay greater heed to dangerous events than to those that augured good news.

Psychologist Paul Slovic studies trust in nuclear power plants. He asked college students to rate the impact of forty-five different hypothetical news stories about a power plant on a scale from 1 to 7, where 1 meant a low impact on trust and 7 would signal a very powerful impact. The stories were designed to either increase trust or decrease trust. Stories to increase trust might say there were no safety problems at the plant last year, employees are carefully trained and selected, managers live near the plant, and the county medical examiner reports that the health of people living near the plant is better than average for the area. Stories to decrease trust included a potential safety problem covered up by plant officials, delayed safety inspections, a plant in another state that had an accident, and the county medical examiner's report that the health of people living near the plant is overall worse than average for the area.[27] Half the respondents gave the negative stories a 6 or 7 impact score. By comparison, less than one out of five respondents gave the positive stories a 6 or 7.[28]

The challenge that a company like Boeing or Wells Fargo faces is that it takes a sustained history of right to wipe out one wrong, and it will be judged by people who change their minds more or less easily. To meet this challenge, the company will have to be on the right side of trust again and again.

The first step for managing a trust breach is understanding the kind of trust breach your company has committed. Tolstoy's famous opening observation in *Anna Karenina* that all happy families are alike but that each unhappy family is unhappy in its own way, provides a useful way for leaders of companies to think about the trust problems they create. While each trust betrayal has its own characteristics, breaking them down into types based on the four dimensions on which trust can be built—competence, motives, means, and impact—can provide a path for moving toward a solution. Betrayals on each of these dimensions have different characteristics, and thus apologies and repair strategies will be more or less effective depending on the dimension violated.

COMPETENCE: TRUST BREACHES DUE TO *ability*. The failure of a product's or service's reliability and fitness for use is a trust breach of competence. The product or service did not work well or failed to live up to the promises you made about it. It's a trust breach that can be easier to fix because an apology and fixing the problem can go a long way toward making amends, as we will see below with the 2017 Academy Awards ceremony.

Apologies aren't always effective but can be an important first step for bridging a competence-trust breach. However, we often shy away from making apologies because we're afraid they will make us seem incompetent or guilty. This is faulty thinking because with a trust breach due to competence, the best course of action is to apologize. (This is not the case for trust breaches due to integrity, and we will explain why later.)

Apologizing indicates a willingness to take ownership for a mistake, a valuable trait we count on when working with others. We are much more likely to take risks with people who own up to mistakes than with those who don't. That's because they are more likely to be candid about problems that may be occurring, meaning you can count on them twice: once to let you know what's going on, and then again because they are willing to acknowledge their own role in what's happened.

Companies often refrain from making apologies out of fear that it will be seen as an admission of guilt and used against them. But apologies enhance, rather than detract from, the perception of the organization that made a mistake.

During the 2017 Academy Awards, PricewaterhouseCoopers mixed up the envelopes for best picture and best actress, leading announcers to mistakenly say *La La Land* had won best picture instead of *Moonlight*.[29] This was clearly a competence issue, rather than one of integrity: PwC didn't switch the envelopes on purpose!

However, PwC still took a lot of grief. Leslie Moonves, the chief executive of CBS, gave an interview to ABC news saying, "If they were my accountant, I would fire them." On Twitter #envelopegate and #Oscarfail trended (it doesn't count as public outrage without a hashtag trending on Twitter). Meanwhile people joked that PwC could stand for "probably wrong card."[30]

PwC responded swiftly. By early morning it had an apology up on its website:

> We sincerely apologize to "Moonlight," "La La Land," Warren Beatty, Faye Dunaway, and Oscar viewers for the error that was made during the award announcement for Best Picture. The presenters had mistakenly been given the wrong category envelope and when discovered, was immediately corrected. We

are currently investigating how this could have happened, and deeply regret that this occurred.

We appreciate the grace with which the nominees, the Academy, ABC, and Jimmy Kimmel handled the situation.[31]

For the 2018 Academy Awards, PwC unrolled a multistep process to prevent a mix-up from happening again. Employees were forbidden from using cell phones, because PwC had discovered that the partner in charge of the envelopes in 2017 had been on his phone shortly before the mix-up. In addition, PwC employees involved with the ceremony were required to memorize all the winners. PwC made a mistake, admitted it, apologized, and fixed it, and society let them move on (and handle the Oscars again). A win all around.[32]

MOTIVES AND MEANS: TRUST BREACHES *due to integrity*. Recovery is much harder when customers, investors, or employees think your trust betrayal is deliberate. Intentional trust betrayals, whether caused by malicious intent or unfair means, are seen as integrity violations. Even unintentional trust betrayals caused by unfair means can be seen as integrity betrayals. Boeing, it goes without saying, did not intend to create planes that killed people. But it prioritized profit over safety by cutting so many corners. The crashes of its 737 Max 8 planes were seen as an integrity issue because of what was motivating their cost-cutting, as well as how they designed, manufactured, and sold the planes. Boeing will have to prove over and over again that it has changed both its motives—why they do what they do—and its means—how they accomplish their goals. However, this will be a much trickier road to recovery, because while apologies are effective for competence errors, they are not as effective for failures of integrity.

In a study about the effectiveness of apologies versus denial, researchers found that in the case of a betrayal of trust due to integrity, it is better to deny if you are innocent. The researchers found that innocent people are seen as having less integrity after an apology even though they are innocent.[33] It turns out, the people who eschew apologies because they think they confirm guilt are onto something. The logic is as follows. Integrity is viewed as a sign of moral character, so when someone denies a problem because they are innocent, that is the kind of consistency that is a hallmark of integrity—I didn't do that thing, so of course I deny it. But if the innocent person instead apologizes, people are, at best, confused, and could conclude that the person can't be trusted if they can't even own up to a situation in which they are innocent!

However, be warned: this is not encouragement to deny instead of apologize. When the researchers gave participants clear evidence that the applicant was guilty, participants were far more willing to hire guilty applicants who apologized than guilty applicants who denied. (And rest assured, in this day and age where anyone can publish online and data are easily available, if someone is guilty, the truth will eventually come out.)

So, when a trust betrayal happens, make sure you understand the type of problem you are dealing with—one of competence or one of integrity—and adjust your strategy accordingly. A trust breakdown can be cast as an error in competence only if it is actually true and can be supported with evidence.

On the other hand, if a company or individual is being accused of wrongdoing and they are innocent, they should deny the charge. Back in 1996, for example, rumors swirled around Tommy Hilfiger, claiming he said he would not have designed his clothes to be "so nice" if he'd known people of color would wear them. Investigations later debunked this, and the Anti-Defamation League confirmed that the rumors were an internet hoax.[34] In 2007, Oprah invited Hilfiger onto her show so they could address the rumor together. While there, Hilfiger set the record straight, and Oprah denounced the rumor as baseless.[35] At the time the brand had a reputation for using a diverse cast of models to advertise its clothes, something not as common as it is today, which was just one sign of the way that Tommy Hilfiger thought about the power of diversity.

You should of course apologize if your company is guilty of an integrity violation, but be prepared for a long and difficult road. Even if your apology is a work of art, it is a necessary step toward rebuilding trust and can still be panned. Yet, if you don't apologize, that will be even worse because you'll be seen as uncaring. Meanwhile, you can expect that it will take a long record of consistency and doing right to regain the public's trust. How hard this is will be determined by the next element: impact.

IMPACT. THE SEVERITY AND FREQUENCY of the trust breach significantly impact how hard it is to repair the problem. The greater the impact someone had suffered, the greater the negative reaction. Which is to say, a good apology is important, but a company is much better off if the impact of their trust betrayal is relatively minor—swapped envelopes at an award ceremony as opposed to death or fraud. This is common sense, and for those of you who love basing your actions on hard research, Debra L. Shapiro, a professor at the University of Maryland, found the most important factor for accepting an explanation was the severity of the harm the individual had suffered.[36]

The persistence of trusted behavior can inoculate a company from a momentary betrayal—up to a point. If a company with a long and rich history of doing right by its customers, employees, and shareholders violates trust, it is more likely that it will be forgiven. However, if trust violations keep happening, each violation creates more evidence that the company is not to be trusted and, taken as a whole, as proof of the true nature of the company. But that decline starts with a single act of betrayal.

In Recruit's case, its salespeople had developed uniquely strong relationships with their customers. Recruit's sales team was trained to visit customers in person to more fully understand their problems, often leading to changes in how they advertised and used the data they received, both of which created greater value for their customers. When the scandal occurred, Recruit did not lose many customers because they felt they had a good relationship with the company and the trust violation of Ezoe's insider trading did not directly impact them. Ezoe's insider trading impacted members of the Japanese elite and some in the overall Japanese public. But its customers did not suffer harm or undergo any additional risk from using Recruit's advertising platform (compared to say a car with a faulty airbag). Moreover, the quality of Recruit's product and services remained unchanged.

The Art of Constructing Apologies

An apology is an important first step. The emphasis is on *first* since both the short- and long-terms effects of a trust betrayal have to be dealt with.

Apologizing is tricky business, and can be a thankless task. If you do it wrong, be prepared to suffer the consequences. When a corporate apology backfires, this can further damage a company's reputation, sometimes even leading to ousting the CEO.

Recall Tony Hayward, the CEO of British Petroleum, and his disastrous apology after the BP oil spill. In 2010, a BP oil drilling rig exploded in the Gulf of Mexico due to the failure of a critical part.[37] The explosion killed eleven workers and spewed 4 million barrels of oil[38] across the wetlands of the Gulf from Texas to Florida.[39] It contaminated an estimated 1,300 miles of coastline.[40] The spill destroyed countless species including killing off half of the bottlenose dolphin population,[41] leading to a 38 percent decline in reef fish diversity,[42] and killing up to 800,000 birds.[43] It was the worst environmental disaster in US history.[44]

In the wake of all of this destruction, Hayward apologized by saying, "I'm sorry. We're sorry for the massive disruption it's caused to their lives. There's no one who wants this thing over more than I do. I'd love my life back."[45] In any situation, this would be an awful apology, but given the extent of the disaster, Hayward's focus on the effects of the oil spill on his own life was especially obnoxious. Hayward made so many missteps in his apologies that he was dismissed shortly after.

If your company has caused great harm as BP did, an apology is necessary, but even so, expect backlash. That said, it's still imperative to give one and to do it right. A bad apology stating you want your life back will make people even angrier and earn you a place in the history books—for all the wrong reasons.

So, what is a good apology? A good apology will take a multi-pronged approach and try to address a variety of different needs, as we'll see below with JetBlue. In 2016, researchers published two studies to understand how 755 participants reacted to different types of apologies. They tested six elements of apologies:[46]

- *Expression of regret*: The offender expresses how sorry they are.
- *Explanation*: The offender describes the reasons for the problem.
- *Acknowledgment of responsibility*: The offender makes a statement that demonstrates they understand their part in the trust betrayal.
- *Declaration of repentance*: The offender promises not to make the same mistake again.
- *Offer of repair*: The offender offers a solution for rebuilding trust.
- *Request for forgiveness*: The offender explicitly asks for pardon.

The most effective apologies contain all six elements. In the event that it is not possible to use all of the elements, the researchers found that the more elements an apology incorporated, the better. Apologies that used only one component were the least effective.

When an apologizer used only a few elements of apology, the most effective combination was acknowledgment of responsibility followed by an offer of repair, then an explanation. For example: "I'm so sorry I didn't invite you to the meeting. Do you have time now for me to tell you what we discussed? I forgot you had joined the team since your division hadn't participated before." The least effective was a request for forgiveness. ("Please forgive me for not inviting you.") The researchers combined different sets of elements and found that some combinations were more powerful than others depending on the scenario they had given subjects. However, combining the most powerful elements (an acknowledgment of responsibility, with an offer of repair and an explanation) was always more powerful than the combination of the least powerful elements (an expression of regret, a declaration of repentance, and a request of forgiveness).

Finally, it's important to keep in mind that the sooner the apology occurs, the more effective it is.[47] It's understandable that companies are tempted to wait before issuing an apology because more facts may come out, but the point is that as a company you *are* deeply sorry for the harm you caused, and while you may not have a fix, an apology shows you understand that there is a problem, which is important to establish as soon as you can.

JetBlue's 2007 apology for its disastrous performance serves as a model. It combined an acknowledgment of responsibility, an explanation, and an offer of repair. On Valentine's Day, an ice storm hit the East Coast. While most airlines canceled flights, JetBlue tried to keep flying. Nine planes were stuck on the tarmac at JFK for up to six hours as their planes waited for conditions to clear.[48] In the following days, JetBlue ended up canceling about 25 percent of its flights anyway.[49] CEO Dave Neeleman offered an unflinching apology for the way they had treated their customers.

Last week was the worst operational week in JetBlue's seven-year history. Following the severe winter ice storm in the

Northeast, we subjected our customers to unacceptable delays, flight cancellations, lost baggage, and other major inconveniences. The storm disrupted the movement of aircraft, and, more importantly, disrupted the movement of JetBlue's pilot and inflight crewmembers who were depending on those planes to get them to the airports where they were scheduled to serve you. With the busy President's Day weekend upon us, rebooking opportunities were scarce and hold times at 1-800-JETBLUE were unacceptably long or not even available, further hindering our recovery efforts.[50]

Neeleman didn't stop there. In the same apology, he announced the creation of a JetBlue Airways Customer Bill of Rights. JetBlue promised customers compensation for delays of over an hour. For delays over four hours, customers were promised a refund on their whole trip, even though JetBlue fares are all one-way.[51] Ultimately, JetBlue's board removed Neeleman. But although Neeleman lost his job, history has been kind to him. *Fast Company*'s headline succinctly summed up public opinion: "Firing Neeleman; JetBlue Just Blew It." The apology has gone down as a textbook case of how to make things right.[52] While even the best apology may not be enough to regain the public's trust or save someone's job, given a choice, it's better to be remembered as a CEO who was unfairly ousted than as one who blew it by asking for his life back.

But Is It Our Leader?

Speaking of ousting leaders, dismissing a leader may be the right thing to do in the face of a trust betrayal, but it needs to be carefully thought through to ensure that this consequential decision doesn't come with unanticipated costs. Business is not a democratic institution. Leaders have the power to make decisions that affect employees through all the levels of the organization's hierarchy. Their actions, and what they choose to praise or turn a blind eye to, go on to shape what is seen as acceptable and unacceptable behavior. This in turn molds the very identity of the company. After all, does anyone think about Apple without bringing up Steve Jobs and the legacy he left there? Letting go of a leader is a quick way to signal to the public that the company's mistakes are in the past and it is turning over a new leaf. However, if the leader has done good work and knows the company inside and out, companies often lose a key resource in the recovery.

One of Recruit's first actions was to promptly get rid of its charismatic founder and CEO, Hiromasa Ezoe (this of course was not hard, as he was going to prison). At the same time, employees were advised by their managers that they could honestly plead ignorance of the situation that had brought disgrace to Recruit. It wasn't their decision to offer the subsidiary's shares in exchange for favors, they told customers. The CEO's mistake had nothing to do with their work together, and the actual quality of the service they provided.

Dismissing the CEO *is often* the right answer. A group of trust researchers examined what happens to organizational trust when a CEO is dismissed.[53] The researchers had participants learn about a fictional CEO trust betrayal. The CEO issued 10 percent pay cuts, and said he too would participate, but did not actually take the cut. The scenario was loosely based on American Airlines CEO Don Carty, who issued pay cuts for 100,000 workers while giving himself and other senior executives hefty bonuses in 2003. Participants were told either that the CEO was dismissed or that there was no action.

Dismissing the CEO resulted in higher trust scores for the organization. But dismissing a CEO is not just good for the company, it's also good for the CEO. When a CEO was dismissed, their trust scores rose too, which isn't as strange as it sounds. The scenario of a CEO who repents and is punished for wrongdoing is a classic example of retributive justice, or having people get what they deserve. It satisfies our need for fairness and reinforces our preference to live in a world where moral rules of cause and effect hold sway.

However, what gets interesting is that the researchers also tested another condition: one where the CEO apologized and was punished (a 20 percent pay cut) instead of being dismissed. Surprisingly, trust scores for the pay cut versus dismissal were similar, showing that our main interest is in seeing the CEO punished, rather than in the particulars of how that occurs.

It's worth keeping in mind that this experiment was limited to one scenario, and the merits of dismissal versus lesser forms of punishment will of course vary according to situation. In a case like Recruit, the need for CEO dismissal was clear-cut: Hiromasa Ezoe committed a crime. He had to serve a jail sentence, and even if he didn't, the scandal was so large that continuing to employ him would have shown that the company "just didn't get it" and undermined any efforts at trust recovery it might take.

However, in the case of JetBlue's Dave Neeleman, who used the Valentine's Day ice storm to actually improve the lot of customers, JetBlue's board would have done well to penalize Neeleman rather than dismiss him, as Neeleman still had plenty to offer. A penalty would have shown that the board found the actions to be unacceptable—Neeleman had made the decision to operate during the blizzard while several other airlines had closed because he didn't want to lose revenue. He had prioritized company profit over customer comfort and safety. On the other hand, his apology and especially his reparation in creating a passenger's bill of rights was groundbreaking. It was a both new and innovative way for customers to hold JetBlue accountable for how they were treated; it also established a system and culture of customer care that JetBlue still relies on today.

The decision to dismiss or punish is highly dependent on the situation, but boards should take into account the scope and severity of the problem, the frequency of the issue, and the CEO's past track record, as well as the perceived potential for redemption.

The Wild Blue Yonder: Long-Term Trust Repair

Change in leadership may be just the first step in the long and rocky journey of rebuilding trust. The big challenge is the crucial process of figuring out where trust was broken and what dimension you have to repair, and then turning inward for repairs to ensure the problem doesn't happen again. PwC didn't simply apologize for flubbing the 2017 Oscars. It instituted a host of new processes in 2018 to try to ensure that 2017 would never happen again.

There is, however, no set of keys to Aladdin's cave that reveal the quick and easy way to rebuild trust. Usually, a trust betrayal is the result of a systemic failure, and it will take nothing short of a system overhaul and delivering continuous positive results to regain trust. But what you need to think about in making these systemic changes is not some exotic or new territory. The elements are the basic building blocks of any organization, and so you have a head start in understanding how important they are and the shape they take in your own organization. This four-step framework for long-term trust repair is in part inspired by the work of two trust researchers, Graham Dietz and Nicole Gilespie, and their extensive study of the academic trust literature, as well as the research we conducted on companies that have successfully recovered from trust breaches.

Recruit didn't recover and become a $20 billion company in the wake of a scandal simply by apologizing and dismissing its CEO. (If only it were that easy!) It recovered after a far-reaching examination of the four fundamental building blocks of companies: strategy; culture and values; structures, policies, and procedures; and external governance.

STRATEGY, THE GOALS A BUSINESS sets, includes plans to allocate resources to different problems and opportunities as well as the specific tactical actions taken to produce results. Changing strategies requires a solid understanding of the industry's future, as well as a very real understanding of the company's capabilities and what it will need to do to execute. A good strategy positions the company a few steps ahead of the competition.

To get past its emissions scandal, Volkswagen went the route of appointing a new leader (more than one, actually) and developing a new strategy. In the past, Volkswagen had become the world's largest carmaker by focusing relentlessly on empire building: more cars, more brands, and more people.[54] Its strategy in the wake of the scandal was a 180-degree pivot: Volkswagen decided to slim down and aim to become one of the first companies to produce affordable electric cars that turn a profit.[55] There's a narrative brilliance to this strategy change. Volkswagen ran into trouble for cheating on emissions, but now aspires to make a name for itself by becoming the gold standard for producing environmentally sound cars. What better redemption story is there?

However, it remains to be seen whether Volkswagen can make good on its strategy. Volkswagen had to delay the launch of its first electric vehicle twice due to software problems.[56] Meanwhile, Volkswagen has faced production problems. It laid off factory workers while hiring software engineers to create its own software in-house, and like companies everywhere, has had to respond to the revenue fallout and employee attendance/safety issues brought on by the coronavirus pandemic.[57] However, there's some hope: it did manage to unveil its first electric SUV in September 2020.[58]

Recruit used two different and very effective strategies during its recovery. On the product and services side, Recruit realized that it was in the print business but digital would be the future. It made a quick pivot to start going digital, and in 1995, during the same month Yahoo went live, Recruit released its first website, Mix Juice.[59]

However, while Recruit had lost very few customers, managers realized Recruit had a bigger problem. Employee morale had plummeted. The children of Recruit employees had trouble at school since they were seen to be tainted by association with the company. In order to retain talent, Recruit would have to make some large changes.

Mitsuru Murai, now chairman of Japan's professional football (soccer) league, was then head of human resources for Recruit. He, along with other senior managers, recognized that Recruit could no longer guarantee lifetime employment—the fundamental promise Japanese employees expected from large employers. Instead, they decided to change strategies and make Recruit a good company to be *from*. If Recruit could no longer promise employees lifelong tenure, it could instead provide employees with the training and skills to make them highly sought after by other employers. "Instead of guaranteeing lifelong employment, we focused on developing employability for your whole life," Murai said.

The strategy change capitalized on Recruit's existing culture and required an overhaul of its policies, but it was worth it. Today, Recruit's alumni network, informally known as the Recruit Mafia, includes people in the top echelons of politics, business, and media and even includes an Olympic medalist. Applying for a job at Recruit is now a highly competitive process. In fact, the Recruit brand and development experience is so valuable that the company created a highly sought-after three-year employment program. This program is geared toward atypical job candidates, such as people who may not have relevant experience or strong academic resumes, or who come from underprivileged backgrounds. During their three-year contracts, they receive the same focus on their development and future employability as regular employees.

Recruit's culture gave it a distinct advantage in carrying out its strategy of becoming a good place to be from. The company had been founded on the premise that the most motivated employees were the ones who believed their work made an impact on the business and for society as a whole. So, Recruit intentionally gave large, high-impact opportunities to young, less experienced employees, so they could learn how to do hard things that stretched them.

Employees would complain that the most common response from an executive of whom they asked a question was, "What do *you* think you should do?" Masumi Minegishi, who was in his mid-twenties at the time and eventually became CEO, pointed out that the scandal only reinforced this culture. Employees created their own solutions to rebuild Recruit. "The scandal made us become autonomous," he said. "The managers thought of the company's survival as their own problem to solve."[60]

BECAUSE CULTURE CAN BE SO hard to pin down and so difficult to see, it's often one of the hardest facets of a company to change, because it permeates every level. A leader can announce that changes are happening, but they have to execute, which requires two elements: buy-in and consistency. If employees don't agree with the changes, they will not implement them, or will be slow to implement them, creating friction between those who comply and those who don't and endangering the future of the new culture. Furthermore, if management doesn't follow through by consistently rewarding and motivating the behaviors that mark the cultural change, the change won't happen.

In 2010, Japan Airlines (JAL) declared bankruptcy. It had once been a top airline, but was taken private in the late 1980s.[61] During its privatization, JAL overspent: it had one of the largest fleets in the world, employed 30 percent more people than the industry average, and had many unprofitable routes.[62] At the time of its bankruptcy, JAL had already been bailed out by the government four times over the course of just ten years.[63] Meanwhile, JAL had a culture problem: employees were divided into factions and there was little accountability.

The government brought in Kazuo Inamori as the new CEO. Inamori, a Buddhist priest, had founded multibillion-dollar electronics and ceramics firm Kyocera.[64] He had zero airline industry experience.

Inamori used methods similar to Recruit's to change JAL's culture: To get buy-in, he focused on employee happiness. He believed it was important for employees to believe that the work they were doing had social impact. He pointed out that JAL had a significant impact on the national economy, keeping the company afloat was necessary for protecting everyone's jobs, and it was employees' duty to provide stable air travel.[65] He also made employee growth a priority. He commented to the *Wall Street Journal*, "We put that at the very beginning of our philosophy statement. 'This is your company, and its goal is to make all of you happy.' To share the idea that the company's goal is to make all employees happy is a prerequisite, before sharing any other ideas. The whole philosophy wouldn't work without this prerequisite."[66]

Inamori printed books for each staff member explaining the social significance of their work, as well as Buddhist principles for how to live, such as being humble and moral.[67] Inamori underscored his commitment to JAL by refusing pay and requiring senior managers to take leadership training courses.[68]

To fix the lack of accountability, he introduced the Amoeba Management System, an invention from Kyocera. Under Amoeba, each division was given autonomy and came up with their own goals and plans for their unit. At the same time, each division head had to share their expenditures and earnings in a monthly meeting so everyone knew just how much each division contributed to JAL's bottom line.[69] Within a year, JAL was profitable again, and by 2012, JAL was the world's most profitable airline.[70]

RECRUIT WAS ABLE TO TURN itself into a company that was good to be from because it also paid close attention to its structure as well as its policies and processes for helping its employees develop themselves.

Recruit scaled back on standard perks like company housing and instead converted those expenditures into increased pay. It started a business college and brought in experts from around the world as speakers. To encourage innovation, it created the New Value Creation Compensation System, which rewarded employees for innovation. It started a "happy exit" program, where employees, beginning in their thirties, who wanted to leave were given a lump sum to help them with their next endeavor. It also created a fellowship program, which allowed employees to work part-time while pursuing another passion.

To this day, Recruit has maintained a number of creative and effective systems for managing employees. Its performance evaluation system, Will-Can-Must, was created with the goal of helping employees clarify their career goals so they can achieve them. Every six months employees are asked about "Will" (what they want to do now and over the next three years), "Can" (their current strengths and weaknesses), and "Must" (what they need to do to bridge the gap between "Will" and "Can"). Recruit also uses this performance system with its contractors to focus them on their career goals so they can be successful when their contract with the company is over.

When Recuit's managers meet twice a year to discuss their direct reports, they are evaluated not only on their ability to comment on the people who report to them but on their knowledge of their peers' reports as well. This forces managers to get to know everyone in more junior positions, not just the people they work with directly, enabling the fast-innovating company to be able to promote talent from throughout the organization as needs arise.

There are times when a scandal or a trust breach doesn't demand a major overhaul of its strategy or culture. Instead, the fixes are at the granular level of policies and procedures that create a new contract between the company and its employees and customers. David Neeleman's passenger's bill of rights at JetBlue is one example. Another is Airbnb's safety guarantee.

In 2011, Airbnb, a platform that allows people to rent their houses and apartments to strangers, had just entered the billion-dollar valuation club. However, investors had identified one of the largest risks as safety: What would happen if a guest destroyed someone's home?[71] Airbnb's business model depended on people trusting strangers to stay in their homes. In late June, investors' fears proved to be well founded. A blogger named EJ wrote about how her home had been completely destroyed by an Airbnb guest.

> They smashed a hole through a locked closet door, and found the passport, cash, credit card and grandmother's jewelry I had hidden inside. They took my camera, my iPod, an old laptop, and my external backup drive filled with photos, journals… my entire life. They found my birth certificate and social security card, which I believe they photocopied—using the printer/copier I kindly left out for my guests' use. They rifled through all my drawers, wore my shoes and clothes, and left my clothing crumpled up in a pile of wet, mildewing towels on the closet floor.[72]

Airbnb bungled its response. First it said that it did not insure hosts against losses and wouldn't reimburse EJ. However, founder Brian Chesky then told a *TechCrunch* reporter that Airbnb would help EJ financially and help her find new housing or anything else that would make her life easier.[73] The day after, EJ posted on her blog that she had not received the promised compensation or accommodation, but Airbnb's cofounder had called and requested she shut down the blog or limit access since it reflected poorly on Airbnb.[74] Airbnb eventually reached a settlement with EJ, but the incident prompted the company to create a new safety policy.[75] Under the new policy Airbnb guaranteed hosts a reimbursement of up to $50,000. (This grew to up to a million dollars the next year.)[76]

Airbnb didn't stop at the policy. They also took steps to create other safety structures including a twenty-four-hour customer service line, expanding the size of its customer service staff, and creating a trust and safety department, as well as working harder to verify users' identities.[77] However, the policy was important for codifying—and putting a dollar value on—Airbnb's commitment to protecting hosts, and regaining trust.

EXTERNAL GOVERNANCE INVOLVES THE WAY a company deals with laws and standards set by other bodies. This, in combination with internal governance, is how a company and its board create an infrastructure of oversight and controls, and work together to make sure the company doesn't go off track.

In a well-regulated industry, stakeholders know what they can and cannot expect from companies. Moreover, they know if the company crosses certain lines, their claims against the company have legal standing. Many companies see regulators as opponents who implement standards and regulations to curb their powers and place obstacles in their path. But companies that view regulators and regulation as antagonists miss a valuable opportunity to build trust.

While it may seem counterintuitive, willingly allowing monitoring by an outside body can increase trust. During his work on studying the risks associated with nuclear power plants, psychologist Paul Slovic found that there was one method that had a "substantial" impact on increasing trust in power plants. When local citizens and environmentalists were allowed to create an advisory board that had the authority to monitor the nuclear plant and shut it down if they thought it was unsafe, the impact on trust was substantial. In fact, trust in the plant doubled.[78] All right, you might be thinking, that's all well and good, but Slovic was studying nuclear power plants. No one trusts them. But there's evidence from other industries that replicates Slovic's results.

Two researchers conducted studies examining the impact of external governance on trust on an unlikely pair of businesses: a piano manufacturer and a chicken restaurant. In both cases, the researchers found the same result: being forced into monitoring did not inspire trust, but voluntarily agreeing to monitoring and offering to shut down facilities if there was any problem went a long way to inspire trust with regulators.[79]

Companies that find themselves in hot water are better off stepping forward to work with regulators and opening themselves up to comply with the results of external monitoring rather than trying to wall themselves off or treat monitors as adversaries. Picture a world where Takata had actually worked with regulators instead of trying to hide the results of its tests. Takata would have saved lives and probably gone down in the textbooks as an example of how you do a recall correctly.

Demonstrating that you believe you have nothing to hide and that you're willing to do all that it takes to fix something wrong goes much further to signal you are trustworthy than being forced to do so by regulators or other forces such as mass demonstrations. In our next chapter, we'll cover Sarah Al-Suhaimi, a young CEO who was faced with the task of turning around Saudi Arabia's largest investment bank. One of the major problems she had was that the regulator had listed several red flags at the firm—far more than average. Instead of trying to hide or stall, Al-Suhaimi decided to work *with* the regulator. She came up with a detailed turnaround plan and timetable that she showed to the regulator and got them to sign off on.

Speaking of transparency, as we were writing this book, we received an email from our contacts at Recruit. Recruit was in hot water again. One of its job websites had sold data to thirty-eight large companies to help them understand how likely it was users would turn down their job offers and take measures to avoid this beforehand.[80] The sale of these data not only violated the privacy of the job seekers, it also created the appearance (or reality) that Recruit was helping companies to cull from their lists employees who had turned down job offers, reducing the number of job opportunities they had access to. While the breach of confidentiality was not on the scale (or even in the domain) of the original scandal, Recruit still went through a soul-searching process to make a longer-term fix.

Immediate steps Recruit took included opening a website where users could read detailed updates about the incident and check to see if and how their personal information had been used. Recognizing that this kind of breach was related to Recruit's culture of innovation, they created new processes to monitor the innovations that were constantly being created in the company. These included developing a multistep checking process for creating new products and services, creating a centralized team to monitor legal risks, strengthening employee training on the proper handling of sensitive data in product and service design, and establishing an advisory committee made up of outside advisors to get a broader perspective on decisions about data utilization.

Trust can be regained, but regaining trust is the result of hard, careful, relentless work that never ceases. One of the most difficult tasks you will face is having to honestly examine what is working in your company and what is not. Just because there's a trust breach doesn't mean everything has to be scrapped. During Recruit's data privacy incident, senior leaders also debated whether they should remain committed to Recruit's bottom-up, employee-driven culture, since a natural response to the problem of a division that exercised poor judgment is to pull back the autonomy that allowed the division to make its own decisions. They ultimately decided not to change the culture, which was responsible for so much of the dynamism, attractiveness of the company as a place to work, and new ideas that benefited their customers. Instead, they focused on building stronger guardrails and checkpoints to ensure that there was greater oversight of the consequences of its support for innovation and for giving employees a chance to grow new skills by taking the risk of developing new products and services.

Recruit's story is a powerful symbol of hope and warning all at once. Trust can be regained, but once it has been regained, it does not mean that a company is in the clear. Trust can be dismayingly easy to lose, and while it is possible to regain it, rebuilding can be the painstaking work of years.

SEVEN

POWER, TRUST, AND LEADERSHIP

*A leader is best when people barely know
he exists... when his work is done, his aim
fulfilled, they will all say: We did it ourselves.*
—LAO TZU

I never dreamed about success. I worked for it.
—ESTÉE LAUDER

WHETHER TRUST TRICKLES OR GUSHES THROUGH AN organization is determined by its leaders since they have the power to set the tone for being trusted—or not. How a leader earns trust is similar to how organizations earn it: on the basis of competence, perceived motives, the means used to achieve goals, and responsibility taken for the impacts of their actions. There is one extra element as well: legitimacy—that is, whether followers believe the leader has earned their position.

When Sarah Al-Suhaimi became the new CEO of NCB Capital, she walked into a challenge. She knew the answers lay in gaining the trust of several groups: customers, employees, regulators, and even her firm's parent company.

NCB Capital is the investment banking and asset management arm of National Commercial Bank (NCB), Saudi Arabia's largest bank in terms of assets. When NCB Capital opened in 2007, it started with a flourish. It generated high profits, benefiting from record-high volumes of trades on the Saudi stock exchange. However, in 2010, NCB Capital began to falter for a number of reasons. Like several of its peers, it struggled with market volatility. Declining brokerage trades ate into NCB Capital's profits, which were based on commissions from trades. Attempts at international partnerships fell apart, demoralizing employees. Over the next four years, NCB Capital went through a CEO and an interim CEO with different visions. NCB Capital struggled internally as well, neglecting several core asset management business lines. Profits declined, and employees began to leave. Meanwhile, NCB Capital began to sustain losses. It would take extraordinary efforts and extraordinary abilities to turn the company around.

Now it was 2014. Al-Suhaimi was the first woman in Saudi Arabia to lead a blue-chip investment firm, and she was young—only thirty-four. When Al-Suhaimi met with employees at NCB Capital, she realized she would have a number of hurdles to overcome. On the one hand were personal factors out of her control. She commented, "I'm a woman, and they don't know who I am—I know they were all thinking, why are you becoming our boss?"

At NCB Capital she discovered a hierarchical environment, with little information sharing, where employees kept their heads down and did their job without much understanding of how they were contributing to the whole. Meanwhile, she had no senior team. Half had been managed out; the other half had quit. This turnover was mirrored all the way down the hierarchy. The environment was toxic, exacerbated by a disorienting combination of neglect and high-handed treatment of people. For example, employees in some of NCB Capital's regional offices hadn't seen anyone from senior management in years.

Even though NCB Capital was still the largest asset manager in Saudi Arabia, with more than 40 billion riyals (about $10.7 billion) of assets under management, the regulator had just finished a periodic inspection, and the firm had been issued one of the largest fines on record at the time. Meanwhile, NCB Capital's relationship with its parent bank was strained at best because several of its most important clients had made investments in NCB Capital funds and projects that had performed poorly.

To have a fighting chance at turning around NCB Capital, Al-Suhaimi would have to convince customers NCB Capital had something unique to offer in an increasingly competitive landscape. She would have to convince regulators to give her enough time to clean up, as well as win back the trust of NCB, NCB Capital's parent bank. Lastly, she would have to win the trust of NCB Capital's employees and attract new talent to execute on these goals. There were a hundred ways to fail and very few to succeed.

In this chapter we will delve into how leaders earn trust from the inside, with their own senior team, managers, and employees; then with their boards of directors; and then in a widening circle of relationships with customers, investors, regulators, government officials, and the general public.

Leading with Trust

Machiavelli proposed nearly 500 years ago that public morality—the morality that should guide leaders—is different from the morality of private individuals because leaders have different responsibilities and powers.

Leaders have powers other people don't. They get to decide (or lead a process of deciding) what products or services a company will offer, how many people to employ and what kinds of jobs they will have, which suppliers to partner with, and even how to interpret laws and regulations. On the flip side, this also means leaders have to make difficult decisions that may mean causing harm in order to preserve the greater good. One senior executive told us, "The fair decisions are easy. My job is to make the difficult decisions."

Because leaders have the responsibility of making decisions, leaders earn trust differently than organizations. Followers want first to know that a leader has earned her power legitimately, and second that she will use it well because she has the power to make decisions that will impact their careers and lives. They rely on their leader to make these difficult decisions with compassion and fairness.

The American philosopher John Rawls divided earning trust into two stages. First, there is "originating consent" where a leader first earns the trust of followers by acquiring power legitimately.[1] Then there is what he calls "joining consent,"[2] the fact that people continuously assess whether they want to keep trusting a leader.

In the first stage of trust, originating consent, followers want to know that leaders acquired their role through the right process, fairly carried out. In other words, how, exactly, did a leader come into their role and get the power that comes with it? In democratic societies we recognize the result of an election by allowing the winning candidate to assume the job of mayor, governor, or president, for example. In corporations, the process is less visible: boards of directors appoint CEOs, and we allow them to lead our organizations.

The process of earning trust, however, does not end with originating consent. Earning trust does not just happen when a leader first acquires power. It's a status that is always being reassessed through joining consent; that is, trust needs to be earned over and over.

Leaders face an uphill battle when it comes to joining consent because it turns out that the very qualities that cause you to earn people's trust in the first place are easily destroyed by acquiring power. Dacher Keltner, a professor of psychology who heads up the University of California–Berkeley Social Interaction Lab, has studied power for decades. He defines power as "one's capacity to alter another person's condition or state of mind by providing or withholding resources…or administering punishments."[3] In his book *The Power Paradox* he describes his research and that of other leading scholars of power.

Power is a paradox because the very behaviors that lead others to trust you with a position of power can be horribly transformed into behaviors that are the *opposite* of what people want in a leader. For instance, leaders often gain their power because of their willingness to listen to others, but once attaining it, they frequently downplay or even refuse to listen to dissenting voices. That is because being in a position of power affects both the way you see yourself and how others see you and the way you act.

Now, the second half of this paradox is not exactly news. There's a reason why you have probably heard some version of the quote, "Power tends to corrupt, and absolute power corrupts absolutely," the famous opinion of the British historian Lord Acton.

Let's start with the first half of the paradox and Keltner's description of the behaviors that lead others to trust you with a position of power. In this view, the road to earning and maintaining power and ultimately trust is paved by actions that show care for others. Groups create leaders.[4] They "give power to those who advance the greater good, construct reputations that determine the capacity to influence, reward those who advance the greater good with status and esteem, and punish those who undermine the greater good with gossip."[5] Keltner's leaders demonstrate empathy, they give to others, and they show gratitude.[6]

Keltner and some colleagues conducted the research that first introduced him to these ideas twenty years ago. He wanted to understand why some people rise to power in a group while others don't. To get at this question, he designed a natural state experiment, which means an experiment that would allow him to interact with participants at home instead of in a lab. He got permission to study the students who lived together in one hall in a first-year dormitory at the University of Wisconsin, Madison.[7] At the beginning of the year, he met students and asked them to rate the amount of influence of each person in the hall. Students also completed a questionnaire that asked them to assess the extent to which their own personalities were defined by five social tendencies: kindness, enthusiasm ("reaching out to others"), focus on shared goals, calmness, and openness ("being open to others' ideas and feelings").[8] He came back at the middle of the academic year, and then at the end, asking students each time to rate the power held by each of their dorm mates.

He tallied the power ratings given to each student. He found that as early as two weeks into the year, some students already had more perceived power than others. He also found that each student's power fluctuated throughout the year. As for the big question, what was it about those who rose to power, here's what he found:

> In my experiment, the strongest predictor of which dorm dwellers rose to the top within the first week of arriving at college, and which ones remained there through the year, was enthusiasm [defined as "reaching out to others"]. The other Big Five mattered as well: kindness, focus, calmness, and openness also related to students' power.[9]

Researchers replicated these results across seventy other studies, finding that all the people who rose to power had all of the Big Five personality traits. The studies were in settings as varied as hospitals, financial firms, manufacturing facilities, schools, and the military. The Big Five were found in people who were promoted, seen as effective leaders, and in military recruits who attained the status of officers.[10] This is overwhelming evidence that if you want to get power, you need to be someone who values others, who cares about the greater good, and who can help a group succeed.

The reason Keltner's book is called *The Power Paradox*, however, is that he goes on to describe how the actions that lead someone to power can disappear under the neurological and psychological effects that wielding power can have on individuals. Keltner calls power a "dopamine high."[11] Dopamine is a neurotransmitter that plays a role in how we feel pleasure, and it is released in our brains when we expect a reward.[12] Keltner found that when people feel powerful they have higher levels of excitement and positive feelings, which lead to more action. Power also makes people more aware of the rewards associated with a course of action. However, these power surges and dopamine highs also make them less aware of the risks associated with an action.

This transformation from a focus on others to a focus on yourself is also a concern of Adam Galinsky, professor of leadership and ethics at Columbia Business School. Galinsky and some colleagues conducted a deceptively easy-looking experiment to illustrate one of the worst effects of power on individuals, which is how it interferes with a person's ability to understand other perspectives.[13] A key component of empathy, perspective-taking, is the proverbial ability to walk in another person's shoes, which means to be able to see, feel, and imagine how someone else experiences the world.

But power can stop us from being able to take other people's perspectives into account. In Galinsky's study of fifty-seven undergraduates, he divided the students into "high-power" and "low-power" groups. Students in the high-power group were asked to write about a personal incident when they had power. In the low-power group, students wrote about a personal situation in which another person had power over them.[14] The students were then taken into a separate room and given a series of tasks: high-power participants were asked to allocate seven lottery tickets to themselves and another participant; low-power participants were asked to guess how many of the seven lottery tickets they would receive from another participant. Students were then given the following instructions: Task 1: With your dominant hand, as quickly as you can, snap your fingers five times. Task 2: With your dominant hand, as quickly as you can, draw a capital E on your forehead with the marker provided.[15]

Here is the amazing thing that happened. The participants in the high-power position wrote the letter E on their foreheads as if *they* were reading it themselves, which meant that the E would be backwards from the perspective of someone looking at them and trying to read it. And the participants in the low-power position wrote the letter so that *a person looking at them* would be able to read it easily. In other words, they wrote it considering the perspective of the other person, whereas the high-power group wrote it from their own perspective.

The experimental process used by Galinsky is called "priming." It refers to the common and well-validated research technique that finds that giving individuals tasks like writing about a personal experience will put them in a frame of mind to think of themselves in a particular way, in this case, as either a person of high power or someone with low power.[16] So, just by being primed to think of yourself as high-power, you look at the world from your own perspective.

CEOs like Travis Kalanick from Uber (he of the toxic culture, never-ending scandals, and bad-boy fame) and Tony Hayward from BP after the Deepwater Horizon oil spill (Mr. I'd love to get my life back) are first-rate examples of what leadership looks like under conditions of power-laced self-focus, an inability to empathize, and indifference to harm imposed on others.

What this comes down to is that as a leader at any level in an organization, or even in your personal life, you must be prepared for the internal battle that awaits. On one side is the focus on others and the good of the group—the actions and beliefs that enable people to gain power and the respect and admiration of others. And on the other side, the well-documented finding that being in a leadership role will pull you toward a focus on yourself, and replace attention to others with an inability to care, understand, or even be curious about the conditions of other people or groups, except those who serve your interests.

Legitimacy

Leaders earn legitimacy—the right to lead and the status and power that come with it—by going through a "proper" process. A monarch may not be the most competent or moral person to lead the country, but he or she will earn the position simply because people accept that the process for the transfer of power is inheritance.

A presidential election is a prime example of how trust in legitimacy works. Depending on the result, there will be a sizable number of people (usually in the opposite party) who believe the new president is incompetent or immoral or both. The new president, however, gets to assume office because the dissenters accept the electoral process, if not the person. That said, if enough people feel strongly about a candidate, they will begin to question the process. During the 2012 presidential election when the Democratic candidate, Barack Obama, was reelected, Republicans' overall confidence in the electoral process was 52 percent. However, during the 2016 election when the Republican candidate, Donald Trump, was elected, it jumped to 71 percent. Meanwhile Democrats' confidence in the electoral process dropped from 76 percent in 2012 to 66 percent in 2016.[17] But we still recognize (if reluctantly) that a president elected by this process is legitimate according to the rules for democratic elections as they have been defined. Similarly, the chairman of NCB and NCB Capital (he had both roles) was in a proper position to offer the job of CEO to Sarah Al-Suhaimi, who, in turn, was regarded by the wary staff at the investment bank as at least having a legitimate role as the new CEO.

There's a reason why we use legitimacy in a political context as our base case. The concept of legitimacy comes from political philosophy, which has a long history of debate about what justifies political authority. Authority in this sense is defined by the British philosopher Fabienne Peters as "a right to rule—a right to issue commands and, possibly to enforce these commands using coercive power."[18]

Until the seventeenth century in Western societies, the right to rule a nation-state was justified based on natural law and divine authority.[19] If you were a king or queen, your authority came from being placed in your role by God. In the sixteenth century, when the Catholic Church wouldn't grant Henry VIII of England a divorce so he could marry Anne Boleyn, he broke from the Catholic Church and established the Church of England. Henry VIII defended himself by claiming that his connection to the divine trumped that of the Catholic Church, whose pope was only "the Bishop of Rome."[20] (The Church excommunicated him, but Henry stayed king.)

In the seventeenth century, the British philosopher Thomas Hobbes and the Dutch philosopher Hugo Grotius turned away from viewing authority as being grounded in the will of God and developed what has become the modern view that authority is justified and made legitimate by *consent*.[21] The British philosopher John Locke agreed, asserting that "no one can be . . . subjected to the political power of another without his own consent."[22]

Legitimacy refers to the process a leader goes through to acquire power. What is more important is whether people support the results of the process. Legitimacy may be the first step for acquiring power and trust, but people consent to a leader's power based on their assessment of the leader's competence, motives, means, and impact.

Competence

Competence is often the most common way for leaders to gain and retain trust. With leaders, we think of technical competence in their field of expertise as the baseline. Equally important is managerial competence, the ability to manage internal and external relationships so they can achieve their company's objectives and adapt to changing circumstances. Competence in leaders allows them to set the vision for producing a product and service as well as manage relationships so the product or service can get off the ground.

Sarah Al-Suhaimi gained trust from the get-go at NCB Capital because of technical competence. Her track record as a top asset manager at her old firm was exemplary, and she brought the same capabilities to her new role as CEO. We'll take a few steps back into Al-Suhaimi's history to understand how she became an un-contested star in an industry that was almost entirely populated by men.

Al-Suhaimi always knew she wanted to get into business and studied accounting at university. She started her career at the Saudi American Bank ("Samba Financial Group" or "Samba Bank"), which was affiliated with Citibank. At the time, few Saudi Arabian women like Sarah worked outside the home, especially in the field of banking. She joined the Investment Management Division, where she was put in an office on a separate floor, because no women were allowed on the floor of the division in which she worked.

At the time, Al-Suhaimi's father was the deputy governor of the Saudi Central Bank and the main person responsible for regulating investment banking in Saudi Arabia before the establishment of the Saudi Capital Market Authority (NCB Capital's current regulator). This connection meant Al-Suhaimi had to work harder to prove she'd earned her position. "They basically gave me no work for a while and the perception, I learned later, was that I was the spoiled daughter of the deputy governor, just coming here to pass time until she gets married. So, no one took me seriously."

Samba Bank had a training center, and Al-Suhaimi asked to go there. There she earned the respect of her coworkers through her stellar performance as a student in the classes. After finishing the program, she elected to join the asset management area. At the time, in 2003 in Saudi Arabia, the asset management function had no data coming through the internet. People worked in a manual world—getting information for public equity research by inputting data into Excel spreadsheets from financial information that was only available in print form.

Al-Suhaimi learned everything she could by volunteering to do the work no one else wanted to do. Over a period of five years there was no job in asset management she didn't do, including overseeing compliance and writing risk reports.[23] And she went beyond that to leading Samba's implementation of a front office asset management system—a first for the kingdom—moving from manual trading activities to a more streamlined, reliable, automated process. She progressed from research analyst, to assistant portfolio manager, to senior portfolio manager.

When Sarah's boss from Samba Bank left to start Jadwa Investment, a midsized boutique investment bank, he asked her to join the new company. And she did—becoming the only female employee at Jadwa where she worked on public equity management. Al-Suhaimi did so well she was made chief investment officer, responsible for sales and wealth management. She was also a member of the committee that decides on private equity investments. There she attracted the attention of the chairman of NCB Capital at the time, who sat on an investment committee that Jadwa managed money for. He was so impressed with her performance that he offered her the position of NCB Capital's CEO.

When Al-Suhaimi arrived at NCB Capital, Wassim Al-Khatib, the current head of investment banking, was then in middle management. He had been working at NCB Capital since 2006 and didn't want to leave. Yet he knew that there was no future for him at NCB Capital if the new leader could not turn it around. He probed into Al-Suhaimi's background and was so reassured by what he found, he decided to stay: "When I asked my professional network about her, there were a lot of good things there. Her old firm was a boutique investment bank, but it was a key player in asset management, private equity and investment banking and what I needed is a string of hope that somebody would come and give our business some attention."[24]

When Al-Suhaimi arrived in 2014, she made good on her reputation for competence by crafting a new strategy for NCB Capital. At the heart of the new strategy was a goal of moving away from volatile revenues, which made it hard to maintain steady growth. The main source of volatile revenues was its brokerage business, where clients pay NCB Capital a transaction fee to buy or sell stocks or bonds on their behalf. When stock and bond prices rise, investors trade more frequently, as had been the case in Saudi Arabia for several years, and the business earns a lot of revenue from transaction fees. The downside is when the stock and bond market does poorly, people stop trading and transaction fee revenue dries up.

Al-Suhaimi and her team created a new strategy to reduce NCB Capital's dependence on volatile revenues such as transaction fees. The first part of the strategy was to create a more dependable revenue base through NCB Capital's asset management businesses. When investment banks sell asset management products such as mutual funds, private equity, or other investment packages they create, they get paid recurring fees for as long as investors stay invested in those products. Since these fees are asset based, the investment bank's revenue only fluctuates if the value of the funds changes or if customers put more money in or take money out. The second part of the strategy was to run the firm more efficiently, so its costs were reduced over time. Because NCB Capital now had lower costs and a more stable source of revenue, even in a terrible year, NCB Capital could aspire to reach 50 percent net profit margins—an ambitious target given that typically investment banks globally have a net profit margin of about 15 percent.[25]

For NCB Capital to grow, it also needed to find a new base of clients to pursue while the firm continued to rebuild its relationship with the parent bank. Going after institutional investors became another pillar of the new strategy. In addition, Al-Suhaimi began a systematic examination of the firm's current asset management products, meeting with product owners for detailed reviews. Over the next two years, NCB Capital either liquidated or scrapped nonperforming products. Only after the product portfolio had been cleaned up did she allow teams to develop new alternative investment products.

For Al-Suhaimi, the first step toward gaining everyone's trust was proving she had the chops to stabilize the business. This required both having an excellent track record (she would have never been given the job without one) and then entering NCB Capital and taking swift action to steer it back to profitability.

As important as technical competence is, it alone is not enough for a leader to establish trust. Equally important is managerial competence, particularly the ability to skillfully manage relationships.

Two weeks before her official start, Al-Suhaimi began to meet with key staff, and Al-Khatib, the employee who had done some research on her past, was one of the first to meet her. He was out-side Riyadh when he got the call, but flew to Riyadh as soon as he received the invitation to talk. Never having met Al-Suhaimi, he had no idea what she was like.

> I walked out onto the floor and there was a lady talking to an-other person with her back to me. When she heard me walk in, she turned around and immediately introduced herself. She invited me into her office and we started talking. Here she was, CEO of what is effectively the Goldman Sachs of Saudi Ara-bia, casually sitting with me having a conversation over coffee. Right away, I was impressed by her humility.[26]

They exchanged stories about their personal lives, backgrounds, and career experiences. Al-Suhaimi asked Al-Khatib to fill her in on the history of the investment banking division at NCBC. "One of the options," she said as he was concluding his description, "is to shut down the investment banking division completely. What do you think of that?" Al-Khatib expressed confidence in the di-vision's potential and was delighted that she agreed. "I appreciated her asking for my opinion," he reported, "and felt this was some-one I could not only relate to, but also work with."[27]

After similar meetings with all the members of the staff, Al-Suhaimi knew her first priority was to build a senior leadership team that could help her turn around the bank while keeping it running, a task she likened to "trying to do a major renovation in your house while you're living in it."[28]

She tried to hire and promote from within whenever she could, focusing especially on drive and fit. Naif Al Mesned described his hiring meeting with Al-Suhaimi:

> I was being interviewed for the head of internal audit; however, I was planning to explore opportunities that would allow me

to move to the business side. Near the interview's end, Sarah said, "You're definitely qualified for the head of internal audit, but I think you're naturally more suited for the business side." I thought, wow, how did she see that! She made me head of risk management, which is much closer to the front of the business since the head of risk is responsible for the assessment of product and investment risk.[29]

After about four years, Al Mesned ended up leading the wealth management business division.

Within a month Al-Suhaimi had a whole new team, who, like Al Mesned, were young and enthusiastic. "Each one of us was given a chance," Al Mesned said. "That first year, I spent four nights a week in different cities, and I did so with pleasure. We all felt we'd do whatever it took to prove we were the right choice."[30]

Her next challenge was to create a connection to the firm's many disillusioned and disheartened employees. "When Al-Suhaimi joined," one executive said, "there was so much conflict between departments that there was no motivation. You'd see people sitting alone in their offices, playing with their phones—everybody thought they were at a dead end. It wasn't a business environment where people wanted to deliver or achieve."[31]

Al-Suhaimi set up town halls across the company to reconnect staff to the business and open up the logjam created by years of a rigid hierarchy that stifled communication and sharing ideas. She visited every branch office to introduce herself and to describe a new vision and ambitious plans for NCB Capital. She recalled the reaction to her message at one town hall meeting in 2015: "I told them I was expecting to double our assets under management by the following year and everyone looked at me like I was crazy. I told them to just trust me and to concentrate on developing good products."[32]

They weren't the only ones who thought she must be kidding. Naif Al Mesned, the new head of wealth management, recounted his first discussion about his own financial goals with Al-Suhaimi. "I remember the first-time targets were assigned to me—I just started laughing. I said, 'Sarah, are you serious? Is this a plan to fail? It's totally unrealistic!' Looking back, I can see how she made us all realize that things we thought were unattainable were actually possible. We learned to think bigger and to push ourselves to achieve our goals."[33]

By the end of Al-Suhaimi's first year, NCB Capital was back in the black and was even earning a profit of $86 million. In 2019 its profits were around $122 million and as of this writing, in 2020, NCB Capital leads the Saudi investment banking and asset management sector on almost every major metric. Al-Suhaimi had more than lived up to her reputation for competence and the trust it inspires.

Motives

Motives are the reasons why a company, or in this case a leader, acts as they do. We care about the motives of leaders because they explain whose interests they serve. Leaders are constantly balancing between their organization's needs (which at times can have their own internal conflicts) and those of other individuals and groups whose interests can conflict.

The late Katharine Graham, as publisher of the *Washington Post*, was faced with a dilemma that called into question her motives. In the eyes of the world, her procedural legitimacy was shaky at best. Her father had purchased the *Washington Post* in 1933, and her husband became the publisher in 1946.[34] After his death in 1963, Katharine Graham inherited the majority stake in the *Washington Post*.[35] In addition, she was living in a world where there were no female top executives in business.

Unlike Sarah Al-Suhaimi, Graham didn't have a long professional track record to inspire trust in her competence. Graham had only a limited journalism education and certainly not much business experience. After graduating from college in 1938, she spent a year working as a reporter for the *San Francisco News*. Then she went back to the *Washington Post* and worked in the editorial and circulation departments, but gave up her career to focus on raising her family in September 1945, when her husband came home from the war in the Pacific.[36] When she started at her position as publisher, Graham went through an exhaustive process of getting to know and understand the *Washington Post* by listening and learning from senior management and reporters at all levels. "What I essentially did was to put one foot in front of the other, shut my eyes, and step off the edge. The surprise was that I landed on my feet," she wrote years later in her memoir.[37]

What Graham was too modest to mention is that not everyone can win the trust and respect of an existing management team, especially if you come in without much expertise. It's clear she was adept at developing good relationships, knowing how to size up people's strengths and weaknesses, and knowing whose advice to listen to and take seriously.

During two difficult periods, Graham earned particular fame for her clear vision and the depth of her trust in those at paper: the decision to publish the Pentagon Papers and the investigation of the Watergate scandal.

In 1971, Daniel Ellsberg, a military analyst, leaked the Pentagon Papers to the *New York Times*. What became known as the Pentagon Papers was a several-thousand-page study in forty-seven volumes on American involvement in Indochina from the end of World War II to the Vietnam War peace talks.[38] After the *New York Times* published its first two stories, the government sued, citing national security, and a judge issued a restraining order against the *New York Times* forbidding it from publishing anything more.[39] After the *Times* had received an injunction and could no longer publish, Ellsberg leaked the papers to the *Washington Post*, and now the *Post* faced an immediate dilemma.[40] Should the paper publish as well? At the time, the *Post* was going through an IPO, and getting a restraining order could have been a death knell for going public.[41] Publishing would also earn the ire of the Nixon administration. On the other hand, the *Post*'s editorial staff and reporters wanted to follow the *Times*'s example and publish, even though that had resulted in the *Times* being barred from publishing. They believed they had a duty to the American public to publish. Not publishing would be "an abdication that would brand the *Post* forever."[42]

Graham gave the paper permission to publish (vividly portrayed in the 2017 movie *The Post*), despite the *Post*'s precarious position. Her agreement was transformative for the paper. It demonstrated that she was committed to ensuring the paper served the American people first and foremost, and placed its business interests and legal fears second. Years later in his memoir, executive editor Ben Bradlee wrote,

> What I didn't understand, when Katharine's "Okay...let's go. Let's publish" rang in my ears, was how permanently the ethos of the paper changed, and how it crystallized for editors and reporters everywhere how independent and determined and confident of its purpose the *Washington Post* had become. In the days that followed, these feelings only increased. A paper that stands up to charges of treason, a paper that holds firm in the face of charges from the president, the Supreme Court, the attorney general.... A paper that holds its head high, committed unshaking to principle.[43]

Just a year after the Pentagon Papers, the *Post* uncovered the Watergate scandal. The story originally started as a description of a break-in at the Democratic Party's headquarters in the Watergate complex in Washington, DC.[44] Amid firm denials of any involvement from the Nixon administration, the *Post*'s reporters began to dig in. Now, Graham had to make a decision.[45] How far to pursue the story—and how? At the time, the *Post* was the only paper covering the story. No one had any idea how far it would go, or if the reporters had even found anything worth chasing.

The *Post* established strict rules for pursuing the Watergate stories. Every piece of information that came from an anonymous source had to be confirmed by another independent source. Meanwhile, the *Post* refused to run anything reported by another paper unless its own reporters had verified and confirmed it. Finally, each word of each story was read by one of the senior editors with a top editor vetting the story before it ran.[46] This may seem like standard practice for journalism, but it's worth noting that when Graham's husband, Philip, was publishing the paper, he used it to achieve his political goals. For instance, Philip Graham once agreed to bury a story about riots at a segregated swimming pool as city and government officials agreed to integrate the pool the following season.[47] Admirable, but not the purpose of a newspaper: newspapers exist to let the public know the truth.

And, as history knows, in service of the public's right to know, the *Post* exposed one of the greatest presidential scandals in US history, which ended the Nixon presidency.

Katharine Graham's dedication to serving readers transformed the *Post* from a local Washington paper to a paper of national prominence that could rival the *New York Times*.[48] This had a financial payoff as well. When Katharine Graham stepped down in 1991 after almost thirty years at the helm, the *Post* had nearly a twenty-fold increase in revenue and its stock during that time was a spectacular performer.[49]

Means

It's often difficult to get a true understanding of a leader's motives in the short term. Certainly, one can ask, but any reasonably socially competent person will know how to discuss (or lie) about their motives so they sound benevolent. It's left to the public and—later—history to evaluate a leader's motives by analyzing their actions—how they behaved and how fairly they treated all of the parties affected by their decisions. Leaders' actions speak louder than their words. The public cannot read minds, so leaders will be scrutinized for the fairness of their actions. If their actions are perceived as unfair, the leader's life from public to private will be further scrutinized in order to understand their motives.

During our earlier discussion of means, a framework of four types of fair action—procedural fairness, distributive fairness, informational fairness, and interpersonal fairness—helped distinguish among different ways that companies can act fairly. That framework applies equally well for distinguishing the ways that leaders can be fair.

The hallmarks of procedural fairness in decision-making are showing consistency in how decisions are made, using a process that creates an accurate picture of the decision and its context, and giving a voice in the process to those impacted by the decision.

Once Al-Suhaimi's senior team was in place, she convened workshops, moderated by her or by outside facilitators, to provide a space for frank assessments of the state of the firm. "She always had an agenda, and relied on data to open discussions and make decisions," one executive recalled. Executives found that Al-Suhaimi would really challenge them, as one remarked, "She has a very strong presence, but she gave everyone the opportunity to speak and made sure everybody felt like their opinion mattered. We felt empowered to express our views and present our ideas."[50] On her part, Al-Suhaimi promised a zero-blame environment where everyone could problem-solve together.[51] Al-Suhaimi also pushed people to make decisions: "I didn't want people to just execute decisions; I needed them to become leaders in their own right, in whatever part of the process we were in."[52] Workshops ended with action points and the people responsible for them identified.

Al-Suhaimi came to these meetings with a point of view about what was going on; however, she did not force it upon the group: "Every time we go into a workshop, even if I knew the answer, it was always designed for people to come up with it and own it.... And people realized quickly that I can change my mind. So it's never me just telling them, 'This is what we're going to do.' Because I realized I needed it to be the success story of every single person."[53]

These workshops were successful because they weren't about confirming a preexisting decision made by the leader, but used a process for subject matter experts to point out problems, discuss solutions, and identify a path forward.

One of the most profound powers of organization leaders is the ability to create processes for deciding who works in the organization, who is promoted, and who should leave. This is a power that can easily make or break trust for leaders because there needs to be distributive fairness in the process. Distributive fairness is the art of allocating both pain and rewards in a manner that is consistent and free from bias.

During her first year at NCB Capital, much of Al-Suhaimi's job involved managing underperforming employees out of the company: a painful task that no leader likes to do. Yet, it must be done; one employee has the potential to ruin an entire team. (A study of financial advisors found that if someone with a history of financial misconduct joins a team, their coworkers are 37 percent more likely to engage in fraudulent behavior.)[54]

Al-Suhaimi created a process for giving people the opportunity to prove themselves. She worked with the employee in question to create a work plan with regular check-ins on progress.

By the time Al-Suhaimi was ready to let the employee know if NCB Capital was the right place for them or not, the employee had already arrived at that conclusion.[55] Al-Suhaimi had to manage out roughly 15 percent of her senior management team, yet when they departed it was their choice and there were no complaints.[56]

INFORMATIONAL FAIRNESS—COMMUNICATING CLEARLY AND truthfully about situations and decisions—was a trademark skill for Al-Suhaimi, and the cornerstone of her ability to establish trusting relationships. She started her tenure by hosting town halls in every office in each of the countries NCB Capital operated in, insisting on visiting not just the office, but each floor of each office, so she could meet people where they worked, and make herself part of their world, rather than insisting that they join hers in a larger and more impersonal whole group meeting. She used these meetings to talk about her vision for NCB Capital and enlist employees in the high-stakes battle to win back the trust of people who worked in the parent bank. Between town halls, Al-Suhaimi used monthly newsletters to share financial results—a striking departure from the past—and to recognize achievements by employees at all levels in the firm.

Al-Suhaimi also created the conditions for honest exchange as the new normal. She first needed to establish herself with the people who didn't know her.

In the beginning it took me one meeting with any person for them to take me seriously; I know what I'm talking about. So, this manager came in and he says we do this, we do that, and then I start asking for details. They cannot hide things. The previous environment discouraged people from being open and honest. They cannot now come and say something about someone else, because I would just call that person in and ask the other person about what they had said in front of the person they were talking about. I did that once, then it never happened again. Then the whole company—everybody—knew.[57]

Interpersonal fairness is the respect and regard we show people when we interact with them. During my earlier research on layoffs I discovered a depressingly large collection of inhumane practices. The worst—and I wish I were making this up—was a company that conducted monthly layoffs by assigning employees to a meeting in one of two rooms that were next to each other. In one room, a sad and somber place, were the people who were being told they were losing their jobs. Just next door, sounds of celebratory music blared out, and people in the layoff room could hear praise for those who got to stay. "YOU ARE WINNERS! YOU ARE HOW WE WILL CONTINUE TO CRUSH THE COMPETITION AND WIN IN THE MARKET PLACE."

It's not surprising that stories of interpersonal *un*fairness abound about layoffs. Interpersonal fairness matters most when the chips are down and you have bad news to convey. The question, then, is how in your interpersonal interactions you can show people the respect they deserve.

Sometimes we show our respect in actions, not words. For example, after Al-Suhaimi had received the board's offer to be CEO of NCB Capital, she needed time to think about what she wanted to do. She called her boss at Jadwa and asked for three weeks of vacation. He had been urging her to take some time off, so this was no problem. She recalled, "I thought three weeks was enough time to assess whether I would go or stay. I also was not going to walk into that office thinking about another company. In addition, we were just starting to fundraise for a product and I didn't want to raise money from clients and then leave them."[58]

After she had made her decision to leave Jadwa, she had to tell the CEO.

My boss...was very disappointed, since we had a good working relationship and I knew that he relied on me for a significant part of Jadwa's growth plans. I was very honest with him and my relationship with him is still amazing. But if you were in that office when we had that conversation, you would think we would never speak to each other again....That's when I learned you cannot hold on to people. People will stay with you once they trust that you are enabling them to do better for themselves with you than they could do with others. I always tell them, "The work you do here, you carry with you for life. It's not mine. Take that as your experience and you'll make decisions correctly, not because you get a title or money."[59]

Impact

Leaders make the call about the impact their company will have. Sometimes it's through their products (think Boeing); at other times it's how they manage their operations (think BP, VW, and Wells Fargo). We look to the leaders who are in charge when serious events occur, and hold them accountable for what happens on their watch.

Sarah Al-Suhaimi was in a different position at NCB Capital. She had to fix mistakes made by the leaders who came before her. Mistakes that were, as she put it, "not my fault, but they are my problem."

In 2017, Al-Suhaimi's success as an investment manager and her performance as CEO at NCB Capital led to her selection as the first woman to chair Tadawul, Saudi Arabia's stock exchange. Her role as chairperson was to set the strategic direction for the exchange, working with Khalid Al-Hussan, CEO of Tadawul, who was responsible for implementation.

Their top initiative was to raise the international standing of the exchange by opening it to foreign investors, becoming part of the network of established capital markets around the world. This required regulatory and operational changes, and coming up with a package of potential investments, products, and communication processes with the Capital Markets Authority, the regulator of the exchange and all capital market activities in the kingdom, that measured up to global standards of transparency and good governance. This would help the exchange earn a place in emerging market indices including the Morgan Stanley Capital Index, S&P Emerging Markets Broad Market Index, and FTSE (Financial Times Stock Exchange Group) Emerging Index.

Being part of an index that tracks stock movements in a sector of the global economy is itself a sign of trust. It signals that in your exchange, the stock prices and their movement are accurately recorded and reliable enough to contribute to the overall picture of how stocks are performing in the global economy. Certain kinds of mutual funds are created on the basis of these indices, promising investors a return that equals the performance of that sector as a whole. They are also used by investors to test the competence of those who invest on their behalf by giving them a point of comparison to determine whether their managers are better than, equal to, or behind the performance of a sector of the global economy as a whole.

All the while, Al-Suhaimi continued to serve as NCB Capital's CEO. In 2019, five years after she started, Al-Suhaimi had righted the course of the investment bank, outperforming all competitors in revenues and net income, and increasing return on equity. In 2019, NCB Capital turned a profit of 458 million riyals ($122 million), its return on equity was 40 percent, and its expenses had dropped by nearly 40 percent.

We've delved deeply into the details of Sarah Al-Suhaimi's story because it illustrates what the work of building trust looks like on the ground. Trust building is a combination of strategy, execution, and the commitment to treating people right. It is difficult to do, but once done the results can be extraordinary.

EIGHT

TRUST AS POTENTIAL

You must trust and believe in people or life becomes impossible.
—ANTON CHEKHOV

THE MAGIC OF TRUST IS THAT IT UNLOCKS A WEALTH OF opportunities that would not be possible otherwise. You are reading this book because of a moment of trust between Shalene and me, one that ultimately grew into a much deeper and more enduring trust. If Shalene had not chosen to trust me, and I to trust her, this would either be an entirely different book or perhaps not exist at all.

As we noted earlier when Shalene challenged me about whether I fully appreciated the scope of my work, trust can result in a book and, on a larger scale, can even transform the lives of millions of people. In 1974, Bangladesh was in the midst of a famine that would ultimately kill 1.5 million people.[1] An economics professor wanted to do something to help his fellow Bangladeshis, but didn't know what. He began to talk to the residents of a nearby village to understand how they lived and the problems they faced. One day he met twenty-one-year-old Sufia Begum, a woman who survived by eking out a living crafting bamboo stools, but with no chance of improving her life in a meaningful way. To purchase materials for making stools Begum had borrowed the equivalent of 25 cents from moneylenders who were charging 10 percent interest per day.[2] Under the terms of the loan, Begum was required to sell her bamboo stools back to the moneylenders well below market level. She made a profit of 2 cents, barely enough to live on. To purchase the raw materials to make more stools, she needed another loan.[3] Begum was trapped in an endless cycle of debts that would keep her in poverty forever.[4]

The professor kept talking to other people in the village of Jobra, and found forty-two other people in the same trap. He decided to lend them each roughly 62 cents, about $27 in total.[5] To his surprise, everyone repaid the loan.

The professor wanted to scale this up to help more people, but knew he couldn't do this on his own. He pitched the idea to a local bank and was turned down flat. The poor had no collateral, the bank's representatives said. Moreover, they were illiterate and wouldn't be able to fill out the proper forms. The professor offered to take care of the forms and guarantee the loans with his own money—about $300—and was finally able to take out a loan on behalf of the group.[6] Once again, he found that the payment of loans from people without collateral was much higher than the repayment of loans from people with collateral. Shortly afterwards, he started a pilot project to lend small amounts to poor people without requiring collateral. The project kept growing and turned into an organization, until finally in 1983 the Bangladeshi government recognized the organization as an official bank.[7] "The poor know that this credit is their only opportunity to break out of poverty," the professor later wrote in his autobiography.[8]

The professor, Mohammad Yunus, the founder of Grameen Bank, received the 2006 Nobel Peace Prize jointly with Grameen Bank for "their efforts to create economic and social development from below."[9] Grameen is a nonprofit that aims to keep interest rates low, and its average loan is about $200.[10] It targeted women and lent to them in groups, where the women would strongly encourage each other to pay back the loans.[11] As of 2019, Grameen Bank had 9.6 million members and 2,568 branches, and it had disbursed about $24 billion in loans.[12] It boasted a repayment rate upwards of 96 percent.[13]

Embedded in the story of Yunus and Grameen is the potential of trust. Yunus's trust in the poor kickstarted the growth of the microloan industry. In Indonesia, Bank Rakyat of Indonesia (BRI) started making microloans in 1984 when it couldn't turn a profit and was on the brink of being shut down. It began turning a profit in 1986.[14] BRI went public in 2003 and was the largest IPO in Asia after the financial crisis of 1997.[15] Meanwhile, in the wake of Grameen, Barclays Bank partnered with Care International UK to create financial services for the poor.[16] By 2013, the number of microloan borrowers grew to 211 million.[17]

In his memoir, Yunus describes one of his success stories: Murshida, a Bangladeshi woman with an abusive husband who sold the roof of their house to pay a gambling debt. When Murshida confronted him, he beat her, threw her out, and then divorced her. Murshida got a microloan of $30 to buy a goat and set up a business to sell its milk. Eventually she was able to take out larger loans and started a sewing and scarf business that employed up to twenty-five women.[18] Not every recipient of a microloan is a Murshida. However, while a microloan doesn't guarantee ending someone's poverty, it provides options and allows for a better quality of life.

Of course, no story is perfect. Grameen Bank and Mohammad Yunus have run into their share of criticism, while microlending has come under fire. In 2010, Andhra Pradesh, a state in India, shut down microfinance organizations after reports of a high suicide rate among borrowers.[19] (A study later found that overall incomes in Andhra Pradesh declined after microfinance organizations were shut down.)[20] Yunus himself ran afoul of Prime Minister Sheikh Hasina of Bangladesh when he started a political party in 2007, and he was ultimately removed from his post of managing director of Grameen Bank in 2011.[21] Grameen Bank was the target of smear campaigns, and Sheikh Hasina accused Yunus of overcharging the poor.[22] She also accused him of misusing aid funds from Norway.[23] Yunus was later cleared after Norway conducted an investigation.[24]

Shadows and clouds aside, Yunus's legacy remains. In the 1970s he chose to trust that a group of impoverished villagers would repay his loan. The villagers, in turn, chose to trust that his loan would not further trap them in poverty. Because of a moment of trust, today, microloans are available for millions of people, giving them choices they otherwise would not have.

IN THE SHORT TERM, PROFITABILITY may seem like it's all that matters, but in the long run, trust is what earns you the customers who keep coming back to you, the employees that put in their best work for you, and the public's tolerance of your ability to operate. This trust is easy to destroy and difficult to rebuild. When you're making any decision, take a second to ask, in the long run, will this make people trust me more or less? It sounds simple, but the tragedy is far too few people are asking themselves this question. Trust us. It will be well worth your time, as Kaspi Bank discovered.

Kaspi Bank, Kazakhstan's third largest,[25] was founded by Vyacheslav Kim and Mikhail Lomtadze, who wanted to create a bank that people loved. Initially Kaspi's goal was to build the largest and most profitable retail bank, which it did with bravado. In 2012, Kaspi was in the top one or two positions for almost all dimensions of retail banking.[26]

However, although Kaspi was flourishing financially, it failed its first trust test. In February 2014, rumors swirled over WhatsApp that the bank was on the verge of collapsing. Even though Kazakhstan insured deposits, terrified customers lined up at branches to withdraw their money. While this might have started out as a rumor, it is the kind of situation that could easily cause a bank to run out of cash. The natural reaction, then, is to limit the amount of money customers can withdraw so the bank stays solvent. For Lomtadze, the bank run was an alarm bell: "If our customers believed in us, they wouldn't be waiting outside our doors. My conclusion was we didn't have their confidence yet," he said.

Instead of limiting cash withdrawals, Kaspi's response was calibrated to win customers' trust. Employees threw open the doors of Kaspi Bank. Management eliminated restrictions on withdrawals and flew in chartered planes with bellies full of cash to ensure that the ATMs and branches had enough money on hand to meet demand. Branches stayed open and employees worked late hours until every customer had been served. Meanwhile Kaspi served pizza and hot beverages to waiting customers. Senior management made a point of being on the ground, accessible and ready to talk with customers. Lomtadze made an appearance on TV to reassure the public that Kaspi was fine. "It took us 72 hours to stabilize things. We didn't sleep at all," he said.

Kaspi took the investment in trust one step further. It refined its mission to "improving people's lives by developing innovative products and services." "Nobody really likes banks," Lomtadze said. "We wanted to build a business which customers love, and the companies people love are the ones that change their lives for the better." To do this, it looked for a metric to measure customers' overall happiness and settled on using net promoter score (NPS), a tool developed by the Bain consulting company, where customers are asked how likely they are to recommend your company to someone else. Kaspi made NPS its top key performance metric, which required redesigning the bank's products and processes to focus on customer happiness.

Kaspi's investment in trust—measured by chartered planes full of cash, employee overtime, as well as the mission rehaul and focus on NPS—paid off when, four years later, Kaspi again became the object of rumors that Lomtadze had disappeared with the bank's money. This time, Kaspi took a photo of Lomtadze holding the current day's Kazakh newspaper and sent it over WhatsApp, telling people to stop believing the rumors. No one showed up at Kaspi asking for their money.[27]

Kaspi had won because it had shored up its vulnerability to rumors, and customers had won because they knew if there ever was a bank run, Kaspi could be trusted to give them their money instead of sitting on it or creating obstacles like fees and limits. Since then, Kaspi has quadrupled the size of its retail deposits and doubled its market share while entering new markets like mobile payments and e-commerce, where it's now a top player. Meanwhile it's still a company that people love: its customer retention rate is 98 percent.

Even though as a global community we are facing challenges from pandemics to climate change that will require us to work together and trust each other if we want to survive, too few companies and leaders are displaying the kind of trust Mohammad Yunus had or recognizing the importance of prioritizing trust the way Kaspi Bank's leaders did. As we mentioned during the introduction, much of this book was written during the COVID pandemic—where unfortunately, all too often, companies stumbled while trying to balance public health and profits.

Amazon is a prime example of a company that excelled on many fronts and yet struggled on others. As COVID-19 was first running wild, in one month, Amazon warehouses had to adjust to massive sales growth.[28] Orders for groceries, for example, grew as much as fifty times in volume.[29] To accommodate this growth, Amazon did many smart things. They prioritized the shipment of medical supplies and household staples, and also slowed the flow of inventory coming in to diminish demand.[30] Meanwhile Amazon's shareholders made out big: in April 2020, Amazon's stock went through the roof, reaching upwards of $2,400 per share. By July, Amazon's stock had passed $3,000.[31]

Amazon also kept a COVID-19 blog,[32] which is a model of how to keep people (employees and others) informed at a critical time. Updated at least several times a week, it cataloged actions we wish more companies had taken, including stopping large gatherings, moving to virtual job interviews, and upping the cleaning of surfaces. Amazon also invested $4 billion in COVID initiatives to keep employees and customers safe, including 150 updates to business processes, providing free masks at all open Amazon and Whole Foods Stores, and launching a $20 million initiative to speed up COVID-19 testing.[33]

But in April, stories about conditions in Amazon's warehouses leaked: in some facilities there was no protective equipment or sanitization supplies, no deep cleaning, and employees were working too close to each other.[34] The absence rate in warehouses was 30 percent[35]—a clear sign that Amazon's employees were voting with their feet.

Amazon did take measures during that time on behalf of warehouse employees: until the end of May 2020, they increased wages by $2 per hour, and overtime improved from time and a half to double the normal rate. Amazon also offered employees unlimited unpaid leave. They also said they would pay anyone two weeks' sick time, on the condition the employee testing positive for COVID was placed in quarantine.[36]

However, on the same day that Amazon was blogging about the shipment of masks to its operations centers, the *New York Times* reported COVID had spread to more than fifty Amazon warehouses in the US,[37] and on April 16, Amazon was forced to close all of its warehouses in France on the grounds that they were not doing enough to keep their workers safe.[38]

We reached out to Amazon for a comment about the warehouse situation in France, and their PR team told us that Amazon had not reported these numbers. However, a few days later, Amazon listed the COVID rates of its frontline workers on its blog. Almost 20,000 workers in the US were infected with COVID.

Amazon reported that this was 42 percent lower than the expected rate of infections based on the general US population.[39]

Trust can't be claimed; it is judged by others and they take a 360-degree view. The public, and its watchdog, the media, are always on alert. Amazon might have gained more trust if it had done a better job of disclosing employee infection rates from the get-go or at least acknowledged what happened with its warehouses. Building and maintaining trust isn't about intentions, it's about fairness and impact as well. And those are judged by *all* the people and groups whose lives we touch.

As Nobel Prize–winning economist Kenneth Arrow once wrote, "Virtually every commercial transaction has within itself an element of trust, certainly any transaction conducted over a period of time. It can be plausibly argued that much of the economic backwardness in the world can be explained by the lack of mutual confidence." Yunus got to the heart of this when he started Grameen Bank, and the leaders of Kaspi Bank recognized the truth of this when they decided to move trust to the forefront of their decision-making. Earning trust can lead to new prospects, such as NCB Capital's incredible turnaround, Michelin's factory transformations, and even the stability that followed Kaspi's customers' refusing to believe a rumor.

Trust is like a kaleidoscope. Each twist and turn creates new and unimagined possibilities. But the red and green and silver and gold parts all have to be aligned to be in the kaleidoscope. We have more power together than apart, and wondrous things happen when we leave ourselves open to twisting and turning with others.

Acknowledgments

WITH TRUST COMES THANKS. THIS book has been a work in progress for the more than twenty years I've spent at Harvard Business School and, as you now know, was baked into being in the years I spent in business before that. The Beatles' "Long and Winding Road" has always been a favorite song of mine, not least because it combines a recognition of long times spent in doing with the feelings of joy, melancholy, and satisfaction that are called up when we contemplate how we got to where we are and whom we should thank for having arrived at this particular destination.

We've told much of the story of how this book came to be as we went along, so what is left now is to thank the people who have played a role in it. That's no small thing, and there is no small list.

First, we are deeply indebted to the many companies and leaders and experts who so generously took the time to talk with us and share their experience and expertise with us. Their stories, insights, and perspectives are on every page of this book. Please join us in thanking them.

Speaking personally, I am thankful to Joe Badaracco and Lynn Paine, who have been principal mentors in all my endeavors at

Harvard Business School. Thanks are due as well to Mike Tushman for responding with encouragement to the first piece I ever wrote as an academic in portrait (i.e., Word) rather than landscape (i.e., PowerPoint), which confirmed the shocking realization that in this kind of communication you actually have to write out *every word*.

The following HBS colleagues (past and current) have offered profoundly useful advice at critical junctures, as well as warm colleagueship and much welcomed friendship: Teresa Amabile, Lynda Applegate, Ted Berk, Jean Cunningham, Tom Delong, Rohit Deshpande, Bob Eccles, Carrie Elkins, Robin Ely, Amy Edmondson, Frances Frei, Lena Goldberg, Jan Hammond, Rebecca Henderson, Steve Kaufman, Dutch Leonard, Joshua Margolis, Nien-he Hsieh, Gautam Mukunda, Kathleen McGinn, Cynthia Montgomery, Mike Norton, Nitin Nohria, Karthik Ramana, Clayton Rose, Arthur Segel, George Serafim, Robert Simons, Hiro Takeuchi, Deb Wallace, and Zeynep Ton.

The HBS research directors have given more than just financial support—my special thanks to Paul Healy, Leslie Perlow, and Jan Rivkin for believing in the work and offering coaching on how to do it. The global scope of this book is in large part due to the indefatigable efforts of the remarkable band of HBS Global Initiative Research Center directors and their staff: they are the best story finders in the world.

Shalene and I are especially grateful to Amy Bernstein and her colleagues at *Harvard Business Review* and HBR.org, who have taught us about excellence by being such great collaborators and editors themselves.

Peter Bernstein, our agent, wins the "unwavering support award" for his patience in seeing us through, after several turns in the road, to this very satisfying moment. John Mahaney, our editor at PublicAffairs, has been incredible to work with, combining well-honed instincts for structure, clarity, and accuracy with passionate devotion to the art of storytelling. With us every step of the way, John has gently pushed us and never held back. We would also like to thank the team at PublicAffairs for their support: Clive Priddle, our publisher; Lindsay Fradkoff, director of marketing; Miguel Cervantes, marketing coordinator; Brynn Warriner, our production editor; and Jocelynn Pedro at PublicAffairs and Mark Fortier and Megan Posco at Fortier, our dedicated publicists. Books are a team effort, and what an incredible team you were. Thank you from the bottom of our hearts.

We are grateful to Adam Davi, our HBS support wizard who has helped in all matters administrative, including locating sources, connecting us to the many people we spoke with, and ably executing the critical task of getting our footnotes in order. Thanks as well to Kelsey Kudak for bringing her fact-checking expertise to a manuscript full of business and nonbusiness stories, current and historical events, social science studies, philosophy, and more. Any errors left are our responsibility. And a special thank-you to Susan Winterberg, the research associate who laid the groundwork for this book by her research into best practices in layoffs, the first area of trust I studied.

And then, Shalene, for all the rest. Working with Shalene is a joy. She is wondrously talented, courageous enough to be trapped in a dark place with, and so kind. I knew none of this in the beginning, and even then, I had hired Shalene in my mind before I met her. Let me explain. All applicants for the position of research associate at Harvard Business School are given a set of facts and asked to write them up as if they are part of a case study. In her write-up, Shalene did something I'd never seen before. She wrote a clear narrative about the facts, but every few sentences, she would add a parenthetical note ("and here I would add data that would back up this assertion") and ("to complete this thought, I would get more information about X"). In other words, Shalene saw what was there, and she also saw *what was not there* and what would be needed to make the story complete. This is a rare skill, and Shalene is a rare combination of big picture, strategic architect, and narrative builder, who wears her miner's hat with a torch light to go fearlessly into tunnels of opportunity. That story about Mao and the four pests? That description of why Quakers earned such trust as businesspeople? All Shalene, along with so much more. In a pre-COVID era, I picture all of us in a big room, and I'm asking Shalene to be celebrated, describing for what, and then we would all applaud. So, let me hear you do that now.

Closer to home, I'm lucky to have a circle of trust of friends I've known, loved, and relied on for decades: Faith Goldshore and Rob Friedman, Karen and Andy Epstein, Jessica Wolfe and Tom Bloch, Carliss Baldwin and Randy Hawthorne, and Julianne and Clayton Rose. Thanks to each and every one of you.

And a loving acknowledgment, last, to the family, where trust began. Jerry and Jean—parents who showed us what true love looked like; Susan and Mark, comrades in arms as we grew up together, and comrades in arms still. Thanks to my husband Richard, the strongest and wisest man I know and the most loving; daughter Libby Jacobson, our tireless, enthusiastic coach; son Andrew Sucher-Jacobson, ever vigilant, who watches over us; gifted and loving daughter-in-law Amy An; and our granddaughters Olivia and Isla: the future unfolding before our eyes. Trust beginning and trust never ending.

—Sandra Sucher

IN ADDITION TO ECHOING SANDRA's heartfelt thanks, I'd like to add some of my own. When I first started at Harvard Business School, the HR manager said, "Oh, Shalene, you're so lucky to be working with Sandra. You're absolutely going to love her. This is going to be a wonderful partnership." If anything, that was an understatement. Sandra excels at bringing out the best in people, because at heart, she trusts that everyone has something to offer and it is her job to unlock it. She listens in a way that I've never heard anyone listen: not only does she hear the words you're saying, she seriously considers the merit of each idea brought before her. I can't imagine many other people in her position would have taken a suggestion from their research associate to reframe a narrative. Not only did Sandra take the suggestion with grace and good humor, she ran with it.

It's been such a privilege to collaborate with her—and a great deal of fun too—whether it's early mornings interviewing sources across the globe, afternoons spent whiteboarding chapters in her office, weekends on the phone redrafting, or exchanging edits late at night. Sandra, it's been such a pleasure getting to know you. I've learned so much from you professionally and personally. There are so many moments when I ask myself, what would Sandra do? And my life is always the better for it. I am so grateful we met.

We interviewed a staggering number of people for this book, and listing everyone we spoke to would fill another book. Our deepest thanks to everyone who talked to us. We were not able to include everyone's stories, but each and every story we heard had an impact on our thinking and shaped this book. Thank you so much for your time and your generosity.

Peter Bernstein, for his endless support, patience, sharp edits, and wonderful stories about the publishing world. John Mahaney, your constant adage to "add more color" had me scurrying to reference books and re-interview sources. Your praise made my day, and your sense of humor was a beacon of light in the trenches. The book is so much better because of you. It's been an honor and a privilege. Kelsey Kudak, thank you so much for scouring each line of our manuscript. Your attention to detail is awe-inspiring. I'd like to add my thanks to the HBS Global Research centers as well for their support in finding stories, coordinating interviews, and acting as sounding boards for all manner of questions. In particular, thank you to Esel Cekin, Gamze Yucaoglu, Fares Khrais, Nobuo Sato, Anjali Raina, and Rachna Tahilyani.

Thank you to Amy Bernstein, for her eagle-eye editorial guidance, sage advice, and deep warmth. Will Hurwitz, officemate, neighbor, and friend. Adam Davi, thank you for being able to solve any problem in a pinch.

I have been deeply lucky in my friendships. My thanks to Garvi Sheth, Denise Lin, Jamie Hittman, Nix Johnston, Chao Cao, Alfred Miller, Younjoo Sang, Manon Verchot, Benjamin Snyder, Lauren Barry, Siri Raasch, Heidi Liu, Alexander Ravich, Kelly Carnahan, Valerie Ollis, and Sandra and Raageen Kanjee, for their wise counsel and support. Thank you for pushing me to do better, picking me up when I fell over, cheering me on, and putting up with copious references to trust and trust research.

My parents, Subhash Gupta and Che Lin Woo, who trusted in my love of words from the very beginning, and sacrificed much so that I could follow my dreams. Words aren't and will never be enough. Thank you for always being there, listening to me when I got stuck, prodding me when I needed to be prodded, and for the several care packages that fueled this manuscript. And finally to Usheer Kanjee, who, with great care, patience, and several pastries, gave me the courage to trust.

—*Shalene Gupta*

Notes

Introduction

1. Federal Deposit Insurance Corporation, "Historical Timeline: The 1980s," accessed August 1, 2020, www.fdic.gov/about/history/timeline/1980s .html.

2. Kathleen Elkins, "A Brief History of the 401(k), Which Changed How Americans Retire," *CNBC*, January 4, 2017, www.cnbc.com/2017/01/04/a -brief-history-of-the-401k-which-changed-how-americans-retire.html.

3. Donald Bernhardt and Marshall Eckblad, "Stock Market Crash of 1987," Federal Reserve History, www.federalreservehistory.org/essays/stock _market_crash_of_1987.

4. Bernhardt and Eckblad, "Stock Market Crash of 1987."

5. Bernhardt and Eckblad, "Stock Market Crash of 1987."

6. Robert Rich, "The Great Recession," Federal Reserve History, accessed August 19, 2020, www.federalreservehistory.org/essays/great_recession_of _200709.

7. Bhargav Srinivasan, "Artificial Intelligence and Ethics Implications" (unpublished manuscript, last modified May 12, 2019), Microsoft Word file.

8. Matt Reynolds, "Biased Policing Is Made Worse by Errors in Pre-Crime Algorithms," *NewScientist*, October 4, 2017, www.newscientist.com

/article/mg23631464-300-biased-policing-is-made-worse-by-errors-in-pre
-crime-algorithms/.

9. Danielle Ensign, Sorelle A. Friedler, Scott Neville, Carlos Scheideg-
ger, and Suresh Venkatasubramanian, "Runaway Feedback Loops in Pre-
dictive Policing," *Proceedings of Machine Learning Research* 81 (2018): 1–12,
https://arxiv.org/abs/1706.09847; Srinivasan, "Artificial Intelligence and
Ethics Implications."

10. Calum Chace, *The Economic Singularity: Artificial Intelligence and
the Death of Capitalism* (Three Cs: 2016).

11. Jonathan Watts, "We Have 12 Years to Limit Climate Change Ca-
tastrophe, Warns UN," *The Guardian*, October 8, 2018, www.theguardian
.com/environment/2018/oct/08/global-warming-must-not-exceed-15c
-warns-landmark-un-report.

12. Watts, "We Have 12 Years."

13. Intergovernmental Panel on Climate Change (IPCC), "Global
Warming of 1.5 ºC," accessed August 2, 2020, www.ipcc.ch/sr15/chapter
/summary-for-policy-makers.

ONE. What Is Trust?

1. Judith Rehak, "Tylenol Made a Hero of Johnson & Johnson: The Recall That Started Them All," *New York Times*, March 23, 2002, www.nytimes
.com/2002/03/23/your-money/IHT-tylenol-made-a-hero-of-johnson
-johnson-the-recall-that-started.html.

2. Rehak, "Tylenol Made a Hero."

3. Clayton S. Rose, Sandra J. Sucher, Rachel Gordon, and Matthew Pre-
ble, "On Weldon's Watch: Recalls from 2009 to 2010" (HBS Case No. 9-311
-029, Harvard Business School, October 21, 2010), 6.

4. Rose et al., "On Weldon's Watch," 3.

5. Roger C. Mayer, James H. Davis, and F. David Schoorman, "An Integrative Model of Organizational Trust," *Academy of Management Review*
20, no. 3 (July 1995): 712; Annette Baier, "Trust and Antitrust," *Ethics* 96,
no. 2 (January 1986): 235.

6. Robert C. Solomon and Fernando Flores, *Building Trust in Business,
Politics, Relationships, and Life* (New York: Oxford University Press, 2001), 236.

7. Solomon and Flores, *Building Trust*, 6.

8. Rose et al., "On Weldon's Watch."

9. Baier, "Trust and Antitrust," 231–260.

10. Baier, "Trust and Antitrust," 232.

11. Baier, "Trust and Antitrust," 234.

12. Baier, "Trust and Antitrust," 238.

13. Goodreads, "Robert C. Solomon," accessed May 28, 2020, www
.goodreads.com/author/show/9704.Robert_C_Solomon.

14. Stephen Knack and Philip Keefer, "Does Social Capital Have an
Economic Payoff? A Cross-Country Investigation," *Quarterly Journal of
Economics* 112, no. 4 (1997): 1251–1288, www.jstor.org/stable/2951271.

15. Knack and Keefer, "Does Social Capital."

16. Kurt T. Dirks, "Trust in Leadership and Team Performance: Evidence from NCAA Basketball," *Journal of Applied Psychology* 85, no. 6
(2000): 1004–1012, https://psycnet.apa.org/record/2000-16508-016.

17. Tony Simons, "The High Cost of Lost Trust," *Harvard Business Review*, September 2002, https://hbr.org/2002/09/the-high-cost-of-lost-trust.

18. Dirks, "Trust in Leadership," 21.

19. Edelman, "2018 Edelman Trust Barometer," accessed July 16, 2018,
www.edelman.com/sites/g/files/aatuss191/files/2018-10/2018_Edelman
_Trust_Barometer_Global_Report_FEB.pdf.

20. Edelman, "2020 Edelman Trust Barometer," accessed July 18, 2020,
www.edelman.com/sites/g/files/aatuss191/files/2020-01/2020%20Edel
man%20Trust%20Barometer%20Global%20Report.pdf, 22.

21. Edelman, "2020 Trust Barometer," 7.

22. Edelman, "2020 Trust Barometer," 12.

23. PricewaterhouseCoopers, "20th CEO Survey," accessed July 16, 2018,
www.pwc.com/gx/en/ceo-survey/2017/pwc-ceo-survey-report-2017.pdf.

24. Troy Segal, "Enron Scandal: The Fall of a Wall Street Darling," *Investopedia*, May 4, 2020, www.investopedia.com/updates/enron-scandal
-summary/.

25. Adam Hayes, "The Rise and Fall of WorldCom," *Investopedia*, May
5, 2020, www.investopedia.com/terms/w/worldcom.asp.

26. PricewaterhouseCoopers, "20th CEO Survey."

27. Niccolò Machiavelli, "Cruelty and Compassion; and Whether It Is Better to Be Loved or Feared, or the Reverse," in *The Prince*, 53–56 (New York: Penguin Classics, 1999).

28. Machiavelli, "Cruelty and Compassion," 54.

29. Jason A. Colquitt and Jessica B. Rodell, "Justice, Trust, and Trustworthiness: A Longitudinal Analysis Integrating Three Theoretical Perspectives," *Academy of Management Journal* 54, no. 6 (2011): 1183.

TWO. Competence

1. Adam Lashinsky, *Wild Ride: Inside Uber's Quest for World Domination* (New York: Penguin, 2017), 80.

2. Uber, "The History of Uber," accessed August 8, 2020, www.uber.com/newsroom/history/.

3. Luz Lazo, "Uber Turns 5, Reaches 1 Million Drivers and 300 Cities Worldwide. Now What?," *Washington Post*, June 4, 2015, www.washingtonpost.com/news/dr-gridlock/wp/2015/06/04/uber-turns-5-reaches-1-million-drivers-and-300-cities-worldwide-now-what/.

4. John Paul Titlow, "Uber to Riders: We Won't Screw You in the Blizzard," *Fast Company*, January 26, 2015, www.fastcompany.com/3041453/uber-to-riders-we-wont-screw-you-in-the-blizzard.

5. Alison Griswold, "Uber's Response to the Chelsea Bombing Says a Lot About Uber," *Quartz*, September 19, 2016, https://qz.com/785585/ubers-response-to-the-chelsea-bombing-says-a-lot-about-uber-and-its-handling-of-surge-pricing/.

6. Davey Alba, "A Short History of the Many, Many Ways Uber Screwed Up," *Wired*, June 21, 2017, www.wired.com/story/timeline-uber-crises/.

7. "Family of 6-Year-Old Girl Killed by Uber Driver Settles Lawsuit," Bay City News, July 15, 2015, https://abc7news.com/san-francisco-uber-driver-syed-muzaffar-muzzafar/852108/.

8. Alba, "Short History."

9. Casey Newton, "This Is Uber's Playbook for Sabotaging Lyft," *Verge*, August 26, 2014, www.theverge.com/2014/8/26/6067663/this-is-ubers-playbook-for-sabotaging-lyft.

10. Susan Fowler, "Reflection on One Very, Very Strange Year at Uber," SusanJFowler.com, February 19, 2017, www.susanjfowler.com/blog/2017/2 /19/reflecting-on-one-very-strange-year-at-uber.

11. Sarah Jeong, "Who Blinked First in Waymo v. Uber?," *Verge*, February 9, 2018, www.theverge.com/2018/2/9/16997394/waymo-v-uber-trial -settlement-explained.

12. Mike Isaac, "How Uber Deceives the Authorities Worldwide," *New York Times*, March 3, 2017, www.nytimes.com/2017/03/03/technology/uber -greyball-program-evade-authorities.html.

13. Kara Swisher and Johana Bhuiyan, "A Top Uber Executive, Who Obtained the Medical Records of a Customer Who Was a Rape Victim, Has Been Fired," *Vox*, June 7, 2017, www.vox.com/2017/6/7/15754316/uber -executive-india-assault-rape-medical-records.

14. Kara Swisher, "Perkins Coie's Lawyer on Uber Firings: 'We Were Very Dogged' in Investigating Misbehavior and It's Still Not Over," *Vox*, June 6, 2017, www.vox.com/2017/6/6/15749216/perkins-coie -lawyer-bobbie-wilson-uber-firings-dogged-investigating-misbehavior -not-over.

15. Meghann Farnsworth, "Read the Full Investigation into Uber's Troubled Culture and Management," *Vox*, June 13, 2017, www.recode.net /2017/6/13/15794412/read-entire-investigation-uber-culture-management -ethics-eric-holder.

16. Kate Conger, "Uber Founder Travis Kalanick Leaves Board, Severing Last Tie," *New York Times*, December 24, 2019, www.nytimes.com /2019/12/24/technology/uber-travis-kalanick.html.

17. Rani Molla, "Lyft Has Eaten into Uber's U.S. Market Share, New Data Suggests," *Vox*, December 12, 2018, www.vox.com/2018/12/12/18134882 /lyft-uber-ride-car-market-share.

18. Molla, "Lyft Has Eaten into Uber's U.S. Market Share."

19. Mike Isaac, Michael J. de la Merced, and Andrew Ross Sorkin, "How the Promise of a $120 Billion Uber I.P.O. Evaporated," *New York Times*, May 15, 2019, www.nytimes.com/2019/05/15/technology/uber-ipo -price.html.

20. Andrew J. Hawkins, "Uber Goes Public: Everything You Need to Know About the Biggest Tech IPO in Years," *Verge*, May 10, 2019, www .theverge.com/2019/5/10/18564197/uber-ipo-stock-valuation-pricing -fares-drivers-public-market.

21. Lauren Feiner, "Uber Ends Its First Day of Trading Down More Than 7%," CNBC, May 10, 2019, www.cnbc.com/2019/05/10/uber-ipo-stock -starts-trading-on-the-new-york-stock-exchange.html.

22. Isaac, de la Merced, and Sorkin, "How the Promise of a $120 Billion Uber I.P.O. Evaporated."

23. Nick Statt, "#DeleteUber Reportedly Led 200,000 People to Delete Their Accounts," *Verge*, February 2, 2017, www.theverge.com/2017/2/2 /14493760/delete-uber-protest-donald-trump-accounts-deleted.

24. Laura M. Holson, "To Delete or Not to Delete: That's the Uber Question," *New York Times*, November 21, 2014, www.nytimes.com/2014/11/23 /fashion/uber-delete-emil-michael-scandal.html.

25. Johana Bhuiyan, "Uber Powered 4 Billion Rides in 2017. It Wants to Do More—and Cheaper—in 2018," *Vox*, January 5, 2018, www.recode .net/2018/1/5/16854714/uber-four-billion-rides-coo-barney-harford-2018 -cut-costs-customer-service.

26. "Aristotle's Rhetoric," Stanford Encyclopedia of Philosophy, accessed July 6, 2020, https://plato.stanford.edu/entries/aristotle-rhetoric/.

27. Roger C. Mayer, James H. Davis, and F. David Schoorman, "An Integrative Model of Organizational Trust," *Academy of Management Review* 20, no. 3 (July 1995): 709–734, www.jstor.org/stable/258792.

28. Shankar Ganesan, "Determinants of Long-Term Orientation in Buyer-Seller Relationships," *Journal of Marketing* 58 (April 1994): 1–19.

29. Daniel J. McAllister, "Affect-Based and Cognition-Based Trust as Foundations for Interpersonal Cooperation in Organizations," *Academy of Management Journal* 38, no. 1 (February 1995): 37.

30. McAllister, "Affect-Based and Cognition-Based Trust," 52.

31. McAllister, "Affect-Based and Cognition-Based Trust," 52.

32. Michael Pirson and Deepak Malhotra, "Foundations of Organizational Trust: What Matters to Different Stakeholders?," *Organization Science* 22, no. 4 (2011): 1092.

33. Brad Stone, *The Upstarts: How Uber, Airbnb, and the Killer Companies of the New Silicon Valley Are Changing the World* (Boston: Little, Brown, 2017), 69–75.

34. Stone, *The Upstarts*, 72.

35. Richard Trenholm, "How's My Driving? Uber to Track Drivers Who Brake Too Hard or Drive Too Fast," *CNET*, June 29, 2016, www.cnet.com /news/hows-my-driving-uber-to-track-drivers-who-brake-hard-or-break -speed-limit/.

36. Douglas MacMillan, "Uber's App Will Soon Begin Tracking Driving Behavior," *Wall Street Journal*, June 29, 2016, www.wsj.com/articles/ubers -app-will-soon-begin-tracking-driving-behavior-1467194404?mod=LS1.

37. Lisa Eadicicco, "Uber Is Tracking Drivers' Phones to Watch for Speeding," *Time*, June 29, 2016, https://time.com/4387031/uber-driver-app -tracking/.

38. Max Chafkin, "Admit It, You Love Uber," *Fast Company*, September 8, 2015, www.fastcompany.com/3050762/admit-it-you-love-uber.

39. Sandra J. Sucher and Stacy McManus, "The Ritz-Carlton Hotel Company" (HBS Case No. 601-163, Harvard Business School, 2001), 12.

40. Sucher and McManus, "The Ritz-Carlton," 28.

41. The Ritz-Carlton, "Gold Standards," www.ritzcarlton.com/en/about /gold-standards, quoted in Sucher and McManus, "The Ritz-Carlton," 28.

42. Sucher and McManus, "The Ritz-Carlton," 15.

43. Sucher and McManus, "The Ritz-Carlton," 29.

44. Sucher and McManus, "The Ritz-Carlton," 13.

45. Sucher and McManus, "The Ritz-Carlton," 13–14.

46. The Ritz-Carlton New York, "Awards, Honors, and Accolades," accessed September 21, 2020, https://s7d2.scene7.com/is/content/ritzcarlton /The_Ritz-Carlton_New_York_Central_Park_-_Awards___Accolades_as _of_Feb._2020pdf.

47. The Ritz Carlton, "Awards," accessed September 21, 2020, www .ritzcarlton.com/en/about/awards.

48. Walter Isaacson, *Steve Jobs* (New York: Simon & Schuster, 2011), 558.

49. Pete Mortenson, "iPod Week: How FireWire Changed Everything," *Wired*, October 24, 2006, www.wired.com/2006/10/ipod-week-how-f/.

50. Rod Adner, "From Walkman to iPod: What Music Tech Teaches Us About Innovation," *The Atlantic*, March 5, 2012, www.theatlantic.com /business/archive/2012/03/from-walkman-to-ipod-what-music-tech -teaches-us-about-innovation/253158/.

51. Sayan Chatterjee and Kayleigh Fitch, "Uber: Leading the Sharing Economy," Ivey Business Publishing case study, February 22, 2016.

52. Stone, *The Upstarts*, 67.

53. M. G. Siegler, "Uber CEO: I Think I've Got 20,000 Years of Jail Time in Front of Me," *TechCrunch*, May 25, 2011, https://techcrunch .com/2011/05/25/uber-airbnb-jail-time/.

54. Virginia Weiler, Paul Farris, Gerry Yemen, and Kusum Ailawadi, "Uber Pricing Strategies and Marketing Communications," Darden School of Business, University of Virginia, Charlottesville, May 2, 2016.

55. Salvatore Cantale and Sarah Hutton, "Uber: An Empire in the Making?," IMD Business School, Lausanne, Switzerland, December 12, 2016, 6.

56. Matt Flegenheimer and Emma G. Fitzsimmons, "City Hall and Uber Clash in Struggle over New York Streets," *New York Times*, July 16, 2015, www.nytimes.com/2015/07/17/nyregion/city-hall-and-uber-clash-in -struggle-over-new-york-streets.html.

57. Fitz Tepper, "Uber Launches 'De Blasio's Uber' Feature in NYC with 25-Minute Wait Times," *TechCrunch*, July 16, 2015, https://tech crunch.com/2015/07/16/uber-launches-de-blasios-uber-feature-in-nyc -with-25-minute-wait-.

58. Matt Flegenheimer, "City Hall, in a Counterattack, Casts Uber as a Corporate Behemoth," *New York Times*, July 20, 2015, www.ny times.com/2015/07/21/nyregion/city-hall-in-a-counterattack-casts -uber-as-a-corporate-behemoth.html?module=inline.

59. Matt Flegenheimer, "De Blasio Administration Dropping Plan for Uber Cap, for Now," *New York Times*, July 22, 2015, www.nytimes .com/2015/07/23/nyregion/de-blasio-administration-dropping-plan-for -uber-cap-for-now.html.

60. Nate Lanxon and Andrew Hoyle, "The Complete History of Apple's iPod," *CNET*, October 25, 2011, www.cnet.com/pictures/the-complete -history-of-apples-ipod/.

61. "iPod Killers That Didn't," *Forbes*, October 23, 2006, www.forbes .com/2006/10/20/ipod-zune-rio-tech-media-cx_rr_1023killers.htm l#27377c9c1a91.

62. "iPod Killers That Didn't."

63. Andrew Greiner, Matt McFarland, Ivory Sherman, and Jen Tse, "A History of Lyft, from Fuzzy Pink Mustaches to Global Ride Share Giant," *CNN Business*, April 2, 2019, www.cnn.com/interactive/2019/03/business /lyft-history/index.html.

64. Newton, "This Is Uber's Playbook."

65. Newton, "This Is Uber's Playbook."

66. Alba, "The Many, Many Ways Uber Screwed Up."

67. Cassandra Khaw, "Uber Accused of Booking 5,560 Fake Lyft Rides," *Verge*, August 12, 2014, www.theverge.com/2014/8/12/5994077/uber -cancellation-accusations.

68. Noam Scheiber, "How Uber Uses Psychological Tricks to Push Its Drivers' Buttons," *New York Times*, April 2, 2017, www.nytimes.com/inter active/2017/04/02/technology/uber-drivers-psychological-tricks.html.

69. Scheiber, "How Uber Uses Psychological Tricks."

70. Sucher and McManus, "The Ritz-Carlton," 12.

71. Sucher and McManus, "The Ritz-Carlton," 23.

72. Dawn Bailey, "Is the Customer Really Always Right? A Hotel Company Invests in Its Employees First," *NIST*, July 27, 2017, www.nist.gov /blogs/blogrige/customer-really-always-right-hotel-company-invests-its -employees-first.

73. Sucher and McManus, "The Ritz-Carlton," 6.

74. Aarian Marshall, "New York City Goes After Uber and Lyft," *Wired*, August 8, 2010, www.wired.com/story/new-york-city-cap-uber-lyft/.

75. Henry Goldman, "NYC Mayor Seeks to Extend Uber, Lyft Limits to Combat Congestion," *Bloomberg*, June 12, 2019, www.bloomberg .com/news/articles/2019-06-12/nyc-mayor-seeks-to-extend-uber-lyft -limits-to-combat-congestion.

76. Andrew J. Hawkins, "New York City Extends Its Cap on New Uber and Lyft Vehicles," *Verge*, August 7, 2019, www.theverge.com/2019/8/7 /20758796/nyc-uber-lyft-cap-extended-tlc-de-blasio.

77. Jonathan Stempel, "Uber Sues New York City over Cruising and Licensing Caps," Reuters, September 20, 2019, www.reuters.com/article /us-uber-new-york/uber-sues-new-york-city-over-cruising-and-licensing -caps-idUSKBN1W52AV.

78. Elizabeth Kim, "Judge Strikes Down De Blasio's Cruising Time Caps on Uber, Lyft," Gothamist, December 24, 2019, https://gothamist.com /news/judge-strikes-down-de-blasios-cruising-time-restrictions-uber-lyft.

79. Holson, "To Delete or Not to Delete."

80. Uber, "Uber Announces Results for Fourth Quarter and Full Year 2019," February 6, 2020, https://investor.uber.com/news-events/news/press -release-details/2020/Uber-Announces-Results-for-Fourth-Quarter-and -Full-Year-2019/.

81. Heather Somerville, "Study Finds Uber's Growth Slows After Year of Scandal; Lyft Benefits," Reuters, May 14, 2018, www.reuters.com/article /us-uber-growth/study-finds-ubers-growth-slows-after-year-of-scandal -lyft-benefits-idUSKCN1IF31A.

82. Somerville, "Study Finds."

83. Rani Molla, "Lyft Has Eaten into Uber's U.S. Market Share, New Data Suggests," *Vox*, December 12, 2018, www.vox.com/2018/12/12/18134882 /lyft-uber-ride-car-market-share.

84. Elizabeth Schulze, "Uber Drivers' Strike Takes Off in Front of Company Headquarters Ahead of $90 Billion IPO," CNBC, May 8, 2019, www.cnbc.com/2019/05/08/uber-drivers-strike-over-low-wages-benefits -ahead-of-ipo.html.

85. Kate Conger, "Uber's First Earnings Report After I.P.O.: $1 Billion Loss," *New York Times*, May 30, 2019, www.nytimes.com/2019/05/30 /technology/uber-earnings-report.html.

THREE. Motives: A Fine Balance

1. Mindy Scheier, "How Adaptive Clothing Empowers People with Disabilities," TED [video], November 2017, www.ted.com/talks/mindy _scheier_how_adaptive_clothing_empowers_people_with_disabilities /transcript.

2. Scheier, "How Adaptive Clothing Empowers."

3. Centers for Disease Control and Prevention, "Disability Impacts All of Us," accessed November 13, 2020, www.cdc.gov/ncbddd/disability andhealth/infographic-disability-impacts-all.html.

4. Cindy Boren, "A Timeline of Colin Kaepernick's Protests Against Police Brutality, Four Years After They Began," *Washington Post*, August 26, 2020, www.washingtonpost.com/sports/2020/06/01/colin-kaepernick -kneeling-history/.

5. The State of Fashion 2019 (New York: McKinsey & Company), 47, accessed April 24, 2020, www.mckinsey.com/~/media/McKinsey /Industries/Retail/Our%20Insights/The%20State%20of%20Fashion %202019%20A%20year%20of%20awakening/The-State-of-Fashion-2019 -final.pdf.

6. Mike Gröndahl, Keith Collins, and James Glanz, "The Dangerous Flaws in Boegin's Automated System," *New York Times*, April 4, 2019, www .nytimes.com/interactive/2019/03/29/business/boeing-737-max-8-flaws .html.

7. David Gelles, "'I Honestly Don't Trust Many People at Boeing': A Broken Culture Exposed," *New York Times*, January 10, 2020, www.nytimes .com/2020/01/10/business/boeing-737-employees-messages.html.

8. Kevin Granville, "Facebook and Cambridge Analytica: What You Need to Know as Fallout Widens," *New York Times*, March 19, 2018, www.nytimes.com/2018/03/19/technology/facebook-cambridge-analytica -explained.html?mtrref=www.google.com, accessed October 2018.

9. Martha C. Nussbaum, *Love's Knowledge: Essays on Philosophy and Literature* (New York: Oxford University Press, 1990), 163.

10. Matthew Huston, "Selfishness Is Learned," *Nautilus*, June 9, 2016, http://nautil.us/issue/37/currents/selfishness-is-learned.

11. David G. Rand, Joshua D. Greene, and Martin A. Nowak, "Spontaneous Giving and Calculated Greed," *Nature* 489, no. 7416 (2012): 427–430.

12. David G. Rand, "Cooperation, Fast and Slow: Meta-Analytic Evidence for a Theory of Social Heuristics and Self-Interested Deliberation," *Psychological Science* 27, no. 9 (2016): 1192–1206.

13. Ernst Fehr and Ivo Schurtenberger, "Normative Foundations of Human Cooperation," *Nature Human Behaviour* 2, no. 7 (2018): 458–486.

14. Daniel L. Ames and Susan T. Fiske, "Intentional Harms Are Worse, Even When They're Not," *Psychological Science* 24, no. 9 (September 2013): 1755–1762.

15. Daniel L. Ames and Susan T. Fiske, "Perceived Intent Motivates People to Magnify Harms," *PNAS* 112, no. 12 (March 2015): 3599–3605.

16. Casey Newton, "This Is Uber's Playbook for Sabotaging Lyft," *Verge*, August 26, 2014, www.theverge.com/2014/8/26/6067663/this-is-ubers-playbook-for-sabotaging-lyft.

17. "Test Act," *Encyclopedia Britannica*, accessed April 30, 2020, www.britannica.com/topic/test-act.

18. Richard Turnbull, Quaker Capitalism: Lessons for Today (Oxford: Centre for Enterprise, Markets and Ethics, 2014), 14, http://theceme.org/wp-content/uploads/2015/07/Quaker-Capitalism.pdf.

19. Niko Matouschek, "If You're Getting Ripped Off, It's Not Surprising," Kellogg School of Management, accessed April 30, 2020, www.kellogg.northwestern.edu/trust-project/videos/matouschek-ep-3.aspx.

20. "Doing Business the Quaker Way," *Forbes*, October 9, 2009, www.forbes.com/2009/10/09/quaker-business-meetings-leadership-society-friends.html#375dfe4e29fa.

21. "Doing Business the Quaker Way."

22. Turnbull, Quaker Capitalism, 29.

23. Hope Leith, "A Community of Exiles: The Quakers in 18th-Century Literature and Society," *Man and Nature* 10 (1991): 96, www.erudit.org/en/journals/man/1991-v10-man0303/1012626ar.pdf.

24. Turnbull, Quaker Capitalism, 9.

25. Leith, "Community of Exiles," 96.

26. Turnbull, Quaker Capitalism, 30.

27. Peter Jackson, "How Did Quakers Conquer the British Sweet Shop?," *BBC News*, January 20, 2010, http://news.bbc.co.uk/2/hi/uk_news/magazine/8467833.stm.

28. Turnbull, Quaker Capitalism, 10.

29. Jackson, "How Did Quakers Conquer the British Sweet Shop?"

30. Turnbull, Quaker Capitalism, 7.

31. "Aviva Agrees Friends Life Takeover," *BBC News*, December 2, 2014, www.bbc.com/news/business-30288738.

32. The Wharton School, "History of Wharton," accessed September 21, 2020, www.wharton.upenn.edu/history/.

33. William T. Allen, "Our Schizophrenic Conception of the Business Corporation," *Cardozo Law Review* 14, no. 2 (1992): 261, https://heinonline -org.ezp-prod1.hul.harvard.edu/HOL/Page?lname=&public=false&col lection=journals&handle=hein.journals/cdozo14&men_hide=false&men _tab=toc&kind=&page=261.

34. John Danley, "Beyond Managerialism: After the Death of the Corporate Statesperson," *Business Ethics Quarterly* (1998): 21–30, www -jstor-org.ezp-prod1.hul.harvard.edu/stable/41968760?pq-origsite=sum mon&seq=1#metadata_info_tab_contents.

35. Allen, "Our Schizophrenic Conception," 269.

36. Thomas M. Garrett, *Ethics in Business* (New York: Sheed and Ward, 1963), 16.

37. Allen, "Our Schizophrenic Conception," 266.

38. Allen, "Our Schizophrenic Conception," 266.

39. Milton Friedman, "The Social Responsibility of Business Is to Increase Its Profits," *New York Times Magazine*, September 13, 1970, http:// umich.edu/~thecore/doc/Friedman.pdf.

40. Allen, "Our Schizophrenic Conception," 266.

41. Andrew Ross Sorkin, "How Shareholder Democracy Failed the People," *New York Times*, August 20, 2019, www.nytimes.com/2019/08/20 /business/dealbook/business-roundtable-corporate-responsibility.html.

42. "Confidence in Major Companies," GSS Data Explorer, accessed May 15, 2020, https://gssdataexplorer.norc.org/trends/Politics ?measure=conbus.

43. "Redefining the C-Suite: Business the Millennial Way," American Express, 2020, www.americanexpress.com/content/dam/amex/uk/staticas sets/pdf/AmexBusinesstheMillennialWay.pdf.

44. Unilever, "Our History," accessed August 15, 2020, www.unilever .com/about/who-we-are/our-history/.

45. "Unilever," *Encyclopedia Britannica*, last modified March 13, 2020, www.britannica.com/topic/Unilever.

46. Unilever, "Dove," accessed August 15, 2020, www.unilever.com /brands/personal-care/dove.html.

47. P. J. Bednarski, "Unilever Chief Says Some of Its Brands Without 'Purpose' May Have to Go," *MediaPost*, July 26, 2019, www.mediapost .com/publications/article/338664/unilever-chief-says-some-of-its-brands -without-pu.html.

48. Unilever, "Unilever's Approach to Corporate Social Responsibility," 2000, www.unilever.com/Images/2000-social-review-of-1999-data_tcm244 -409696_en.pdf.

49. Andrew Ross Sorkin, "World's Biggest Investor Tells C.E.O.s Purpose Is the 'Animating Force' for Profits," *New York Times*, January 17, 2019, www.nytimes.com/2019/01/17/business/dealbook/blackrock-larry-fink -letter.html.

50. Berkeley Lovelace Jr., "Billionaire Sam Zell: BlackRock's Larry Fink Is 'Extraordinarily Hypocritical' to Push Social Responsibility," *CNBC*, January 16, 2018, www.cnbc.com/2018/01/16/sam-zell-blackrock-ceo-fink-is -hypocritical-to-push-social-responsibility.html/.

51. Sorkin, "World's Biggest Investor."

52. Business Roundtable, "Members," accessed August 15, 2020, www .businessroundtable.org/about-us/members.

53. Business Roundtable, "Statement on the Purpose of a Corporation," August 2019, https://opportunity.businessroundtable.org/wp-content /uploads/2019/08/BRT-Statement-on-the-Purpose-of-a-Corporation-with -Signatures.pdf.

54. Sumantra Ghoshal, Gita Piramal, and Sudeep Budhiraja, "Housing Development Finance Corporation," in *World Class in India: A Casebook of Companies in Transformation* (New York: Penguin Books), 592.

55. Lynn S. Paine, Carin-Isabel Knoop, and Suma Raju, "HDFC" (HBS Case No. 301-093, Harvard Business School, March 2001).

56. Paine, Knoop, and Raju, "HDFC."

57. Joydeep Ghosh, "40 Years Ago…and Now: Home Loan: A Tale of Three Institutions," *Business Standard*, October 30, 2014, www .business-standard.com/article/pf/40-years-ago-and-now-home -loan-a-tale-of-three-institutions-114091400747_1.html.

58. Ghosh, "40 Years Ago."

59. Ghosh, "40 Years Ago."

60. Paine, Knoop, and Raju, "HDFC," 3.

61. Paine, Knoop, and Raju, "HDFC," 3.

62. Ghoshal, Piramal, and Budhiraja, "Housing Development Finance Corporation."

63. Paine, Knoop, and Raju, "HDFC," 5.

64. Paine, Knoop, and Raju, "HDFC," 5.

65. Manu Balachandran, "The Satyam Scandal: How India's Biggest Corporate Fraud Unfolded," *Quartz*, April 9, 2015, https://qz.com /india/379877/the-satyam-scandal-how-indias-biggest-corporate-fraud -unfolded/.

66. Tamal Bandyopadhyay, "Deepak Parekh: Satyam Was Rescued to Preserve India's Image," Mint, January 6, 2010, www.livemint.com /Companies/rerv1jG2O5YD6C0I50oZgL/Deepak-Parekh--Satyam-was -rescued-to-preserve-India8217s.html.

67. Alissa de Carbonnel, "EU Seeks More Powers over National Car Regulations After VW Scandal," Reuters, January 27, 2016, www.reuters .com/article/us-volkswagen-emissions-eu-regulations/eu-seeks-more -powers-over-national-car-regulations-after-vw-scandal-idUSKCN 0V51IO.

68. Matthew Campbell, Christopher Rauwald, and Chris Reiter, "How Volkswagen Walked Away from a Near-Fatal Crash," *Bloomberg*, March 29, 2018, www.bloomberg.com/news/features/2018-03-29/how-volkswagen -walked-away-from-a-near-fatal-crash.

69. Julia Kollewe, "VW Profits Down 20% After Diesel Emissions Scandal," *The Guardian*, May 31, 2016, www.theguardian.com/business/2016 /may/31/vw-volkswagen-profits-down-20-diesel-emissions-scandal.

70. Jae C. Jung, "The Volkswagen Emissions Scandal and Its Aftermath," *Global Business and Organizational Excellence* 38, no. 4 (May 2019): 9, www.researchgate.net/publication/332327135_The_Volkswagen_emissions_scandal_and_its_aftermath.

71. Stephen Wilmot, "The Long-Term Cost of Volkswagen's Emissions Scandal," *Wall Street Journal*, September 24, 2019, www.wsj.com/articles/the-long-term-cost-of-volkswagens-emissions-scandal-11569343060.

72. Ivana Kottasová, "German Prosecutors Charge Former Volkswagen CEO Martin Winterkorn with Fraud," *CNN Business*, April 15, 2019, www.cnn.com/2019/04/15/business/winterkorn-volkswagen-diesel-fraud-charges/index.html.

73. Edward Taylor and Jan Schwartz, "German Prosecutors Charge 6 VW Employees over Emissions Scandal," *Automotive News*, January 14, 2020, www.autonews.com/automakers-suppliers/german-prosecutors-charge-6-vw-employees-over-emissions-scandal.

74. Christopher Rauwald, "VW Fires 204 Staff for Breaching Rules in Compliance Crackdown," *Automotive News*, August 23, 2019, www.autonews.com/automakers-suppliers/vw-fired-204-staff-breaching-rules-compliance-crackdown.

75. David Cote, *Winning Now, Winning Later: How Companies Can Win in the Short Term While Investing for the Long Term* (Nashville: HarperCollins Leadership, 2020), xi.

76. Sandra J. Sucher and Susan J. Winterberg, "Honeywell and the Great Recession (A)" (HBS Case No. 315-022, Harvard Business School, October 2014), 4.

77. Sucher and Winterberg, "Honeywell," 5.

78. Cote, *Winning Now, Winning Later*, xi.

79. Sucher and Winterberg, "Honeywell," 3.

80. Sucher and Winterberg, "Honeywell," 6.

81. Sucher and Winterberg, "Honeywell," 7–8.

82. Cote, *Winning Now, Winning Later*, 65.

83. Cote, *Winning Now, Winning Later*, 66.

84. Sandra Sucher and Susan Winterberg, "Leadership Lessons of the Great Recession: Options for Economic Downturns," *Harvard Business*

School Working Knowledge, September 9, 2015, https://hbswk.hbs.edu /item/leadership-lessons-of-the-great-recession-options-for-economic -downturns/.

85. Sucher and Winterberg, "Leadership Lessons."

86. Center on Budget and Policy Priorities, "Great Recession Created an Unusually Large and Long-Lasting Gap Between Actual and Potential GDP," June 6, 2019, www.cbpp.org/research/economy/chart-book-the -legacy-of-the-great-recession.

87. Till von Wachter, Jae Song, and Joycee Manchester, "Long-Term Earnings Losses Due to Job Separation During the 1982 Recession: An Analysis Using Longitudinal Administrative Data from 1974 to 2004" (Columbia University discussion paper, April 2009), https://doi.org/10.7916 /D8WM1RPR.

88. Sandra J. Sucher and Susan J. Winterberg, "Furloughs: An Alternative to Layoffs for Economic Downturns" (Harvard Business School note 314-097, February 2014).

89. Cote, *Winning Now, Winning Later*, 233.

90. Morgan Stanley Research North America, "Honeywell International: Trick Is in the Doing; Initiate at Overweight," January 4, 2012.

91. Sucher and Winterberg, "Honeywell," 4.

92. Steven Bushgong, "Honeywell's David Cote Selected 'CEO of the Year,'" *Windpower*, July 3, 2013, www.windpowerengineering.com /honeywells-dave-cote-selected-ceo-of-the-year/.

93. Honeywell, "Five Years in a Row! Dave Cote on Barron's World's Best CEOs," March 30, 2017, www.honeywell.com/en-us/news room/news/2017/03/five-years-in-a-row-dave-cote-on-barrons-worlds -best-ceos.

94. Alex Ismail, interview by Susan J. Winterberg, December 20, 2013.

FOUR. **Means: When All Is Fair**

1. Sandra J. Sucher and Susan J. Winterberg, "Michelin: Socially Responsible Restructuring" (Harvard Business School research report, 2016), 11.

2. Sucher and Winterberg, "Michelin," 10–11.

3. Corine Védrine, "Des espaces disciplinaires aux espaces de jouissance: Les transformations de Michelinville," *Espaces et sociétés* 158, no. 3 (January 2014): 135–149.

4. Herbert L. Lottman, *The Michelin Men: Driving an Empire* (London: I. B. Tauris, 2003), 235.

5. Katherine McAuliffe, Peter R. Blake, and Felix Warneken, "Do Kids Have a Fundamental Sense of Fairness?," *Scientific American*, August 23, 2017, https://blogs.scientificamerican.com/observations/do-kids -have-a-fundamental-sense-of-fairness/.

6. Maria Szalavitz, "Even Babies Can Recognize What's Fair," *Time*, February 20, 2012, http://healthland.time.com/2012/02/20/even-babies -can-recognize-whats-fair/.

7. Matteo Tonello, "CEO and Executive Compensation Practices: 2017 Edition," *Conference Board, Inc.*, October 4, 2017, https://corpgov.law.harvard .edu/2017/10/04/ceo-and-executive-compensation-practices-2017-edition/.

8. David F. Larcker and Brian Tanyan, "Does Your CEO Compensation Plan Provide the Right Incentives?," *McKinsey Quarterly*, April 1, 2012, www.mckinsey.com/business-functions/organization/our-insights/does -your-ceo-compensation-plan-provide-the-right-incentives.

9. Jeff Cox, "CEOs See Pay Grow 1,000% in the Last 40 Years, Now Make 278 Times the Average Worker," *CNBC*, August 16, 2019, www.cnbc .com/2019/08/16/ceos-see-pay-grow-1000percent-and-now-make-278 -times-the-average-worker.html.

10. Jordan Crook, "Netflix Learns from Past Mistakes, Increases Prices the Right Way," *TechCrunch*, May 9, 2014, https://techcrunch.com /2014/05/09/netflix-learns-from-past-mistakes-increases-prices-the-right -way/.

11. Daniel Indiviglio, "Netflix to Lose a Million Subscribers: It's Worse Than It Looks," *The Atlantic*, September 15, 2011, www.theatlantic.com /business/archive/2011/09/netflix-to-lose-a-million-subscribers-its-worse -than-it-looks/245175/.

12. Crook, "Netflix Learns from Past Mistakes."

13. Matthias Heinze, Sabria Jeworrek, Vanessa Mertins, Heiner Schumacher, and Matthias Sutter, "Indirect Effects of Employer Behavior on

Workplace Performance," *Vox*, December 15, 2017, https://voxeu.org/article /when-employers-are-unfair-even-unaffected-workers-underperform.

14. Heinze et al., "Indirect Effects."

15. Heinze et al., "Indirect Effects."

16. Tess Riley, "Just 100 Companies Responsible for 71% of Global Emissions, Study Says," *The Guardian*, July 10, 2017, www.theguardian.com /sustainable-business/2017/jul/10/100-fossil-fuel-companies-investors -responsible-71-global-emissions-cdp-study-climate-change.

17. Susan Fowler, "Reflection on One Very, Very Strange Year at Uber," SusanJFowler.com, February 19, 2017, www.susanjfowler.com/blog /2017/2/19/reflecting-on-one-very-strange-year-at-uber.

18. Fowler, "Reflection."

19. Tom L. Beauchamp and James F. Childress, *Principles of Biomedical Ethics* (New York: Oxford University Press, 2001); John C. Fletcher, Paul A. Lombardo, Mary Faith Marshall, Franklin G. Miller, eds., Introduction to Clinical Ethics, 2nd ed. (Haggerstown, MD: University Publishing Group, 1997).

20. Jodi Kantor and David Streitfeld, "Inside Amazon: Wrestling Big Ideas in a Bruising Workplace," *New York Times*, August 15, 2015, www .nytimes.com/2015/08/16/technology/inside-amazon-wrestling-big -ideas-in-a-bruising-workplace.html.

21. Jason A. Colquitt, "On the Dimensionality of Organizational Justice: A Construct Validation of a Measure," *Journal of Applied Psychology* 86, no. 3 (June 2001): 386–400.

22. Sandra Sucher and Susan Winterberg, "Leadership Lessons of the Great Recession: Options for Economic Downturns," *Harvard Business School Working Knowledge*, September 9, 2015, https://hbswk.hbs.edu /item/leadership-lessons-of-the-great-recession-options-for-economic -downturns/.

23. Sandra J. Sucher and Stacy E. McManus, "The Ritz-Carlton Hotel Company" (HBS Case No. 601-163, Harvard Business School, rev. September 20, 2005), 10.

24. Sucher and Winterberg, "Michelin," 9.

25. Sucher and Winterberg, "Michelin," 14.

26. Jason A. Colquitt, Donald E. Conlon, Michael J. Wesson, Christopher O. L. H. Porter, and K. Yee Ng, "Justice at the Millennium: A Meta-Analytic Review of 25 Years of Organizational Justice Research," *Journal of Applied Psychology* 86, no. 3 (2001): 426.

27. Colquitt et al., "Justice at the Millennium," 426.

28. Colquitt et al., "Justice at the Millennium," 426.

29. Emmanuel Egloff, "Michelin veut en finir avec les fermetures d'usines en France," *Le Figaro*, May 21, 2015, www.lefigaro.fr/societes/2015/05/19/20005-20150519ARTFIG00358-michelin-veut-en-finir-avec-les-fermetures-d-usines-en-france.php.

30. Laurent Poillot, "Comment Michelin a réussi à préserver l'usine de Roanne," *Les Echos*, May 29, 2015, https://business.lesechos.fr/directions-ressources-humaines/comment-michelin-a-reussi-a-preserver-l-usine-de-roanne-111391.php.

31. Poillot, "Comment Michelin a réussi."

32. Leventhal published two book chapters in 1980 in which he described his criteria for what makes a process fair. Gerald S. Leventhal, "What Should Be Done with Equity Theory? New Approaches to the Study of Fairness in Social Relationships," in *Social Exchange: Advances in Theory and Research*, ed. Kenneth J. Gergen, Martin S. Greenberg, and Richard H. Willis, 27–55 (New York: Plenum, 1980); Gerald S. Leventhal, Jurgis Karuza, and William R. Fry, "Beyond Fairness: A Theory of Allocation Preferences," in *Justice and Social Interaction*, ed. Gerold Mikula, 167–218 (New York: Springer-Verlag, 1980).

33. Definitions quoted from Jason A. Colquitt and Jessica B. Rodell, "Justice, Trust, and Trustworthiness: A Longitudinal Analysis Integrating Three Theoretical Perspectives," *Academy of Management Journal* 54, no. 6 (2011): 1183; and Colquitt et al., "Justice at the Millennium," 426.

34. Rachel Botsman, *Who Can You Trust?* (New York: PublicAffairs, 2017), 59–60.

35. Botsman, *Who Can You Trust?*, 59–60.

36. Botsman, *Who Can You Trust?*, 59–60.

37. Michael O'Grady, "Walmart Is Currently the World's Largest Retailer, but Alibaba and Amazon Are Closing In," *Forrester*, August 20, 2018,

https://go.forrester.com/blogs/walmart-is-currently-the-worlds-largest -retailer-but-alibaba-and-amazon-are-closing-in/.

38. Colquitt and Rodell, "Justice, Trust, and Trustworthiness."

39. Colquitt and Rodell, "Justice, Trust, and Trustworthiness," 1183.

40. Sucher and Winterberg, "Michelin," 17.

41. Lauren Collins, "How the BBC Women Are Working Toward Equal Pay," *New Yorker*, July 23, 2018, www.newyorker.com/magazine/2018/07/23 /how-the-bbc-women-are-working-toward-equal-pay.

42. Collins, "How the BBC Women Are Working Toward Equal Pay."

43. Carrie Grace, "'Enough Is Enough': Carrie Grace's Letter on Pay Inequality in Full," *The Guardian*, January 8, 2018, www.theguardian.com /media/2018/jan/08/carrie-gracie-letter-in-full.

44. Collins, "How the BBC Women Are Working Toward Equal Pay."

45. Collins, "How the BBC Women Are Working Toward Equal Pay."

46. Julian Lamont and Christi Favor, "Distributive Justice," *Stanford Encyclopedia of Philosophy* (Winter 2017), https://plato.stanford.edu/en tries/justice-distributive/#Opportunity; John Danaher, "Principles of Distributive Justice," Philosophical Disquisitions blog, September 30, 2010, https://philosophicaldisquisitions.blogspot.com/2010/09/principles-of -distributive-justice.html.

47. Leif Wenar, "John Rawls," *Stanford Encyclopedia of Philosophy* (Spring 2017), https://plato.stanford.edu/archives/spr2017/entries/rawls/.

48. Jack Welch, *Winning* (New York: HarperCollins, 2005), 71.

49. Robin Bleiweis, "Quick Facts About the Gender Wage Gap," Center for American Progress, March 24, 2020, www.americanprogress.org/issues /women/reports/2020/03/24/482141/quick-facts-gender-wage-gap/.

50. Office for National Statistics (UK), "Gender Pay Gap in the UK: 2019," October 29, 2019, www.ons.gov.uk/employmentandlabourmarket /peopleinwork/earningsandworkinghours/bulletins/genderpaygapintheu k/2019#:~:text=The%20gender%20pay%20gap%20among,2019%2C%20 and%20continues%20to%20decline.

51. Aleksandra Wisniewska, Billy Ehrenberg-Shannon, Cale Tilford, and Caroline Nevitt, "Gender Pay Gap: Women Still Short-Changed in the

UK," *Financial Times*, April 23, 2019, https://ig.ft.com/gender-pay-gap-UK -2019/.

52. Carrie Gracie, "About," accessed September 26, 2020, https://carriegracie.com/about.html.

53. Collins, "How the BBC Women Are Working Toward Equal Pay."

54. Sucher and Winterberg, "Michelin," 18.

55. Sucher and Winterberg, "Michelin," 19.

FIVE. Impact: Our Actions Speak

1. John Platt, "The Great Sparrow Campaign Was the Start of the Greatest Mass Starvation in History," *Treehugger*, July 30, 2019, www.treehugger.com/the-great-sparrow-campaign-was-the-start-of-the-greatest -mass-4864032.

2. "Great Leap Forward," *Encyclopedia Britannica*, accessed July 17, 2020, www.britannica.com/event/Great-Leap-Forward.

3. Louisa Lim, "A Grim Chronicle of China's Great Famine," NPR, November 10, 2012, www.npr.org/2012/11/10/164732497/a-grim-chronicle -of-chinas-great-famine.

4. Rebecca Kreston, "Paved with Good Intentions: Mao Tse-Tung's 'Four Pests' Disaster," *Discover*, February 26, 2014, www.discovermagazine.com/health/paved-with-good-intentions-mao-tse-tungs-four-pests -disaster.

5. Kreston, "Paved with Good Intentions."

6. Michael Greshko, "Maybe Rats Aren't to Blame for the Black Death," *National Geographic*, January 15, 2018, www.nationalgeographic.com/news /2018/01/rats-plague-black-death-humans-lice-health-science/.

7. George Dvorsky, "China's Worst Self-Inflicted Environmental Disaster: The Campaign to Wipe Out the Common Sparrow," *Gizmodo*, July 18, 2012, https://io9.gizmodo.com/china-s-worst-self-inflicted-environmental -disaster-th-5927112.

8. "Eliminate the Four Pests (1958)," ChinesePosters.net, accessed July 17, 2020, https://chineseposters.net/themes/four-pests.php.

9. "Eliminate the Four Pests (1958)."

10. Kreston, "Paved with Good Intentions."

11. Tania Branigan, "China's Great Famine: The True Story," *The Guardian*, January 1, 2013, www.theguardian.com/world/2013/jan/01/china-great-famine-book-tombstone.

12. Lim, "Grim Chronicle."

13. Branigan, "China's Great Famine."

14. Lim, "Grim Chronicle."

15. Lim, "Grim Chronicle."

16. Zheping Huang, "Charted: China's Great Famine, According to Yang Jisheng, a Journalist Who Lived Through It," *Quartz*, March 10, 2016, https://qz.com/633457/charted-chinas-great-famine-according-to-yang-jisheng-a-journalist-who-lived-through-it/.

17. James D. Tracy, "Erasmus," *Encyclopedia Britannica*, accessed July 8, 2020, www.britannica.com/biography/Erasmus-Dutch-humanist#ref59230.

18. Dominic Baker-Smith, "Thomas More," *Stanford Encyclopedia of Philosophy* (Winter 2019), https://plato.stanford.edu/entries/thomas-more/#Uto.

19. Tracy, "Erasmus."

20. Germain P. Marc'hadour, "Thomas More," *Encyclopedia Britannica*, accessed July 2, 2020, www.britannica.com/biography/Thomas-More-English-humanist-and-statesman.

21. Sandra J. Sucher, *The Moral Leader: Challenges, Insights, and Tools* (New York: Routledge, 2007), 115.

22. Isaiah Berlin, *Against the Current: Essays in the History of Ideas* (Princeton: Princeton University Press, 1955), 25–79.

23. Niccolò Machiavelli, *The Prince*, trans. W. K. Marriott (2006), chap. 18, www.gutenberg.org/files/1232/1232-h/1232-h.htm#link2HCH0018.

24. American Psychology Association, "Mach Scale," accessed August 1, 2020, https://dictionary.apa.org/mach-scale.

25. Machiavelli, *The Prince*.

26. Climate Accountability Institute, "Carbon Majors," accessed October 11, 2020, https://climateaccountability.org/carbonmajors.html.

27. Mike Gröndahl, Keith Collins, and James Glanz, "The Dangerous Flaws in Boegin's Automated System," *New York Times*, April 4, 2019, www.nytimes.com/interactive/2019/03/29/business/boeing-737-max-8-flaws.html.

28. David Gelles, "'I Honestly Don't Trust Many People at Boeing': A Broken Culture Exposed," *New York Times*, January 10, 2020, www.nytimes .com/2020/01/10/business/boeing-737-employees-messages.html.

29. Chris Hamby, "A Decade Later, Dutch Officials Publish a Study Critical of Boeing," *New York Times*, January 21, 2010, www.nytimes.com /2020/01/21/business/boeing-737-crashes.html.

30. Gelles, "Broken Culture Exposed."

31. Hamby, "A Decade Later."

32. Gelles, "Broken Culture Exposed."

33. Sidney Dekker, Report of the Flight Crew Human Factors Investigation (Lund, Sweden: Lund University School of Aviation, July 2, 2009), www.onderzoeksraad.nl/nl/media/inline/2020/1/21/human_factors_re port_s_dekker.pdf.

34. Hamby, "A Decade Later."

35. Hamby, "A Decade Later."

36. "How Millennials Want to Work and Live," Gallup, accessed July 19, 2020, www.gallup.com/workplace/238073/millennials-work-live.aspx.

37. McKinsey & Company, "Purpose: Shifting from Why to How," April 22, 2020, www.mckinsey.com/business-functions/organization/our -insights/purpose-shifting-from-why-to-how#.

38. McKinsey, "Purpose."

39. McKinsey, "Purpose."

40. Emily Chasan, "Global Sustainable Investments Rise 34 Percent to $30.7 Trillion," Bloomberg, April 1, 2019, www.bloomberg.com/news /articles/2019-04-01/global-sustainable-investments-rise-34-percent-to-30 -7-trillion.

41. Goldman Sachs, "Impact Investing," accessed July 19, 2020, www.goldmansachs.com/what-we-do/investing-and-lending/impact -investing/.

42. Dean Hand, Hanna Dithrich, Sophia Sunderji, and Noshin Nova, "2020 Annual Impact Investor Survey," Global Impact Investing Network, June 11, 2020, https://thegiin.org/research/publication/impinv-survey -2020.

43. Lubasha Heredia, Simon Bartletta, Joe Carrubba, Dean Frankle, Katsuyoshi Kurihara, Benoit Mace, Edoardo Palmisani, Neil Pardasani, Thomas Schulte, Ben Sheridan, and Qin Xu, "Global Asset Management 2020: Protect, Adapt, and Innovate," Boston Consulting Group, May 19, 2020, www.bcg.com/en-us/publications/2020/global-asset-management-protect-adapt-innovate.

44. McKinsey, "Purpose."

45. Jeff Beer, "Exclusive: Patagonia Is in Business to Save Our Home Planet," *Fast Company*, December 12, 2018, www.fastcompany.com/9028 0950/exclusive-patagonia-is-in-business-to-save-our-home-planet.

46. "EEMBC and Volkswagen to Develop Benchmarking Standards to Quantify Microcontroller Energy Efficiency," BusinessWire, May 21, 2013, www.businesswire.com/news/home/20130521005030/en /EEMBC-VOLKSWAGEN-Develop-Benchmarking-Standards-Quantify-Microcontroller.

47. Phil LeBeau, "Volkswagen Makes a Big Push to Be No. 1," *CNBC*, March 12, 2015, www.cnbc.com/2015/03/12/volkswagen-makes-a-big-push-to-be-no-1.html.

48. Andrew Hoffman, "Volkswagen's Clean Diesel Dilemma" (William Davidson Institute case study no. W04C84, University of Michigan, Ann Arbor, 2016).

49. Andreas Cremer and Tom Bergin, "Fear and Respect: VW's Culture Under Winterkorn," Reuters, October 10, 2015, www.reuters.com/article/us-volkswagen-emissions-culture/fear-and-respect-vws-culture-under-winterkorn-idUSKCN0S40MT20151010.

50. Cremer and Bergin, "Fear and Respect."

51. Jack Ewing, "Six Years Ago, He Helped Expose VW's Diesel Fraud. This Year, GM Let Him Go," *New York Times*, May 6, 2019, www.nytimes.com/2019/05/06/business/hermanth-kappanna-vw-emissions-gm.html.

52. Sonari Glinton, "How a Little Lab in West Virginia Caught Volkswagen's Big Cheat," NPR, September 24, 2015, www.npr.org/2015 /09/24/443053672/how-a-little-lab-in-west-virginia-caught-volkswagens-big-cheat.

53. Ewing, "Six Years Ago."

54. Gwyn Topham, Sean Clarke, Cath Levett, Paul Scruton, and Matt Fidler, "The Volkswagen Emissions Scandal Explained," *The Guardian*, September 23, 2015, www.theguardian.com/business/ng-interactive/2015/sep/23/volkswagen-emissions-scandal-explained-diesel-cars.

55. Alana Semuels, "'Rampant Consumerism Is Not Attractive': Patagonia Is Climbing to the Top—and Reimagining Capitalism Along the Way," *Time*, September 23, 2019, https://time.com/5684011/patagonia/.

56. Patagonia, "1% for the Planet," accessed October 8, 2020, www.patagonia.com/one-percent-for-the-planet.html.

57. Semuels, "'Rampant Consumerism.'"

58. Patagonia, "Hey How's That Lawsuit Against the President Going?," accessed October 7, 2020, www.patagonia.com/stories/hey-hows-that-lawsuit-against-the-president-going/story-72248.html.

59. Semuels, "'Rampant Consumerism.'"

60. Forest Reinhardt, Ramon Casadesus-Masanell, and Hyun Jin Kim, "Patagonia" (HBS Case No. 9-711-020, Harvard Business School, October 19, 2010).

61. Semuels, "'Rampant Consumerism.'"

62. Forest Reinhardt, Ramon Casadesus-Masanell, and Lauren Barley, "Patagonia (B)" (HBS Case No. 9-714-465, Harvard Business School, February 4, 2014).

63. Jeff Beer, "How Patagonia Grows Everytime It Amplifies Its Social Mission," *Fast Company*, February 21, 2018, www.fastcompany.com/40525452/how-patagonia-grows-every-time-it-amplifies-its-social-mission.

64. Josh Sanburn, "Walmart's On-Again, Off-Again Relationship with Guns," *Time*, January 11, 2013, https://business.time.com/2013/01/11/walmarts-on-again-off-again-relationship-with-guns/.

65. Nathan Layne, "Wal-Mart to Stop Selling AR-15, Other Semi-Automatic Rifles," Reuters, August 27, 2015, www.reuters.com/article/us-wal-mart-stores-rifles/wal-mart-to-stop-selling-ar-15-other-semi-automatic-rifles-idUSKCN0QV26520150827.

66. Chris Canipe and Lazaro Gamio, "What the Deadliest Mass Shootings Have in Common," *Axios*, September 7, 2019, www.axios.com/deadliest -mass-shootings-common-4211bafd-da85-41d4-b3b2-b51ff61e7c86.html.

67. Aaron Smith and Christina Alesci, "Walmart to Stop Selling AR-15 Guns," *CNN Business*, August 26, 2015, https://money.cnn.com/2015/08/26 /news/companies/walmart-ar-15-guns/index.html.

68. Layne, "Wal-Mart to Stop Selling AR-15."

69. Smith and Alesci, "Walmart to Stop Selling AR-15 Guns."

70. Elizabeth Chuck, Alex Johnson, and Corky Siemaszko, "17 Killed in Mass Shooting at High School in Parkland, Florida," *NBC News*, February 14, 2018, www.nbcnews.com/news/us-news/police-respond-shooting -parkland-florida-high-school-n848101.

71. Jen Kirby, "Walmart Raises the Minimum Age to Buy Firearms to 21," *Vox*, February 28, 2018, www.vox.com/2018/2/28/17065210/walmart -dicks-guns-21-age-limit.

72. Jason Silverstein, "There Were More Mass Shootings Than Days in 2019," *CBS News*, January 2, 2020, www.cbsnews.com/news/mass-shootings -2019-more-than-days-365/.

73. Hayley Peterson, "Walmart Corporate Employee Sends Mass Email Urging Workers to Go on Strike Until the Company Stops Selling Guns," *Business Insider*, August 6, 2019, www.businessinsider.com/walmart -shooting-corporate-employee-urges-strike-to-stop-gun-sales-2019-8.

74. David Williams, "A Walmart Worker Sent a Mass Email Urging Thousands of Associates to Strike over Gun Sales," *CNN Business*, August 7, 2019, www.cnn.com/2019/08/07/business/walmart-gun-sales-walkout -trnd/index.html.

75. Hayley Peterson, "I Tried to Buy a Gun at Walmart Twice, and Roadblocks Left Me Empty-Handed Both Times," *Business Insider*, August 21, 2019, www.businessinsider.com/walmart-gun-buying-review-virginia -store-2019-8.

76. Clare Duffy, "How Walmart Became an Unlikely Champion of Gun Safety," *CNN Business*, September 4, 2019, www.cnn.com/2019/09/04 /business/walmart-gun-policy-reactions/index.html.

77. John Gramlich, "What the Data Says About Gun Deaths in the U.S.," Pew Research Center, August 16, 2019, www.pewresearch.org/fact -tank/2019/08/16/what-the-data-says-about-gun-deaths-in-the-u-s/.

78. Rachel Treisman, "Poll: Number of Americans Who Favor Stricter Gun Laws Continue to Grow," NPR, October 20, 2019, www.npr .org/2019/10/20/771278167/poll-number-of-americans-who-favor-stricter -gun-laws-continues-to-grow.

79. Peterson, "I Tried to Buy a Gun at Walmart."

80. Peter Löscher, "The CEO of Siemens on Using a Scandal to Drive Change," *Harvard Business Review*, November 2012, https://hbr .org/2012/11/the-ceo-of-siemens-on-using-a-scandal-to-drive-change.

81. Cary O'Reilly and Karin Matussek, "Siemens to Pay $1.6 Billion to Settle Bribery Cases," *Bloomberg News*, December 16, 2008, www.wash ingtonpost.com/wp-dyn/content/article/2008/12/15/AR2008121502926 .html.

82. US Securities and Exchange Commission, "SEC Charges Siemens AG for Engaging in Worldwide Bribery," December 15, 2008, www.sec.gov /news/press/2008/2008-294.htm.

83. Löscher, "CEO of Siemens."

84. Löscher, "CEO of Siemens."

85. Liz Polley, "Introducing the New Footprint Chronicles on Patagonia.com," Pagatonia, accessed October 7, 2010, www.patagonia .com/stories/introducing-the-new-footprint-chronicles-on-patagoniacom /story-18443.html.

86. Patagonia, "The Footprint Chronicles: Methodology, Environmental Cost Calculations," accessed October 7, 2020, www.patagonia.com/on /demandware.static/Sites-patagonia-us-Site/Library-Sites-PatagoniaShared /en_US/PDF-US/method_for_cost5.pdf.

87. Kang Hsu, Sahil Malkani, Patrick Shanahan, and Christopher S. Tang, "Supply Chain Transparency: A New Competitive Strategy," UCLA Anderson Global Supply Chain Blog, March 31, 2015, https://blogs.anderson .ucla.edu/global-supply-chain/2015/03/supply-chain-transparency-a-new -competitive-strategy.html.

88. Patagonia, "Factories, Farms, and Mills," accessed October 7, 2020, www.patagonia.com/factories-farms-mills/.

89. George Serafeim and Katie Trinh, "A Framework for Product Impact-Weighted Accounts" (Harvard Business School Working Paper 20-076, 2020).

90. Vodafone, "Environmental Profit and Loss," 2014–2015, www.vodafone.nl/_assets/downloads/algemeen/environmental_profit_and_loss_account_2014_2015.pdf, 14.

91. Wells Fargo, "Who We Are," accessed July 17, 2020, www.wellsfargo.com/about/corporate/vision-and-values/.

92. Jim Zarroli, "Wells Fargo's Unauthorized Accounts Likely Hurt Customers' Credit Scores," NPR, September 26, 2016, www.npr.org/2016/09/26/495501008/wells-fargos-unauthorized-accounts-likely-hurt-customers-credit-scores.

93. Stacy Cowley and Emily Flitter, "Wells Fargo's Ex-Chief Fined $17.5 Million over Fake Accounts," *New York Times*, January 23, 2020, www.nytimes.com/2020/01/23/business/wells-fargo-ceo-fine.html.

94. Cowley and Flitter, "Wells Fargo's Ex-Chief Fined."

95. Cowley and Flitter, "Wells Fargo's Ex-Chief Fined."

96. Zarroli, "Wells Fargo's Unauthorized Accounts."

97. Emily Flitter, "The Price of Wells Fargo's Fake Account Scandal Grows by $3 Billion," *New York Times*, February 21, 2020, www.nytimes.com/2020/02/21/business/wells-fargo-settlement.html.

98. Flitter, "The Price of Wells Fargo's Fake Account Scandal."

99. Kevin Wack, "OCC Drops Hammer on Stumpf, Seven Other Ex-Wells Fargo Execs," *American Banker*, January 23, 2020, www.americanbanker.com/news/occ-drops-hammer-on-stumpf-seven-other-ex-wells-fargo-execs.

100. Gillian B. White, "All Your Clothes Are Made with Exploited Labor," *The Atlantic*, June 3, 2015, www.theatlantic.com/business/archive/2015/06/patagonia-labor-clothing-factory-exploitation/394658/.

101. Patagonia, "Migrant Workers," accessed October 9, 2020, www.patagonia.com/our-footprint/migrant-workers.html.

102. Patagonia, "Migrant Workers."

103. Jason Judd and Sarosh Kuruvilla, "Why It's So Hard to Find Clothing That's Ethically Made," *Fast Company*, May 5, 2020, www.fastcompany .com/90500556/why-its-so-hard-to-find-clothing-thats-ethically-made.

104. US Library of Congress, "Black Monday Stock Market Crash," April 2008, www.loc.gov/rr/business/businesshistory/October/blackmonday.html.

105. Jerry B. Harvey, "The Abilene Paradox: The Management of Agreement," *Organizational Dynamics* 3, no. 1 (Summer 1974): 63–80, www.sciencedirect.com/science/article/pii/0090261674900059.

106. Harvey, "Abilene Paradox," 63–80.

107. Harvey, "Abilene Paradox," 63–80.

108. Anglo American, "Socio-Economic Assessment Toolbox: Version 3," accessed May 17, 2020, www.angloamerican.com/~/media/Files /A/Anglo-American-PLC-V2/documents/communities/seat-overview -english.pdf.

109. Jan Klawitter, "Take Your Seat, Please!" (Anglo American internal document).

110. BMW Group, "Sustainable Value Report 2018," 2, accessed July 15, 2020, www.bmwgroup.com/content/dam/grpw/websites/bmwgroup_com /responsibility/downloads/en/2019/2019-BMW-Group-SVR-2018-Eng lisch.pdf.

111. BMW Group, "Sustainable Value Report 2018," 2.

112. BMW Group, "Sustainable Value Report 2018," 13.

113. BMW Group, "Sustainable Value Report 2018," 22.

114. Megan Michelson, "Want Ethically Sourced Wool? Buy from Patagonia," Outside, July 29, 2016, www.outsideonline.com/2101871/want -ethically-sourced-wool-buy-patagonia.

115. Josh Constine, "How Facebook Stole the News Business," Tech-Crunch, February 3, 2018, https://techcrunch.com/2018/02/03/facebooks -siren-call/.

116. Constine, "How Facebook Stole."

117. Nicholas Thompson and Fred Vogelstein, "Inside the Two Years That Shook Facebook—and the World," *Wired*, February 2, 2010, www .wired.com/story/inside-facebook-mark-zuckerberg-2-years-of-hell/.

118. Thompson and Vogelstein, "Inside the Two Years."

119. Bryan Clark, "Facebook Confirms: Donald Trumped Hillary on the Social Network During 2016 Election," *The Next Web*, April 3, 2018, https://thenextweb.com/facebook/2018/04/04/facebook-confirms-trumps -ads-bested-clintons-during-presidential-bid/.

120. Kevin Granville, "Facebook and Cambridge Analytica: What You Need to Know as Fallout Widens," *New York Times*, March 19, 2018, www.nytimes.com/2018/03/19/technology/facebook-cambridge-analytica -explained.html?mtrref=www.google.com.

121. Carole Cadwalladr and Emma Graham-Harrison, "Revealed: 50 Million Facebook Profiles Harvested for Cambridge Analytica in Major Data Breach," *The Guardian*, March 17, 2018, www.theguardian.com /news/2018/mar/17/cambridge-analytica-facebook-influence-us-election.

122. Steven J. Vaughan-Nichols, "How Cambridge Analytica Used Your Facebook Data to Help Elect Trump," *ZDNet*, March 20, 2018, www.zdnet .com/article/how-cambridge-analytica-used-your-facebook-data-to-help -elect-trump/.

123. Mike Isaac, "Facebook Mounts Effort to Limit Tide of Fake News," *New York Times*, December 15, 2016, www.nytimes.com/2016/12/15/tech nology/facebook-fake-news.html.

124. Thompson and Vogelstein, "Inside the Two Years."

125. Isaac, "Facebook Mounts Effort."

126. Evan Osnos, "Can Mark Zuckerberg Fix Facebook Before It Breaks Democracy?," *New Yorker*, September 10, 2018, www.newyorker .com/magazine/2018/09/17/can-mark-zuckerberg-fix-facebook-before-it -breaks-democracy.

127. Zach Winter, "2 Days, 10 Hours, 600 Questions: What Happened When Mark Zuckerberg Went to Washington," *New York Times*, April 12, 2018, www.nytimes.com/2018/04/12/technology/mark-zuckerberg-test imony.html.

128. Kevin Roose and Cecilia Kang, "Mark Zuckerberg Testifies on Facebook Before Skeptical Lawmakers," *New York Times*, April 10, 2018, www.nytimes.com/2018/04/10/us/politics/zuckerberg-facebook-senate -hearing.html.

129. John Constine, "Facebook Asks for a Moat of Regulations It Already Meets," *TechCrunch*, February 17, 2020, https://techcrunch.com /2020/02/17/regulate-facebook/.

130. Issie Lapowsky, "The 21 (and Counting) Biggest Facebook Scandals of 2018," *Wired*, December 20, 2010, www.wired.com/story/facebook -scandals-2018/.

131. Mark Scott, "Facebook to Tell Millions of Users They've Seen 'Fake News' About Coronavirus," *Politico*, April 16, 2020, www.politico .com/news/2020/04/16/facebook-fake-news-coronavirus-190054.

132. Scott, "Facebook to Tell Millions."

133. Robert McMillan and Daniela Hernandez, "Pinterest Blocks Vaccination Searches in Move to Control the Conversation," *Wall Street Journal*, February 20, 2019, www.wsj.com/articles/next-front-in-tech-firms -war-on-misinformation-bad-medical-advice-11550658601?mod=hp _lead_pos2.

134. McMillan and Hernandez, "Pinterest Blocks Vaccination Searches."

135. McMillan and Hernandez, "Pinterest Blocks Vaccination Searches."

136. Erin Brodwin, "How Pinterest Beat Back Vaccine Misinformation— and What Facebook Could Learn from Its Approach," STAT, September 21, 2020, www.statnews.com/2020/09/21/pinterest-facebook-vaccine-misinfor mation/.

137. McMillan and Hernandez, "Pinterest Blocks Vaccination Searches."

138. Pinterest, "Community Guidelines," accessed July 17, 2020, https://policy.pinterest.com/en/community-guidelines.

139. Osnos, "Can Mark Zuckerbig Fix Facebook?"

140. Barbara Ortutay, "Does the Naked Body Belong on Facebook? It's Complicated," *USA Today*, January 19, 2020, www.usatoday.com/story /tech/2020/01/19/facebook-nudity-policies/4483805002/.

141. Herb Weisbaum, "Trust in Facebook Has Dropped 66 Percent Since the Cambridge Analytica Scandal," *NBC News*, April 18, 2018, www.nbc

news.com/business/consumer/trust-facebook-has-dropped-51-percent
-cambridge-analytica-scandal-n867011.

142. Weisbaum, "Trust in Facebook Has Dropped."

143. Casey Newton, "The Verge Tech Survey 2020," *Verge*, March 2, 2020, www.theverge.com/2020/3/2/21144680/verge-tech-survey-2020-trust
-privacy-security-facebook-amazon-google-apple.

144. Brian X. Chen, "I Downloaded the Information That Facebook Has on Me. Yikes," *New York Times*, April 11, 2018, www.nytimes.com
/2018/04/11/technology/personaltech/i-downloaded-the-information-that
-facebook-has-on-me-yikes.html.

145. Mark Murray, "Poll: Americans Give Social Media a Clear Thumbs-Down," *NBC News*, April 5, 2019, www.nbcnews.com/politics
/meet-the-press/poll-americans-give-social-media-clear-thumbs-down
-n991086?curator=TechREDEF.

SIX. Recovery

1. Glassdoor, "Recruit Holdings Announces Completion of Glassdoor Acquisition," June 20, 2018, www.glassdoor.com/about-us/recruit-holdings
-announces-completion-of-glassdoor-acquisition/.

2. Recruit Holdings Co. Ltd., "Consolidated Financial Results for FY2019," May 27, 2020, https://recruit-holdings.com/ir/library/upload
/report_202003Q4_er_en.pdf.

3. "Sayonara, Salaryman," *Economist*, January 3, 2008, www.economist
.com/briefing/2008/01/03/sayonara-salaryman.

4. "Sayonara, Salaryman."

5. "Sayonara, Salaryman."

6. William Nester, "Japan's Recruit Scandal: Government and Business for Sale," *Third World Quarterly* 12, no. 2 (1990): 91–109, www.jstor.org
/stable/3992261.

7. "Recruit Founder, '80s Bribe-Giver Ezoe Dies at Age 76," *Japan Times*, February 10, 2013, www.japantimes.co.jp/news/2013/02/10/nati
onal/recruit-founder-80s-bribe-giver-ezoe-dies-at-age-76/.

8. Nester, "Japan's Recruit Scandal."

9. Peter J. Herzog and Iwao Hoshii, *Japan's Pseudo-democracy* (Abingdon: Routledge, 1993), 207.

10. "Why BP Is Paying $18.7 Billion," *New York Times*, July 2, 2015, www.nytimes.com/interactive/2015/07/02/us/bp-oil-spill-settlement-background.html.

11. Siv Padhy, "What Was the BP Stock Price Before the Deepwater Horizon Spill?," *Investing News*, August 9, 2017, https://investingnews.com/daily/resource-investing/energy-investing/oil-investing/bp-oil-stock-price-before-spill/.

12. Andrew Ward, "BP: Rebuilding Trust After Disaster," *Financial Times*, April 29, 2018, www.ft.com/content/3e09d84a-489f-11e8-8ee8-cae73aab7ccb.

13. Ward, "BP: Rebuilding Trust."

14. "Getting a Handle on a Scandal," *Economist*, March 28, 2018, www.economist.com/business/2018/03/28/getting-a-handle-on-a-scandal.

15. Hiroko Tabuchi, "Takata Saw and Hid Risk in Airbags in 2004, Former Workers Say," *New York Times*, November 6, 2014, www.nytimes.com/2014/11/07/business/airbag-maker-takata-is-said-to-have-conducted-secret-tests.html?_r=0.

16. Tabuchi, "Takata Saw and Hid Risk."

17. "Air Bag Recalls Deadly Slow: Our View," *USA Today*, November 9, 2014, www.usatoday.com/story/opinion/2014/11/09/takata-air-bags-honda-national-highway-traffic-safety-administration-editorials-debates/18776045/; Clifford Atiyeh, "Honda and Takata Allegedgly Knew About Deaths, Injuries from Exploding Airbags for Years Before Recall Expansion," Car and Driver, September 15, 2014, www.caranddriver.com/news/a15361948/honda-taking-heat-for-hiding-deaths-injuries-from-exploding-airbag-recalls/.

18. National Highway Traffic Safety Administration (NHTSA), "Supplemental Statement for the Record: NHTSA's Historical Timeline of Events Regarding Takata Inflator Ruptures," October 22, 2015, 2, www.nhtsa.gov/sites/nhtsa.dot.gov/files/documents/nhtsa_historical_timeline_takata_inflators.pdf.

19. NHTSA, "Supplemental Statement," 3.

20. NHTSA, "Fact Sheet: Takata Recall History and Key Terms," May 4, 2016, www.nhtsa.gov/sites/nhtsa.dot.gov/files/documents/20160504-fact _sheet-takata-recall-history-key-terms.pdf.

21. "Takata Settles with Injured Drivers to Exit Bankruptcy," Associated Press, February 12, 2018, www.usatoday.com/story/money/cars/2018/02/12 /takata-settles-injured-drivers-exit-bankruptcy/328396002/.

22. Charisse Jones and Nathan Bomey, "Timeline: How Takata's Air-Bag Scandal Erupted," *USA Today*, June 25, 2017, www.usatoday.com /story/money/2017/06/25/takata-air-bag-scandal-timeline/103184598/.

23. "Takata Settles with Injured Drivers."

24. Amanda Ripley, "How to Get Out Alive," *Time*, April 25, 2005, http://content.time.com/time/magazine/article/0,9171,1053663,00.html.

25. Ripley, "How to Get Out Alive."

26. Michael Haselhuhn, Maurice E. Schweitzer, Laura Kray, and Jessica A. Kennedy, "When Trust Is Easily Broken, and When It's Not," *Harvard Business Review*, February 17, 2016, https://hbr.org/2016/02/when -trust-is-easily-broken-and-when-its-not.

27. Paul Slovic, "Perceived Risk, Trust, and Democracy," *Risk Analysis* 13, no. 6 (1993): 675–682.

28. Slovic, "Perceived Risk."

29. Dave McNary, "After Oscars Mishap, PricewaterhouseCoopers Tightens Envelope Procedure," *Variety*, January 22, 2018, https://variety .com/2018/film/news/oscars-new-envelope-procedures-pricewaterhouse coopers-1202672294/.

30. David Gelles and Sapna Maheshwari, "Oscars Mistake Casts Unwanted Spotlight on PwC," *New York Times*, February 27, 2017, www.ny times.com/2017/02/27/business/media/pwc-oscars-best-picture.html.

31. Oscars, "Statement from PricewaterhouseCoopers," February 27, 2017, www.oscars.org/news/statement-pricewaterhousecoopers.

32. Joanna Robinson, "The Oscars Have an Intense, Six-Step Plan to Avoid Another Envelope Disaster," *Vanity Fair*, January 22, 2018, www.vanityfair.com/hollywood/2018/01/oscars-envelope-new-rules -moonlight-la-la-land.

33. Peter H. Kim, Donald L. Ferrin, Cecily D. Cooper, Kurt T. Dirks, "Removing the Shadow of Suspicion: The Effects of Apology Versus Denial for Repairing Competence- Versus Integrity-Based Trust Violations," *Journal of Applied Psychology* 89 (February 2004): 104–118.

34. Anti-Defamation League, "ADL Letter to Tommy Hilfiger," July 11, 2001, www.adl.org/news/letters/adl-letter-to-tommy-hilfiger.

35. "Did Oprah Winfrey Throw Tommy Hilfiger Off Her Show for Making a Racist Comment?," *Snopes*, February 12, 2000, www.snopes.com /fact-check/tommy-hilfiger-oprah/.

36. Debra L. Shapiro, "The Effects of Explanations on Negative Reactions to Deceit," *Administrative Science Quarterly* 36, no. 4 (December 1991): 614–630.

37. Mika Gröndahl, "Investigating the Cause of the Deepwater Horizon Blowout," *New York Times*, June 21, 2010, https://archive.nytimes.com /www.nytimes.com/interactive/2010/06/21/us/20100621-bop.html.

38. Environmental Protection Agency, "Deepwater Horizon—BP Gulf of Mexico Oil Spill," accessed July 14, 2020, www.epa.gov/enforcement /deepwater-horizon-bp-gulf-mexico-oil-spill.

39. Debbie Elliott, "5 Years After BP Oil Spill, Effects Linger and Recovery Is Slow," NPR, April 20, 2015, www.npr.org/2015/04/20/400374744/5 -years-after-bp-oil-spill-effects-linger-and-recovery-is-slow.

40. Alejandra Borunda, "We Still Don't Know the Full Impacts of the BP Oil Spill, 10 Years Later," *National Geographic*, April 20, 2020, www.na tionalgeographic.com/science/2020/04/bp-oil-spill-still-dont-know-effects -decade-later/#close.

41. National Ocean Service, "Deepwater Horizon Oil Spill," April 20, 2017, https://oceanservice.noaa.gov/news/apr17/dwh-protected-species.html.

42. Justin P. Lewis, Joseph H. Tarnecki, Steven B. Garner, David D. Chagaris, and William F. Patterson III, "Changes in Reef Fish Community Structure Following the Deepwater Horizon Oil Spill," *Scientific Reports* 10, no. 1 (April 2020), https://doi.org/10.1038/s41598-020-62574-y.

43. Richard Pallardy, "Deepwater Horizon Oil Spill," *Encyclopedia Britannica*, accessed July 9, 2010, www.britannica.com/event/Deepwater-Horizon-oil-spill/Environmental-costs.

44. Debbie Elliott, "The BP Oil Disaster, 10 Years Later," NPR, April 20, 2020, www.npr.org/2020/04/20/839138445/the-bp-oil-disaster-10-years-later.

45. "Hayward—Life Back," CNN, July 21, 2016, YouTube video, www .youtube.com/watch?v=EZraCNZZ7U8.

46. Roy J. Lewicki, Beth Polin, and Robert B. Lount Jr., "An Exploration of the Structure of Effective Apologies," *Negotiation and Conflict Management Research* 9, no. 2 (April 2016): 177–196, https://doi.org/10.1111 /ncmr.12073.

47. Edward C. Tomlinson, Brian R. Dineen, and Roy J. Lewicki, "The Road to Reconciliation: Antecedents of Victim Willingness to Reconcile Following a Broken Promise," *Journal of Management* 30, no. 2 (2004): 165– 187, https://doi.org/10.1016/j.jm.2003.01.003.

48. Chris Isidore, "JetBlue's Winter Nightmare," *CNN Business*, January 7, 2014, https://money.cnn.com/2014/01/07/news/companies/jetblue/.

49. Joseph Avila, "The JetBlue Post Morterm, Part 1: What Went Wrong?," *CBSD News*, February 22, 2007, www.cbsnews.com/news/the -jetblue-post-mortem-part-1-what-went-wrong/.

50. Public Apology Central, "JetBlue Airways," accessed July 15, 2020, http://publicapologycentral.com/apologia-archive/corporate-2/jet-blue/.

51. JetBlue, "JetBlue Announces the JetBlue Customer Bill of Rights," February 20, 2007, http://mediaroom.jetblue.com/investor-relations/press -releases/2007/02-20-2007-015119917.

52. Adam Hanft, "Firing Neeleman; JetBlue Just Blew It," *Fast Company*, May 14, 2007, www.fastcompany.com/660116/firing-neeleman-jetblue-just -blew-it.

53. Donald L. Ferrin, Cecily D. Cooper, Kurt T. Dirks, and Peter H. Kim, "Heads Will Roll! Routes to Effective Trust Repair in the Aftermath of a CEO Transgression," *Journal of Trust Research* 8, no. 1 (2018): 7–30.

54. Matthew Campbell, Christoph Rauwald, and Chris Reiter, "How Volkswagen Walked Away from a Near-Fatal Crash," *Bloomberg*, March 29, 2018, www.bloomberg.com/news/features/2018-03-29/how-volkswagen -walked-away-from-a-near-fatal-crash.

55. Edward Taylor and Jan Schwartz, "Bet Everything on Electric: Inside Volkswagen's Radical Strategy Shift," Reuters, February 6, 2019, www.reuters

.com/article/us-volkswagen-electric-insight/bet-everything-on-electric
-inside-volkswagens-radical-strategy-shift-idUSKCN1PV0K4.

56. Jonathon Ramsey, "Volkswagen ID.3 Reportedly Suffering Software Problems," *Autoblog*, December 27, 2019, www.autoblog.com/2019/12/27 /vw-id3-ev-software-issue-fix/; William Boston, "Volkswagen Delays Key Electric Car Launch amid Software Troubles," *Wall Street Journal*, June 10, 2020, www.wsj.com/articles/volkswagen-delays-key-electric-car-launch -amid-software-troubles-11591809421#:~:text=William%20Boston,-Bio graphy&text=BERLIN%E2%80%94%20Volkswagen%20AG%20VOW%20 1.20,after%20software%20glitches%20delayed%20production.

57. Sean O'Kane, "VW's First Mass-Market EV Suffers Delay Thanks to Software Struggles," *Verge*, June 11, 2020, www.theverge .com/2020/6/11/21288572/volkswagen-id3-ev-delay-software-vw-herbert -diess.

58. Peter Valdes-Dapena, "Volkswagen Unveils the ID.4, Its New All-Electric SUV," CNN, September 23, 2020, www.cnn.com/2020/09/23/suc cess/volkswagen-id-4-electric-suv-unveiled/index.html.

59. Mitsumaru Murai, interview by Sandra Sucher and Shalene Gupta, Tokyo, January 11, 2017.

60. Matsumi Minegishi, interview by Sandra Sucher and Shalene Gupta, Tokyo, January 13, 2017.

61. "Japan Airlines," *Encyclopedia Britannica*, accessed July 15, 2020, www.britannica.com/topic/Japan-Airlines.

62. Philip Zerrillo, Sheetal Mittal, Havovi Joshi, and Akira Mitsumasu, "Japan Airlines: Turning Around to Take Off Again" (Singapore Management University case SMU310, December 14, 2016).

63. Mayumi Negishi and Mariko Katsumura, "Japan Airlines Files for $25 Billion Bankruptcy," Reuters, January 18, 2010, www.reuters.com /article/us-jal/japan-airlines-files-for-25-billion-bankruptcy-idUSTRE 60H4NA20100119.

64. Takako Taniguchi, "Kyocera Founder's Secret: Make Workers Happy," *Japan Times*, November 5, 2015, www.japantimes.co.jp/news/2015 /11/05/business/kyocera-founders-secret-make-workers-happy/#.Xjm1 Ny2ZNt8.

65. Julian Ryall, "Kyocera Founder Explains His Strategy to Revive JAL," *Japan Today*, September 24, 2013, https://japantoday.com/category /business/kyocera-founder-explains-his-strategy-to-revive-jal.

66. Kenneth Maxwell, "'Mikoshi' Management: How Kazuo Inamori Lifted Japan," *Wall Street Journal*, July 30, 2012, https://blogs.wsj.com /japanrealtime/2012/07/30/mikoshi-management-how-kazuo-inamori -lifted-japan-airlines/.

67. Taniguchi, "Kyocera Founder's Secret."

68. Ryall, "Kyocera Founder Explains His Strategy."

69. Zerrillo et al., "Japan Airlines."

70. Derrick A. Paulo, "How a Buddhist Monk Turned CEO Revived Japan Airlines from Bankruptcy," *Channel News Asia*, December 15, 2018, www.channelnewsasia.com/news/cnainsider/buddhist-monk-ceo-kazuo -inamori-save-japan-airlines-jal-bankrupt-11033866.

71. Stone, *The Upstarts*, 267.

72. EJ, "Violated: A Traveler's Lost Faith, A Difficult Lesson Learned," *Around the World and Back Again* blog, June 29, 2011, https://ejroundthe world.blogspot.com/2011/06/violated-travelers-lost-faith-difficult.html.

73. Michael Arrington, "The Moment of Truth for Airbnb as User's Home Is Utterly Trashed," *TechCrunch*, July 27, 2011, https://tech crunch.com/2011/07/27/the-moment-of-truth-for-airbnb-as-users -home-is-utterly-trashed/.

74. EJ, "Airbnb Nightmare: No End in Sight," *Around the World and Back Again* blog, July 28, 2011, https://ejroundtheworld.blogspot.com/2011/07/.

75. Stone, *The Upstarts*, 290.

76. Stone, *The Upstarts*, 287.

77. Stone, *The Upstarts*, 286.

78. Slovic, "Perceived Risk," 675–682.

79. Kazuya Nakayachi and Motoki Watabe, "Restoring Trustworthiness After Adverse Events: The Signaling Effects of Voluntary 'Hostage Posting' on Trust," *Organizational Behavior and Human Decision Processes* 97, no. 1 (2005): 1–17, https://doi.org/10.1016/j.obhdp.2005.02.001.

80. Tsuyoshi Tamehiro and Hideki Sinohara, "Japan's Recruit Sold Job-Seeker Data to Honda in Privacy Scandal," *Nikkei Asian Review*, August

10, 2019, https://asia.nikkei.com/Business/Companies/Japan-s-Recruit-sold
-job-seeker-data-to-Honda-in-privacy-scandal.

SEVEN. Power, Trust, and Leadership

1. John Rawls, *Lectures on the History of Political Philosophy* (Cambridge: Harvard University Press, 2007), 124.

2. Rawls, *Lectures on the History of Political Philosophy*, 124.

3. Dacher Keltner, "The Power Paradox," Greater Good Magazine, accessed August 8, 2020, https://greatergood.berkeley.edu/article/item/power_paradox.

4. Keltner, "The Power Paradox," 43.

5. Keltner, "The Power Paradox," 16.

6. Keltner, "The Power Paradox," 16–17.

7. Cameron Anderson, Oliver P. John, Dacher Keltner, and Ann M. Kring, "Who Attains Social Status? Effects of Personality and Physical Attractiveness in Social Groups," *Journal of Personality and Social Psychology* 81 (2001): 116–132.

8. Keltner, "The Power Paradox," 48.

9. Keltner, "The Power Paradox," 49.

10. T. A. Judge, J. E. Bono, R. Ilies, and M. W. Gerhardt, "Personality and Leadership: A Qualitative and Quantitative Review," *Journal of Applied Psychology* 87 (2002): 465–480.

11. Keltner, "The Power Paradox," 7.

12. "How Does Dopamine Affect the Body?," Healthline, accessed August 8, 2020, www.healthline.com/health/dopamine-effects#how-it-makes-you-feel.

13. Adam D. Galinsky, Joe C. Magee, M. Ena Inesi, and Deborah H. Gruenfeld, "Power and Perspectives Not Taken," *Psychological Science* 17 (2006): 1068–1074.

14. Galinsky et al., "Power and Perspectives Not Taken," 1070.

15. Galinsky et al., "Power and Perspectives Not Taken," 1070.

16. Adam D. Galinsky, Deborah H. Gruenfeld, and Joe C. Magee, "From Power to Action," *Journal of Personality and Social Psychology* 85 (2003): 453–466.

17. "Measuring Confidence; Figure 2, Voter Confidence," MIT Election Data + Science Lab, accessed August 1, 2020, https://electionlab.mit.edu/research/voter-confidence.

18. Fabienne Peter, "Political Legitimacy," *Stanford Encyclopedia of Philosophy* (Summer 2016).

19. Peter, "Political Legitimacy," 17.

20. Robert Bolt, *A Man for All Seasons* (New York: Vintage Books, 1960), 116.

21. Peter, "Political Legitimacy," 17.

22. John Locke, *Second Treatise on Civil Government*, ed. C. B. MacPherson (Indianapolis: Hackett, 1990 [1690]).

23. Sarah Al-Suhaimi, online interview, by Sandra Sucher, Shalene Gupta, Gamze Yucaoglu, and Fares Kharis, April 13, 2020.

24. Wassim Al-Khatib, online interview, by Sandra Sucher, Shalene Gupta, Gamze Yucaoglu, and Fares Kharis, April 15, 2020.

25. Sandra J. Sucher, Shalene Gupta, Gamze Yucaoglu, Fares Khais, "The NCB Capital Turnaround: Waking the Sleeping Giant" (unpublished Harvard Business Publishing Case), 10.

26. Sucher et al., "NCB Capital Turnaround," 7.

27. Sucher et al., "NCB Capital Turnaround," 7.

28. Al-Suhaimi interview, April 15, 2020.

29. Naif Al Mesned, online interview by Sandra Sucher, Shalene Gupta, Gamze Yucaoglu, and Fares Khrais, April 14, 2020.

30. Naif Al Mesned interview.

31. Sucher et al., "NCB Capital Turnaround," 7.

32. Sucher et al., "NCB Capital Turnaround," 8.

33. Sucher et al., "NCB Capital Turnaround," 8.

34. *Washington Post*, "General Information," www.washingtonpost.com/wp-srv/polls/washpost/gi_hi.htm.

35. *Washington Post*, "General Information."

36. "Katharine Graham," *Encyclopedia Britannica*, accessed July 13, 2020, www.britannica.com/biography/Katharine-Graham.

37. Katharine Graham, *Personal History* (New York: Vintage, 1998), 340–341.

38. "Pentagon Papers," History.com, August 21, 2018, www.history .com/topics/vietnam-war/pentagon-papers.

39. "Pentagon Papers," History.com.

40. Graham, *Personal History*, 447.

41. Graham, *Personal History*, 448.

42. Ben Bradlee, *A Good Life: Newspapering and Other Adventures* (New York: Simon & Schuster, 1995), 315.

43. Bradlee, *A Good Life*, 307.

44. Graham, *Personal History*, 460.

45. Graham, *Personal History*, 465.

46. Graham, *Personal History*, 471.

47. Graham, *Personal History*, 186.

48. J. Y. Smith and Noel Epstein, "Katharine Graham Dies at 84," *Washington Post*, July 18, 2001, www.washingtonpost.com/wp-dyn/content /article/2005/08/04/AR2005080400963.html.

49. Smith and Epstein, "Katharine Graham Dies at 84."

50. Sucher et al., "NCB Capital Turnaround," 8.

51. Sucher et al., "NCB Capital Turnaround," 7.

52. Sucher et al., "NCB Capital Turnaround," 8.

53. Al-Suhaimi interview, April 15, 2020.

54. Stephen Dimmock and William C. Gerken, "Research: How One Bad Employee Can Corrupt a Whole Team," HBR.org, March 5, 2018, https:// hbr.org/2018/03/research-how-one-bad-employee-can-corrupt-a-whole -team.

55. Al-Suhaimi interview, April 15, 2020.

56. Al-Suhaimi interview, April 15, 2020.

57. Al-Suhaimi interview, April 13, 2020.

58. Al-Suhaimi interview, April 13, 2020.

59. Al-Suhaimi interview, April 13, 2020.

EIGHT. **Trust as Potential**

1. Evaristus Mainsah, Schuyler R. Heuer, Aprajita Kalra, and Qi- ulin Zhang, "Grameen Bank: Taking Capitalism to the Poor" (Columbia

Business School course paper, 2004), 1, www0.gsb.columbia.edu/mygsb/fac ulty/research/pubfiles/848/Grameen_Bank_v04.pdf.

2. Muhammad Yunus, *Banker to the Poor: Micro-Lending and the Battle Against World Poverty* (New York: PublicAffairs, 1999), 48.

3. Yunus, *Banker to the Poor*, 48.

4. Mainsah et al., "Grameen Bank."

5. Mainsah et al., "Grameen Bank."

6. Yunus, *Banker to the Poor*, 55.

7. Katharine Esty, "Lessons from Muhammad Yunus and the Grameen Bank," *OD Practitioner* 43, no. 1 (2011): 24–28, https://cdn.ymaws.com /www.odnetwork.org/resource/resmgr/364.pdf.

8. Yunus, *Banker to the Poor*, 58.

9. "The Noble Peace Prize 2006," NoblePrize.org, accessed August 20,2020, www.nobelprize.org/prizes/peace/2006/summary/.

10. Mainsah et al., "Grameen Bank," 4.

11. Mainsah et al., "Grameen Bank," 4.

12. Grameen Bank, "Grameen Bank," accessed August 20, 2020, www .grameen.com/introduction/.

13. Stephanie Wykstra, "Microcredit Was a Hugely Hyped Solution to Global Poverty. What Happened?," *Vox*, January 15, 2019, www.vox.com /future-perfect/2019/1/15/18182167/microcredit-microfinance-poverty -grameen-bank-yunus.

14. Marguerite S. Robinson, "Why the Bank Rakyat Indonesia Has the World's Largest Sustainable Microbanking System" (presented at the International Seminar on BRI's Microbanking System, Bali, December 4, 2004), 3, www.ruralfinanceandinvestment.org/sites/default/files/1117473611572_Rob inson_BRI_Paper_Revised_April_2005.pdf.

15. Mainsah et al., "Grameen Bank," 15.

16. Anne Perkins, "A Short History of Microfinance," *The Guardian*, June 3, 2008, www.theguardian.com/katine/2008/jun/03/livelihoods.project goals1.

17. Wykstra, "Microcredit Was a Hugely Hyped Solution."

18. David Roodman, "Microcredit Doesn't End Poverty, Despite All the Hype," *Washington Post*, January 20, 2012, www.washingtonpost.com/opin

ions/microcredit-doesnt-end-poverty-despite-all-the-hype/2012/01/20/gIQAtrfqzR_story.html.

19. Soutik Biswas, "India's Micro-Finance Suicide Epidemic," *BBC News*, December 16, 2010, www.bbc.com/news/world-south-asia-11997571.

20. Wykstra, "Microcredit Was a Hugely Hyped Solution."

21. Alastair Lawson, "How Grameen Founder Muhammad Yunus Fell from Grace," BBC News, April 5, 2011, www.bbc.com/news/world-south-asia-12734472.

22. "Saint Under Siege," *The Economist*, January 5, 2011, www.economist.com/newsbook/2011/01/05/saint-under-siege.

23. "Grameen Bank's Yunus Cleared in Aid Probe," *Economic Times*, https://economictimes.indiatimes.com/news/international/grameen-banks-yunus-cleared-in-aid-probe/articleshow/7068230.cms.

24. "Grameen Bank's Yunus Cleared in Aid Probe."

25. Abhinav Ramnarayan and Arno Schuetze, "Kazakj Financial Firm Kaspi Revives Plans for London Float—Sources," Reuters, February 25, 2020, www.reuters.com/article/kaspi-kz-ipo/kazakh-financial-firm-kaspi-revives-plans-for-london-float-sources-idUSL5N2AP3NF.

26. Victoria Ivashina and Esel Cekin, "Kaspi.kz IPO" (Harvard Business School Case N9-220-007, July 5, 2019), 4.

27. Ivashina and Cekin, "Kaspi.kz IPO."

28. Karen Weise, "When Even Amazon Is Sold Out of Exploding Kittens," *New York Times*, April 17, 2020, www.nytimes.com/2020/04/17/technology/amazon-coronavirus.html.

29. Karen Weise and Kate Conger, "Gaps in Amazon's Response as Virus Spreads to More Than 50 Warehouses," *New York Times*, April 5, 2020, www.nytimes.com/2020/04/05/technology/coronavirus-amazon-workers.html.

30. Weise, "When Even Amazon."

31. "Amazon, Inc." Yahoo Finance, September 26, 2020.

32. Amazon, Amazon's COVID-19 Blog, https://blog.aboutamazon.com/company-news/amazons-actions-to-help-employees-communities-and-customers-affected-by-covid-19.

33. Amazon, Amazon's COVID-19 Blog.

34. Weise and Conger, "Gaps in Amazon's Response."

35. Weise and Conger, "Gaps in Amazon's Response."

36. Weise and Conger, "Gaps in Amazon's Response."

37. Weise and Conger, "Gaps in Amazon's Response."

38. Liz Alderman, "Amazon to Suspend Operations in France over Coronavirus Dispute," *New York Times*, April 15, 2020, www.nytimes .com/2020/04/15/business/amazon-france-covid.html.

39. "Update on COVID-19 Testing," Amazon's COVID-19 Blog, October 1, 2020, https://blog.aboutamazon.com/operations/update-on-covid -19-testing.

Index

EVGENIA ELISEEVA

SANDRA J. SUCHER is a professor of management practice and Joseph L. Rice III Faculty Fellow at Harvard Business School, where she has been teaching for the last twenty years. At Harvard, Sucher has studied how organizations can change and improve while retaining stakeholder trust and the vital role that leaders can play in the process.

She is an advisor to the Edelman Trust Barometer and provides expert commentary for *Bloomberg*, the *New York Times*, the *Washington Post*, the *Wall Street Journal*, NPR, and *Fortune*. Prior to teaching at Harvard, Sucher had a two-decade career as a senior-level executive at Filene's and Fidelity specializing in uncovering complex organization problems and creating new ways to address them.

USHEER KANJEE

SHALENE GUPTA is a research associate at Harvard Business School. Previously she was a *Fortune* reporter covering diversity in Silicon Valley, big data, and smart cities. Prior to *Fortune* she worked at the US Department of Treasury and had a Fulbright grant in Malaysia. Her work has appeared in the *Jakarta Post*, the *New Strait Times*, *Kirkus Reviews*, *Fortune*, and ESPN.

PublicAffairs is a publishing house founded in 1997. It is a tribute to the standards, values, and flair of three persons who have served as mentors to countless reporters, writers, editors, and book people of all kinds, including me.

I. F. Stone, proprietor of *I. F. Stone's Weekly*, combined a commitment to the First Amendment with entrepreneurial zeal and reporting skill and became one of the great independent journalists in American history. At the age of eighty, Izzy published *The Trial of Socrates*, which was a national bestseller. He wrote the book after he taught himself ancient Greek.

Benjamin C. Bradlee was for nearly thirty years the charismatic editorial leader of *The Washington Post*. It was Ben who gave the *Post* the range and courage to pursue such historic issues as Watergate. He supported his reporters with a tenacity that made them fearless and it is no accident that so many became authors of influential, best-selling books.

Robert L. Bernstein, the chief executive of Random House for more than a quarter century, guided one of the nation's premier publishing houses. Bob was personally responsible for many books of political dissent and argument that challenged tyranny around the globe. He is also the founder and longtime chair of Human Rights Watch, one of the most respected human rights organizations in the world.

• • •

For fifty years, the banner of Public Affairs Press was carried by its owner Morris B. Schnapper, who published Gandhi, Nasser, Toynbee, Truman, and about 1,500 other authors. In 1983, Schnapper was described by *The Washington Post* as "a redoubtable gadfly." His legacy will endure in the books to come.

Peter Osnos, *Founder*